Just City

Just City

JUST CITY

Growing Up on the Upper West Side When Housing Was a Human Right

Jennifer Baum

EMPIRE STATE EDITIONS

AN IMPRINT OF FORDHAM UNIVERSITY PRESS

NEW YORK 2024

Excerpts of this book were previously published as "A Different Set of Rules" in *Newfound Journal* (2014); "She Liked to Save Things" in *MUTHA* (2016); "Soot" in *Guernica* (2016); "Comfort Zone: Jennifer Baum on Leaving New York, Regrets, and Home" in *MUTHA* (2017); "Growing Up in the 'Just City'" in *Jacobin* (2018); "When Housing Was a Human Right" in *Guernica* (2021); and "Shoplifting in Bloomingdale's" in *MUTHA* (2021).

Fordham University Press has no responsibility for the persistence or accuracy of URLs for external or third-party Internet websites referred to in this publication and does not guarantee that any content on such websites is, or will remain, accurate or appropriate.

Fordham University Press also publishes its books in a variety of electronic formats. Some content that appears in print may not be available in electronic books.

Visit us online at www.fordhampress.com/empire-state-editions.

Library of Congress Cataloging-in-Publication Data available online at https://catalog.loc.gov.

Printed in the United States of America

26 25 24   5 4 3 2 1

First edition

To my mother, Judith Baum, who stayed true to her common
good values as the world changed around her

CONTENTS

Photographs follow page 132

PREFACE

When I started writing this book, I didn't know if I wanted to write about myself or my building—RNA House, the subsidized, integrated cooperative where I was raised on Manhattan's Upper West Side. But I found as I continued that the two subjects were inextricably linked. RNA House had long been my muse. I made two films set there and photographed it endlessly. I wrote numerous essays about its socialist system, one where cooperators got apartments according to family size and paid maintenance based on income. Yet I felt uncomfortable telling my own story. Who would care about my life? What made my circumstances exceptional?

Growing up as a public school kid living in subsidized housing seemed nothing out of the ordinary. It wasn't until I transferred to a private school and learned about class divisions that my circumstances seemed unique. As an adult moving around the world for school, a husband, and work, I realized even more that being raised in an integrated collective was special—as integration was the exception, not the norm. I yearned for RNA House, where I felt anchored, my true self, and I cherished visiting my mother there.

Losing my RNA House apartment upon my mother's death unmoored me. Apartment 14E was where my mother, father, sister, and I lived happily until my father's sudden death when I was ten; the place embodied a feeling of wholeness that took me years to regain. It seemed my whole adult life I'd been searching for stability, for a physical and emotional place to call home. My own experiences with housing dislocation heightened my awareness of the city's affordable housing crisis, where New York was transforming into a playground for the rich, leaving everyone else behind. More and more, I felt a pressing urge to write about the era of the common good when politicians, urban planners, and architects combined forces to build affordable housing en masse. The result of my efforts is *Just City: Growing Up on the Upper West Side When Housing Was a Human Right*, a hybrid memoir about housing history and my search for home.

Just City

INTRODUCTION

"GIRLS. WE BOUGHT a new apartment. It has three bedrooms and a terrace with a great view. There's a huge backyard with a playground. Lots of young families are moving in. You'll have plenty of kids to play with."

In 1967, when I was four years old, my family moved into our brand-new co-op at RNA House, one of numerous brutalist-style middle-income Mitchell-Lama buildings being constructed on New York's Upper West Side at a time when the idea that housing is a human right was a guiding principle of politics, urban design, and planning. *Just City: Growing Up on the Upper West Side When Housing Was a Human Right* is about the benefits and crucial necessity of affordable housing told through the lens of my experience growing up at the peak of the progressive housing movement. It is about what that era meant to me and to my generation of New Yorkers. And it offers the ideas and values of that era as a lesson, model, and hope for the current affordable housing crisis.

Just City outlines my own shifting personal relationship with RNA House. As a public school child, living there imbued me with different values than those of America's individualistic society. I explore how I became ashamed of the building once my parents later enrolled me in a private school and then, as I grew into a young adult, learned to appreciate the real worth of social housing as a salve against soaring rents and the ultra-rich takeover of the city. It focuses on my personal struggle—coping with my father's sudden death, adapting to life with a single working mother, fleeing 1980s New York City in search of a new form of utopia, my longing to

1

return to RNA House, and finally, my subsequent devastation when losing my childhood apartment upon my mother's death in 2013.

Just City traces over fifty years of RNA House history, from the early socialist ethos of the original cooperators to the push to privatize by some residents looking to profit versus efforts by others to resist and remain public. Weaving memoir with interviews, archival material, history, and policy, the book illustrates how my family, along with families in neighboring co-ops and New York City Housing Authority (NYCHA) public housing, similarly shaped by a collectivist, integrationist spirit, lived with dignity and thrived, despite the dramas and trauma that we lived through in that period.

It flips the script on failed social housing. In this "just city," low- and middle-income tenants paid reasonable maintenance and rents, had housing security, knew our neighbors, formed committees to beautify our building grounds, and organized activities for children to keep them off the streets. These cooperative actions buttressed our everyday experiences, molded our lives inside the building, our worldviews, and our approach to society, breeding tolerance and activism.

Just City tells the story of the rise and fall—or teetering—of public housing and the democratic principle of a decent home for all that had once made New York a model for the nation. Looking at the current affordable housing crisis, *Just City* advocates for a massive intervention from the federal government on the scale of the 1949 Housing Act, not only to return to the value of housing as a human right, but to address systemic racism, which plays a major role in United States housing inequality.

Finally, *Just City* illustrates how growing up in Mitchell-Lama housing shaped my sense of what "home" can and should be. My life, and that of my family and friends, were improved socially, culturally, economically, and spiritually by living in a subsidized, integrated cooperative. I would like others to have the same opportunities that I did.

Chapter 1

Moving into the Just City

MY PARENTS CAME of age in 1950s New York City believing in the dream of equality through architecture. My mother, a secular Jew raised in Brooklyn, and my father, a moderately observant Jew from the Bronx, both found God in modernism. They believed the homes we build could change the world for the better. At their core, they embraced the Bauhaus ideology of "architecture as the collective, satisfying all vital needs with the exclusion of personal demands,"[1] which could "create a human brotherhood, with organic community ties."[2] On their tall functional bookcase, my parents prominently displayed a black-and-white hardcover tome titled *Bauhaus* the way others exhibited a bible.

In 1967, their fervor was fulfilled when we relocated to RNA House, at 150–160 West 96th Street between Amsterdam and Columbus Avenue, one of the first in a series of no-frills super-slabs conceived by urban planners and politicians committed to the belief that every American deserves a decent home. The building was financed by the Mitchell-Lama Housing Program, sponsored by New York State Senator MacNeil Mitchell and Assemblyman Alfred Lama and made into law in 1955 as the Limited-Profit Housing Companies Act. Its mission was to provide affordable rentals and cooperative apartments for thousands of middle-income New Yorkers like my family. The state gave developers low-interest loans, mortgages, and tax exemptions to build apartments contingent upon controlled rents and sales prices below market value for a twenty-year period. Once the twenty years passed, the buildings could either opt out of the program and privatize or refinance under the same conditions and remain public.

At the time, the Upper West Side was considered slummy, crime-ridden, and graffiti-scarred, and many Whites were fleeing to the suburbs. But families like ours, attracted to the integrationist social agenda of the West Side Urban Renewal Area, were thrilled by the proximity of Central Park, bookstores, movie theaters, and the opportunity to live their engineered utopian vision.

My parents bought our subsidized RNA House apartment below market rate for $3,800.[3] Because we had a family of four, we were allotted three bedrooms and charged maintenance adjusted to our family income. Those with earnings above a certain amount were ineligible. At the time, my father was a Mechanical Engineering Professor at Manhattan College, and we qualified. RNA House also set aside a share of "skewed" apartments on the second and third floors, with reduced maintenance charges, for those in the neighborhood displaced by development. Thus, the subsidized middle class subsidized the working poor. The idea was not to make a profit but to live an affordable, safe, communal life in an integrated community in which everybody had a stake.

It was a liberal scheme of its time and place—postwar America, when the economy was booming, and fair play and collectivism were dogmas.

Turning the key on the stiff #14E lock, my father, Charles, held the door open for us as we entered for the first time our spanking-clean modern apartment, painted a bright glossy white with linoleum floors, so new it had no dishwasher, stove, refrigerator, or air conditioners. As RNA House's first cooperators, we had the pick of apartments. We chose #14E, high up on the fourteenth floor with a southern exposure, opposite the noisy 96th Street thoroughfare. The apartment had an open-air floor plan with a connected living room, galley kitchen, dining room, and terrace off the eating area. Large bare windows lined the walls of the living room and three bedrooms, all in a row. On the other side of the narrow hallway were two small bathrooms.

"Girls! There's the Empire State Building!" Pointing, my mother, Judy, walked over to have a look. My father handed her the binoculars hanging around his neck. We each took a turn, my dad hoisting me onto his shoulders so I could see. My father was the kind of man who always had viewing objects at his disposal, a man who liked to share his perceptions with anybody who'd listen.

We explored the apartment, opening and closing plywood cabinet doors and discovering mouse droppings in corners. "With new construction, mice bring their suitcases," my father said. He chose the smallest middle room as his workspace, where he'd build telescopes, design machine models, and store wine. The back bedroom was the largest. "You girls will share this room," my mother said. "You're too young to sleep alone."

Back then, my family was a cohesive unit. Whole. We acted as one. So would our burgeoning RNA House community.

We headed to the basement garage to pick out a parking space, waiting in the drab fluorescent-lit hallway until the elevator plodded along to retrieve us. When the door opened, two White men were inside, holding hands and leashes, each attached to a gray shorthaired schnauzer. They introduced themselves as Scott and James and told us they lived on the fifteenth floor, just above us, and were going out to walk their dogs.

My sister, Elizabeth, and I petted the schnauzers while my parents and the couple chatted. Other neighbors got on as we descended. That's when I met Angela, a Black girl, four years old, like me, and her mother, Nicole. Soon the elevator grew crowded and noisy with folks getting to know each other, eventually exiting at the lobby, except for our family, headed to the garage, an empty concrete cave. Elizabeth and I shouted *echo echo echo* at the top of our lungs and played hide-and-seek behind the rectangular cement pillars festooned with sand-filled fire buckets.

My father chased and tickled us while my mother stood watching, arms crossed, an amused smile on her face.

"C'mon, girls," my father said after he tired of the game. "I want to show you the spot I've chosen for the car."

We had an olive-green Studebaker Lark, which until now had been left on the street. He pointed at space eighteen. "It's close to the elevator. More importantly, I chose eighteen because the number in Hebrew, *Chai*, means life. It's made up of two letters, Chet ח and Yod י ." He laughed and kissed the three of us. Taking a notepad and pen from his pocket, he drew the letters, showing us how they combined to get חי *Chai*. I studied the writing in the weak fluorescent light. It seemed like a complicated cosmic math equation. "Even a parking spot needs meaning," he said.

Little did I know, at the time, that a cement parking space would come to signify life, life cycles, and continuity, and that, for me, the kabbalistic cosmology of a Hebrew number would forever be connected with the values of community and inclusiveness my dad instilled in us.

That first summer at RNA House, my family went to a party at Frank and Lillian's apartment on the west side of the building. While Elizabeth and I ran up and down the hallway in our sunflower A-line jumpers, my parents rang the bell. Lillian, sporting hip-hugging orange bell-bottoms and a sequined, yellow low-cut blouse, greeted us with hugs and kisses, "¿Qué tal?" She led us through a black-and-red beaded curtain into a smoke-filled living room filled with neighbors sitting on chrome bar stools with red vinyl seats, sipping sangria and puffing cigarettes.

She handed my parents drinks, and they mingled with other couples—Puerto Rican, Black, Jewish, Chinese, and interracial—while we played with their kids and a fluffy white cat named Ethan. Every now and then, Elizabeth and I snuck some liquor-soaked fruit from the Sangria bowl and sucked it dry.

My mother laughed and pushed her black cat-eye eyeglasses up the bridge of her nose. "The kids are getting drunk."

"It's good for them," my father said, draping his arm around her. They were nearly the same size, my father five foot six, my mother five foot three, both with black hair, though my mother's was thin and straight, cut into a pageboy, my father's thick and tightly curled; my father was swarthy, my mother more olive-skinned.

My mother was au courant, though not in Lillian's sexy swinging '60s mode. Instead, she wore a loose green, pink, and blue-circled Marimekko frock, hanging just above her knees, the latest style for liberated women. My father dressed more conservatively in his gray polo shirt with white and black vertical stripes and black knit trousers, though he was by no means staid. Rather, he was gregarious and funny. "A watched pot *does* boil," he liked to say and then explained the laws of quantum mechanics to whoever would listen.

Lillian put a Willie Colón record on the turntable, cranked up the volume, and broke into salsa steps, her long dark hair swinging from a ponytail crowning her head. Soon a large group joined in, including Scott and his boyfriend, James, our neighbors on the fifteenth floor. The couple kicked, turned, dipped, and gyrated their hips to the rhythm of the clave and Colón's spirited, elegant trombone.

My parents weren't ones to let loose on the dance floor, so they watched contentedly from the sidelines, clapping to the beat. The movements reminded my mother of the euphoric Horah dancing at Jewish weddings—participatory, exuberant, unabashed, communal engagement.

RNA House, designed by Saul Edelbaum and Ida Webster—one of the first women to make partner in an architecture firm—was a fifteen-story, low-rise, concrete block, more wide than tall, with beehive windows, terraces along the corners, and a tree-lined garden in front. It was set back from the street, giving tenants and pedestrians breathing room from the rumbling, screeching traffic. Our building was cozier than the other high-rise Mitchell-Lamas we watched shoot up on Columbus and Amsterdam in the late '60s and '70s, obscuring our view. It resembled Kips Bay Towers on the east side of Manhattan, designed by the great modernist architect I. M. Pei, a Chinese American informed by Le Corbusier, and the Bauhaus architects Walter Gropius and Marcel Breuer. Le Corbusier coined the term "brutalism," derived from the French words *Béton Brut*, meaning "raw concrete." RNA House also brought Mondrian to mind, not his primary-colored Broadway Boogie Woogie painting, but a more subdued, less known cubist painting, Tableau No. 2/ Composition No. VII, with black intertwining lines, the spaces filled in with dabs of gray and ocher.

My parents loved the clean, angular lines and the spare, geometric grid of the windows on the building's facade. They slowly and deliberately filled the apartment with finely crafted minimalist Danish Modern furniture, matching the building's design, laying down cherrywood floors in the living/dining room area and in the hallway. Our living room was small but still big enough for teak shelving units, a console with a turntable and receiver, a liquor cabinet, a winged chair with a footstool, a brown sofa with slanted arms and tapered hairpin legs, and an inherited baby grand piano. Even our cutlery was simple, functional Danish Modern design. Lots of art hung on the walls—cool abstract expressionist art, optical art, and paintings by Black Harlem Renaissance artists Jacob Lawrence and Charles Alston, Lawrence's teacher and mentor, that my parents bought at a benefit for the local music school we attended before the artists were well-known and modern art big business. The Jacob Lawrence, I believe, was from *The Builders* series. The abstract work, tempera on hardboard, depicts men holding up wooden planks, their silhouetted dark and light, brown-skinned faces staring up at the beams, their bold-colored vertically linked bodies illustrating the collectivist toil of the American people.

My parents were raised in prewar buildings with decorative moldings, high ceilings, and hardwood floors: my mother on Eastern Parkway in Brooklyn and my father on the Grand Concourse in the South Bronx, when it was, in fact, grand. After the Cross Bronx Expressway was completed in 1963, displacing thousands and destroying the neighborhood, the middle and upper classes abandoned the Concourse, many Whites moving to the suburbs, leaving only the poor to suffer as the South Bronx succumbed to decay and pollution.

Owning a suburban home was never my parents' dream. Enjoying New York was their priority. In the 1950s, my mother won a Regents Scholarship to Barnard, Columbia University's women's college. She commuted from Brooklyn to Barnard's Morningside Heights campus, tasting Manhattan's modernity. My father remained on the Grand Concourse with his widowed mother and uncle, enrolling at NYU's Bronx campus. They met through a mutual friend. During their six-month courtship, they took turns taking the long subway ride across the boroughs to visit each other, often arriving home late at night. When they married in 1958, they lived in the Bronx. As soon as they could, they moved to the Upper West Side of Manhattan.

They rejected the outer boroughs, searching for the morality of modernism in Manhattan, reading the world through the maxims of English American poet W. H. Auden, who wrote, "More even than in Europe, here / The choice of patterns is made clear / Which the machine imposes, what / Is possible and what is not, / To what conditions we must bow/ In building the Just City now."[4]

To this day, it's hard for me to understand their choice. Our apartment was contained in its smallness and predictability. I lived in a different fantasy, a parallel child's narrative influenced by my novels nestled beneath my parents' architectural journals. I envied the kids I knew who lived in older buildings with high ceilings, wooden floors, vast hallways, large bedrooms, character, and history, like apartments in *Rosemary's Baby*: "Old, black, and elephantine . . . prized for their fireplaces and Victorian detail."[5] I coveted getting lost in dark, cavernous rooms that went on and on, mazelike, with seemingly endless bedrooms off hallways off maid's rooms off kitchens off pantries off trapdoors, like in *The Lion, the Witch and the Wardrobe*. "And then came three steps down and five steps up, and then a kind of little upstairs hall and a door that led out onto a balcony, and then a whole series of rooms that led into each other and were lined with books—most of them very old books."[6]

At that time, you didn't have to be rich to rent or even buy a spacious prewar apartment on West End Avenue or Riverside Drive above 96th Street. But for my mother, older buildings meant poor heating and faulty plumbing. She grew up in a two-bedroom apartment where the toilet frequently clogged. Older buildings also didn't have a community room, a day-care center, a bicycle room, a parking garage, a backyard, or a cooperative spirit—the latter being a direct result of modernist urban planning promoting integration and fairness.

Though the vision governing our lives was idealistic, the disparity in the neighborhood was harsh. Still, we worked together to solve problems, confronting them head-on, never pushing people away or isolating ourselves in the suburbs. Many homeless people lived in the neighborhood, but they weren't criminalized or disdained. We called them hobos or bums, like the Bowery Bums, in a good-natured way. One such scraggly bum, with pink whiskey cheeks and long graying hair and beard, sat a few seats down from us on the #7 bus, his rag-like shirt and jeans falling off his skinny body. My mother and I were headed south on Columbus Avenue to Adventure Playground, a newly opened revolutionary play space in Central Park at 67th Street, with pyramids, enormous slides, and mazes made from wood and brutalist cement. The playground encouraged kids to explore and create, like the "real world, fraught with challenges to overcome,"[7] said the renowned Adventure Playground landscape designer M. Paul Friedberg, which aligned with my parents' worldview.

I was happily licking a chocolate Carvel soft ice cream cone, drips staining my red and blue striped T-shirt and jeans, while my mother, comfortable in a yellow smock dress, tackled the Sunday *New York Times* crossword puzzle. The bus was full but not overly crowded. It was steamy, nonetheless, even with the windows wide open.

"That ice cream looks good," the man said to me.

I smiled at him and lapped up some more.

He came closer. "Can I have a taste?"

I gave him my cone, he took a lick, and returned it.

The passengers, a mix of older Black women wearing long skirts, blouses buttoned to their necks, and bright felt church hats and White women in cropped jackets, pencil skirts, and pillbox hats, gasped.

"I'm proud of you. That was very generous," my mother said and went back to her puzzle.

Soon after we'd installed ourselves at 96th Street, we came home from a weekend in the country to find all the lights on in the apartment. Though we lived on the fourteenth floor, the clamor of the city tore through the rooms as if we were on street level. A cool gush of air made us shiver.

"Quiet," my father warned. "Stay right here." His tone petrified us. My mother, sister, and I huddled together in the hallway, terrified and shaking, as he crept through the apartment.

"The TV is gone," he reported when he returned. "So is some of Mommy's jewelry." He motioned for us to follow him into the dining room; the sliding glass door was wide open. "The robbers must've climbed down from the roof and in through the terrace." He closed the door, the noise subsiding. "Very clever."

When the police came, my parents told them they should check out the apartment next door, connected to ours by a partitioned terrace. Instead, they left.

"Ludicrous." My mother shook her head. "The cops have given up. There's too much petty crime around here."

The next day we found out our neighbors had been robbed too.

On the terrace the robbers had broken in through, my mother wiped black soot off the glass table and wrought iron chairs with a washcloth. She wrung out the dirty rag in the sink, scrubbed it with dish soap, and then went outside to rub some more. "Girls," she called. "Lunchtime."

Hungry, we darted outside and clutched the grimy metal railing, pressing our bodies against the blackened bars, soiling our matching smiley face

T-shirts. Looking south on Columbus Avenue, we saw an excavation where a building was going up with skeletal frames disappearing in the smog, soon to be new Mitchell-Lama towers like ours. One would be Jefferson Towers, a high-rise slab around the corner from RNA House. Just after it opened in 1968, my maternal grandmother, Helen, moved into a one-bedroom there. In the '60s, after Grandpa Leon died, leaving Grandma Helen penniless, she went to work as a legal secretary, earning a modest living. Fortunately, middle-income Mitchell-Lama housing was widely available. Unlike today, there were no wait-lists or lotteries. Postwar, 138,000 Mitchell-Lama apartments were built in New York City,[8] 4,900 of which were scheduled for the West Side Urban Renewal Area,[9] stretching from 87th to 97th Street, between Amsterdam Avenue and Central Park West.

While our mother focused on cleaning, oblivious to the soot blending into her black pencil trousers and matching Danskin shirt, we picked up pebbles from her flower box and tossed them over the railing, hoping they'd fly above the white cement wall dividing our building from a row of burnt-out brownstones. Instead, they landed in our concrete backyard, where children played. A few kids pointed up at us, shouting, *Mira! Mira!*

Our father caught us. "What are you girls doing? You should know better. You could hurt someone."

Reprimanded, we sat down, covering our mouths to muffle our giggles. Our mother served tuna fish and tomato sandwiches on Pepperidge Farm bread, sliced in half. We tried to eat, but soot from incinerators burning day and night kept raining onto our food. Sighing, my mother brushed away the black ash, leaving a dark residue on the white bread. "Eat it anyway. I hate to waste food." A Depression baby, she always conserved. Plus, she had a laissez-faire attitude toward hygiene.

"Gross." Elizabeth pushed her plate away. "I'm not eating this."

"Me neither." I shoved my plate, too, mimicking my big sister.

Determined to utilize the terrace, my mother relented and made us new sandwiches, but the soot kept falling, so we decided to go inside. The construction exacerbated the city's already poor air quality.

My father tried to reassure us. "Pollution is bad today. But a thunderstorm's coming. It'll clear things up. We can try again tomorrow."

Happy to be living in Manhattan, my parents tolerated the foul air and constant drilling, rumbling, crashing construction cacophony, the background soundtrack of our lives for the next decade. They were committed to living in New York City and making it a better place for their daughters to grow up. My sister and I knew nothing else. We sprouted out of the cement along with the budding buildings in the neighborhood, cubist children with fractured, artistic sensibilities.

In 1967 the Public Health Service in Washington, DC, declared New York City to have "the most severe pollution problem of any metropolitan area in the nation."[10] In 1969, according to the New York Department of Air Resources, when the city began its daily air pollution index, not one day was labeled "good."[11] New York still burned garbage in incinerators, and it was routine to see smokestacks releasing black plumes of sulfur dioxide, smoke shade, and carbon monoxide.[12]

The flakes of black soot that drifted onto our terrace like snow were particulate matter comprised mostly of carbon and sulfur dioxide—the result of burning fossil fuels. The interior of our apartment was dirty, too, with black soot coating our windowsills, baseboard heaters, and the bottoms of our feet. The asthma I developed as a kid and still suffer from today might well have resulted from breathing in "suspended particulates . . . settling into the deep recesses of the lungs."[13]

If we Upper West Side kids had it bad, kids from the South Bronx had it worse, living and attending schools near waste transfer facilities and expressways to the suburbs—a result of funds from the inspired yet flawed 1949 Housing Act, which greatly expanded federal Whites-only mortgage insurance and public housing construction, aiding white flight and destroying Bronx neighborhoods. The unrelenting truck traffic spewed elemental carbon or black soot, exposure to which can increase the risk of asthma. To this day, "the Bronx has the highest age-adjusted asthma death rate among all counties in New York State: 43.5 deaths per million residents in the Bronx, as opposed to the state average of 13.1 deaths per million."[14]

In 1965, Tom Lehrer, a New York City singer-songwriter, wrote and performed his satirical song "Pollution":

Just go out for a breath of air
And you'll be ready for Medicare
The city streets are really quite a thrill
If the hoods don't get you, the monoxide will
Pollution, pollution!
Wear a gas mask and a veil

Then you can breathe
Long as you don't inhale!

In 1968, the musical *Hair* opened on Broadway. One of its many hit songs was "Air":

Welcome, sulfur dioxide
Hello, carbon monoxide
The air, the air
Is everywhere
Breathe deep
While you sleep
Breathe deep

The air in New York City was so bad that an activist hippie troupe staged a "soot-in" in front of Consolidated Edison, the local electric company, showering black mist and giving out befouled flowers.[15]

This was in the late 1960s before the Clean Air Act, the Environmental Protection Agency, and Earth Day were established, all in 1970. According to a 1992 EPA publication, Earth Day may have started with the first moon landing when astronauts took photos of the Earth, creating a new appreciation for the planet.[16] That perspective resonated with my father, who had a lifelong love of astronomy, and he taught my sister and me to prize and care for the planet as much as he did.

I jumped to reach #14 but hit the off switch instead. The elevator jerked to a halt halfway between the lobby and the second floor.

Crying, I banged on the gray metal panel until I saw Scott peer at me through the elevator window. "Don't worry, Jenny. The repairman's coming."

Eventually, the repairman arrived and fixed the problem. By then, a group of concerned cooperators had gathered with Scott to watch.

More often than not, it was a malfunction, not a misstep of mine, that caused the elevator to break down. Sometimes when both elevators on the 150 side were out of order, we took the elevators on the 160 side, got out on the fifteenth floor, climbed the staircase to the roof, and walked back to our side, descending the steps to our respective apartments. In the evening, folks returning from work streamed across the top, the roof as busy as the sidewalk.

When I was young, being alone up on the roof was magical, like a private world floating above the city, the rooftop wall low, the metallic and wood water towers like giant bells, the hazy sun softening the light, warming the cool concrete, masking the chimneys spewing black smoke. Sometimes the asphalt was sticky from the heat or icy from the cold, but always sooty. It was easy to get filthy up there. Even closing the door handle left a residue of grime.

It was remarkable we had roof access back then. That's how the robbers had broken in. I tried to imagine replicating the experience myself, stretching my small body so my legs or arms could hook onto the railing of the fifteenth-floor terrace, inching my way down onto ours, breaking open the flimsy lock. The second time we were robbed via the terrace, my father drilled a hole in the sliding door and inserted a removable nail as a barrier. After my father died, my mother, sister, and I guarded that nail, which had secured our home and reminded us of him.

Years later, while dismantling the apartment after my mother's death, I discovered that very same nail. I hadn't thought about keeping it until we had to turn over the apartment to the co-op board. Should I leave the nail for the next family so they too could be protected? Would they understand what it was for? Would they care?

I rolled the tiny, weathered silver nail back and forth with my fingers, then tossed it in my bag.

Chapter 2

∭

Community, Collectivism, and Tolerance

BECAUSE SO MANY kids from RNA attended P.S. 75, it was like an extension of life in the building. Together we walked down the hill to school on West End Avenue between 95th and 96th Street, a communal sea—Black, White, Puerto Rican, Asian, and all variations of mixed races. The gang—me, Elizabeth, Nina, Gina, Emily, Julie, Angela, Debbie, Dore, Robby, Gary, Carlos, Tom, Rosalinda, Clifford, Clyde, Peter, George, Benji, Lourdes—interacted at P.S. 75, returned home together, and were in and out of each other's apartments. We hung out in the staircases and hallways and held birthday parties in the community room with a piñata suspended from the ceiling. In the backyard, a wide-open area flanking the building, we cycled, roller-skated, played handball, tag, hopscotch, and double Dutch, and climbed on a space-age cement jungle gym.

The chauffeur to King Curtis, the blues, funk, and soul jazz saxophonist, lived at RNA House. While waiting to work, he double-parked his black Cadillac in front of the building and sauntered to the backyard, draped in an ankle-length white fur coat, a gold medallion, and sporting an Afro.

"Hey, it's the fur man," Dore said.

"Got any candy?" Gina called out.

The chauffeur tickled us in the stomach, reached into his pockets, and handed out chocolate kisses.

In the evening, mothers from the lower floors stuck their heads out their windows, calling kids home for supper. Our apartment was too high up to hear our mother, no matter how loud she cried. My cue to go home was when, through the broad lobby window, I glimpsed my father in his black suit and tie, leather briefcase in hand, unlocking the 150 side door. I tore into the lobby, and we hugged, then waited for the elevator.

On Halloween, my sister and I, clutching pillowcases and orange UNICEF boxes, set out door-to-door asking for change, merging with the hordes of kids trick or treating. We took over the hallways and staircases, marching around in our mothers' homemade costumes, a merry band of pranksters. Tenants invited us in to marvel at our getups and gave us too much candy.

We weren't always angels. Sometimes we threw apples, viewed as expendable, down the stairs, making a mess for the adults to clean later. When we got home, our parents didn't bother to inspect our goods, unconcerned about razors or poisoned candy.

When torrential downpours clogged the drains, flooding the slanted sidewalk at Amsterdam and 96th Street, we rolled up our jeans, kicked off our Keds, and took to the street barefoot, wading in the knee-deep water, side-stepping syringes and coke cans, free, fearless in our murky neighborhood seashore.

I dipped my hand in the water, foraging for coins.

"Got one." Stuffing it in my pocket, dipping down for more, I collected a dollar in change and went upstairs to show my mother.

"Put it in your piggy bank," she said, kissing me.

After Nixon went on his historic China trip to open up relations with the Communist regime, the Chinese champion Ping-Pong players toured the US, performing at P.S. 75, part of Ping-Pong diplomacy engineered by Mao Zedong. The entire school assembled in the auditorium to watch the champions play. Standing far from the table, the players dazzled us, bouncing the ball back and forth quickly and rhythmically, like a mechanized dance. When we cheered, they backed up even further. Soon after, a P.S. 75 teacher who lived at RNA set up a community Ping-Pong table in the backyard, on loan from the Riverside Table Tennis Courts, Marty Reisman's Ping-Pong Palace on 96th Street between Broadway and West End Avenue, near P.S. 75. We rushed home after school, stood in line to take turns, and taught ourselves how to play. Even the adults joined in.

We RNA House kids were in and out of other neighborhood Mitchell-Lamas, especially 711 Amsterdam Avenue, officially called Goddard

Towers, a massive redbrick and cement middle-income co-op on Amsterdam between 94th and 95th, built, as was RNA, in 1967 during Stage I of the West Side Urban Renewal Area plan. We went to visit our P.S. 75 friends who lived there and to hear neighborhood concerts by the African drumming circle and the Jazzmobile.

Over the years, I lost touch with my 711 friends, so when I wanted to interview them for this book, I put out a call to my Facebook groups *Growing Up on the Old Upper West Side* (10,000+ members), and *Upper West Side Natives* (4,000+ members). At the time, I was living in Arizona because my husband, Jacob, was teaching at Arizona State University. Many of the members came of age in the '60s and '70s, as did I, and yearn for a time when our beloved neighborhood was funky, affordable, bohemian, and communal. They, like me, are left bereft, spiritually homeless, longing for the sense of community we once had. Those who've remained on the Upper West Side understand its transformation. Few perceive the change as positive.

Folks lucky enough to grow up in Mitchell-Lama housing enjoyed a collective Upper West Side experience. I didn't find my old 711 friends on Facebook, but I made some new ones, albeit virtually, people with whom I must've mingled, shared backyards, schools, stores, public spaces, and streets.

The themes that emerged during the interviews with original 711 co-operators were their diverse backgrounds and how they valued integration and went to local public schools. Jill Bargonetti's family moved into 711 in 1967 when she was five:

> My father is a first-generation Italian American, and my mother is descended from African slaves on both sides. There were beautiful, integrated playgroups. On Halloween, twenty-seven floors of kids all trick or treated together, knocking on doors. CANDY!!! I loved the neighborhood. It was contiguous with Harlem. It was great, not fashionable like it is today. I remember in front of the building finding the most special thin and lovely paper. I sprayed it with perfume and took it to P.S. 75 to give to my favorite teacher. I didn't realize it was rolling paper for marijuana until years later when talking with my mother about how wonderful my teacher was. Haha . . . There were lots of people doing drugs in the 711 backyard, but I did not see this. I saw wonderful community and home. Being mixed-race, growing up in Upper West Side Mitchell-Lama housing with other mixed-race families, and attending public schools with diverse populations helped me navigate different worlds.

Elissa Vecchione Scott's father is also a first-generation Italian American, born in New Jersey to immigrant parents. Her mother is an Irish Canadian from Newfoundland and did not become an American citizen until Elissa was an adult:

> My parents still live in 711, and I still call it home, although I have been in Oregon for twenty-plus years. We moved in when I was twelve–eighteen months old. My father worked at the *New York Times* and said the housing writer there told him about the Mitchell-Lama program. The demographics were very heterogeneous. We all played together, and we were like one big family, separated by age levels, but everyone got along. We walked to P.S. 75 together, and our mothers protested education budget cuts by blocking traffic. When we went outside, we used the lobby buzzer system to communicate with each other and our parents. My favorite memory was roller skating with other girls in the building in the 1970s. We were allowed to go in front of the building between 94th and 95th and could only go "up the block" on 94th to the end of the building property, and we were not allowed to cross Amsterdam Avenue.

Another theme to surface from these interviews was the connection between Jewish cooperators and the labor movement, which not only advocated for better living conditions but also sponsored and built co-op housing as an alternative to slummy, crowded tenements. Hilary Roberts's father, Seymour Roberts, was a union organizer:

> My father was also a Freedom Rider, going into the Deep South on interstate buses to protest segregated transportation. Trained as an engineer, he was a major player in getting the building built, which took eight years, and he made sure those displaced by construction got first dibs on new apartments. My dad moved us out of the Bronx because he said it was unrealistic to live in an all-White Jewish neighborhood. So, he chose the Upper West Side. I was ten when we moved in. I think many people I knew at 711 had come from an "outer" borough. The Bronx was where Jews moved upon leaving the Lower East Side as they assimilated.

Laurie Nelson's family moved into 711 on June 5, 1967, the day the Six-Day War broke out:

> My parents were Ashkenazi Jews, second generation, middle class, both from Brooklyn. My dad ran a labor union and was the president

of the Riverside Democrats. All very "pink diaper" progressive, so I think the chance to move to Mitchell-Lama Co-ops was common knowledge in my folks' circles. First, from 1956–61, when I was very young, we lived on the Lower East Side in East River Houses, a middle-income rental built by the AFL-CIO—now known as The Grand Street Co-ops. Then we moved to Seward Park Houses, also AFL-CIO, I believe.

Like Hilary, she noted that her parents also relocated to the Upper West Side for its diversity:

We left there in 1967 because my parents thought the neighborhood was too White, LOL. They wanted their kids to grow up in a more diverse neighborhood. Also 711 Amsterdam presented a buy opportunity that wasn't available then on the Lower East Side. The joke, of course, was that soon after we left Seward Park, the area became more diverse, and after we moved to the Upper West Side, it progressively became less diverse and more gentrified.

In contrast to Jill, Elissa, and Hilary, Laurie identified a social hierarchy among playgroups at 711:

When I first moved in, the demographics were totally heterogeneous. The apartments below the seventh or eighth floors were more subsidized, and generally the kids, almost exclusively minorities, who lived there played apart, but other than that, my entire social life was kids in the building. No hostility in any case that I recall. There were plenty of minority families on the middle and upper tower floors as well, but interestingly all my friends who were minorities were from the upper floors—more middle-class. My closest friend in the building was a Black guy, John, whose father, John R. Strachan, was the first African American Postmaster of New York City. I don't recall that there were separate areas in the playground where people hung out in different groups, but I simply know that the diverse gangs of kids I hung out with hardly ever included anyone from the lower floors. So maybe that says that there were class divisions without racial divisions. Who the hell knows?

I replied that RNA House also had apartments on the lower floors with skewed designation, but it didn't affect who we played with. Apparently, some Orthodox Jewish families lived in second- and third-floor skewed apartments because they wanted to be Shabbos observant and walk up and down stairs rather than take the elevator.

Meeting these 711 folks lifted a heaviness and satisfied a longing in me, especially living in Arizona, where I had few friends, felt isolated in car-dependent suburbia, and was a political and cultural outsider. They reinforced that my experience growing up in RNA house wasn't a mirage. It was a unique, united existence—one that's been almost impossible to replicate, at least in terms of housing.

We spent time with Latino kids from the old-law tenements across the street on the north side of 96th, which had somehow escaped renovation. These were next door to a Mitchell-Lama tower housing a methadone clinic, where a long line of addicts waited for their compromised fix. Ivan, from Cuba, lived on the ground floor; we climbed through his kitchen window to play with him, as well as Fernando from Ecuador and Frederico from the Dominican Republic.

The boys visited us in our backyard, too. I borrowed Ivan's bicycle. He was older and taller than me, and his bike was too big. It didn't matter. If he could do it, so could I.

I hefted the bike and climbed on. "*Mírame, mírame,*" I said, showing off my newly acquired Spanish. "*Me gusta.*"

"*Cuidado,*" Ivan yelled, but I crashed anyway into a bolt on the metal jungle gym and fell on the cement.

As I stared vacantly up at the kids and the building cranes high above, someone said, "*¿Tu estás* okay?"

I thought I was fine. I stood up and got on the bike again, but Ivan stopped me. He checked my head and saw a bloody gash on one side. Before I knew it, a group of kids was examining me. By committee, the gang decided I had to go to the hospital. Emily buzzed the intercom to summon my family. My mother and sister came down, and my dad drove the car out front. We piled in and were off to the hospital.

I was never alone at 96th Street. Even though I grew up on cement, in a harsh, polluted environment, I was nurtured by the people around me, an integrated tolerant group who played by a different set of rules.

The backyard was nearly empty, only a few older tenants mingling on a cement bench near the lobby, and I was bored. I climbed the jungle gym, straddling the curves and negative spaces of a concrete structure resembling the two-pronged Danish modern cutlery my parents bought for special occasions. I wore my customary tomboy outfit—jeans and Mets T-shirt, with my hair in pigtails and feet in Keds. Lourdes showed up in her Catholic schoolgirl uniform—blue sweater over a white blouse, plaid skirt barely covering her butt, and knee-high white socks, along with black-and-white Oxfords, a gold headband, and pink rhinestone earrings, her only distinguishing wardrobe features. She went to Holy Name Catholic School, attached to the church, catty-corner from RNA on 96th and Amsterdam.

She climbed onto a small cement slab and, standing with her hands on her hips, asked: "Do you believe in God?"

"No." I mounted an adjacent metal cylinder and perched on the rim. "Do you?"

She nodded. "You're going to hell," she said.

"What do you mean?"

"If you don't believe in God, you'll go to hell. Everybody knows that."

I didn't. It was the first I'd ever heard of it.

"My mother knows it, my father knows it, my brothers know it, my *abuelita* knows it."

Skeptical, I said: "I'm going to ask my mother."

I leaped down onto the concrete and went upstairs.

My mother was making hamburgers in our tiny kitchen, Walter Cronkite was discussing the aftermath of the Munich Olympics massacre, and my sister was lying on the couch, legs crossed, reading *The Phantom Tollbooth*.

My mother formed raw kosher ground meat into clumps, stuffed them into ramekins, and gave one to each of us. I stood next to her on a stool, nibbling away. "If I don't believe in God, will I go to hell?"

My mother, chopping onions, said, "What are you talking about?"

"Lourdes said we'd go to hell if we don't believe."

"That's her opinion. It's not what we think."

"What do we think?"

"We don't believe in God. This is true for us. Lourdes believes in God and that she'll go to hell if she loses faith. This is true for her."

"How can both be true?"

"I could say what we believe is true and what she believes is false, but life doesn't work this way," my mother said.

"But she's certain."

"I'm certain, too."

I accepted the answer and stared out the glass terrace door. There I saw Christina, also in a Catholic schoolgirl uniform, jumping at her apartment window in the tall brick, prewar building facing ours, her blonde pigtails bouncing up and down. *There she goes again*, I thought. Growing up, I was fascinated by Christina's perpetual peculiar habit. After a while, I plopped down next to my sister and devoured the raw meat.

My mother and Kaila, sweaty in T-shirts and jeans, pushed carts full of big cartons overflowing with fruits and vegetables into the RNA laundry room, a windowless box with dreary gray walls, droning industrial-sized washing machines and fans, an alcove with a couple of stacked bookshelves that acted as an informal lending library, and a bathroom lacking toilet paper. My mother and Kaila were childhood friends from Crown Heights, Brooklyn, back then a mostly White, Jewish neighborhood, and had moved into RNA House at the same time. I became instant best friends with Kaila's daughter, Nina. When Nina's father was a baby, he escaped Hitler's Berlin with his family at the very last moment, landing on Manhattan's Upper West Side. Her father and mine also formed a close friendship.

Before dawn, our mothers had driven up to Hunts Point Terminal Market in the Bronx, buying fruits, vegetables, and meat from wholesalers. They were members of a fifteen-woman food co-op, including those living in other neighborhood Mitchell-Lamas and brownstones, who took turns shopping for the group. When the shoppers returned, they used the RNA laundry room to distribute food. The members purchased basic food items from a set list—lettuce, carrots, bananas, apples—and were allowed to buy two more items not on the list.

Women of all colors, shapes, and sizes lined up, chatting, milling about, and riffling through library books from the laundry room's exchange library bookshelves.

"What's this?" Kaila sniffed an unrecognizable leafy green vegetable, then handed it to Nicole, a tall and regal woman in a full-length African print dress, her natural hair styled into an Angela Davis afro.

"Arugula," Nicole said, putting it in her tote bag.

While the bevy of cooperators waited for their weekly allotments, Nina, Angela, and I climbed in and out of oversized washing machines and dryers, played Jacks on the floor, or ran up and down the hallway, laughing and crashing into other kids. After all the members claimed their food, an outside group of women bought the remainder at a slightly higher price.

In addition to the food co-op, Kaila and my mother were also part of a nighttime babysitting co-op with RNA House women, who distributed index cards as money and paid each other using this neighborly economy. My parents had an active social life, going out every weekend, which they could afford because they had a community, a support system.

Kaila was my favorite and most frequent babysitter, though I was a pain in the ass.

"Time to go to sleep," Kaila would say.

"No." Dressed in my Snoopy nightshirt, I perched on the brown Papa Bear chair, refusing to budge. Kaila, who wore a flower print caftan, hemline above the knee, her hands on her slim hips, stood in the hallway at the edge of the living room, irritated.

"I'm not kidding, Jenny."

I crossed my arms in defiance. This exchange continued until Kaila had enough. She grabbed my T-shirt and dragged me down the hallway to the bedroom I shared with my sister. I was on better behavior with the other sitters, but Kaila was like a second mother to me, so I felt comfortable acting out.

After my mother died, Kaila told me that once when a co-op member babysat at her apartment, the woman commented, *When I looked inside your refrigerator, I knew you were rich.* "This made me so mad. I remember it to this day. Fifty years later."

Class divisions did exist at RNA, but they were minimized. People got apartments according to the size of their families, not because money bought them a bigger space. Maintenance was based on income, with the more affluent paying a surcharge and the lower-income paying public housing rates. Those with incomes either too high or too low didn't qualify to live in Mitchell-Lama housing.

RNA House cooperators also acted collectively in other ways, bringing down prices by making group purchases of dishwashers, stoves, refrigerators, and air conditioners. My father was elected to the board of directors, which formed committees to manage the garden, cleaning, garbage, and each floor in the building. He lobbied unsuccessfully to allow tricycle storage in the hallways outside the apartments rather than the already jampacked bicycle room, and he negotiated the hours kids could play in the backyard, appeasing the older folk who objected to noise. Conflicts arose at RNA, but they weren't based on race, religion, or sexual preference.

My mother, sister, and I came downstairs headed for P.S. 75, my mother carrying a sleeping bag, pillow, and small suitcase. There we met Kaila and Nina, Kaila also toting supplies to spend the night so our mothers could occupy the school to keep it open during the 1968 NYC Teachers' Strike. The strike was the largest in American history, involving sixty thousand teachers and directly affecting residents at 96th Street.[1] Both my sister's teacher, mine, and Nina's opposed the walkout and wanted to hold classes in the school.

The strike came about over the "local control" issue in the public schools, stemming primarily from the Black community's perception that the White power structure was not providing an adequate education for its children, which was certainly true: The black community felt it could do a much better job if they controlled school districts in which they were the majority. A pilot district in Ocean-Hill Brownsville, Brooklyn, formed to pave the way for decentralizing the school system, fired teachers (mostly Jewish) and replaced them with Black teachers. The United Federation of Teachers was hostile to community control, fearing the union would be undermined. During the strike, an anonymous anti-Semitic flyer was placed in the mailboxes of some Brooklyn teachers, referring to Jewish educators as "Blood-sucking Exploiters and Murderers" who taught Black children 'Self-Hatred.'"[2]

When we walked outside, we saw cooperators with linked arms on the RNA House steps, blockading the main lobby to prevent a group of teachers who supported the strike from gaining access to the community room as they'd done during a previous strike. This time RNA House was off-limits. Progressives at RNA objected to how the union thwarted the local school boards, pitting Blacks and Jews, teachers and parents against one another. The strike also marked the beginning of the deteriorating relations between the Black and Jewish communities, historical allies.

As the teachers tried to push through the blockade, Black and Jewish protestors chanted, "Don't divide us, don't divide us."

We got caught up in the shoving, and I almost fell, but my mother caught me and whisked us away to the eastern entrance of the building. Somehow, in the chaos, we lost Kaila and Nina.

"What's going on?" I asked, scared and confused.

"It's complicated, honey." My mother put her arm around me. "The strike is divisive. Black people and Jewish people in the city are fighting."

She pointed at the blockade. "Our neighbors are trying to stop the fight, but I don't like their extreme tactics, whatever the cause."

When my mother first told me about this, I expected her to side with the union, as she always did. But in this case, the union wanted control over communities it was serving poorly, so she was against it. "It was counterintuitive for progressives to be against unions," my mother explained. "But in those days, unions were discriminating against Blacks by keeping them out of well-paying jobs as construction workers, police officers, and firefighters. And the unions supported the Vietnam War."

My parents were politicized by these group actions. Instead of living in a typical New York City building where tenants were isolated from one another, they belonged to a community where the collective action of the building's residents underpinned their everyday experiences, shaping their lives inside the building, their worldviews, and their approach to society.

My life, too, was profoundly influenced by my collectivist, integrationist experiences, a time when my family was unbroken, as was our community. I didn't realize my circumstances were unique until I went to private school and met kids who didn't have friends in their buildings or backyards. While I desired their luxury, I didn't envy their isolation.

Chapter 3

On the Street

THE EGALITARIAN PRINCIPLES we lived by in the building often didn't apply when we walked through the lobby door, out into the street. Once our gang of kids turned seven or eight, we went to P.S. 75 unescorted. On the "pervert block" between Amsterdam and Broadway, Nina and I held hands and avoided eye contact with the Puerto Rican men who sat on tenement stoops calling out, *Mamacita puta, muy bonita madre, dame beso* (Mama whore, very pretty mother, give me a kiss). When we got to Broadway, we hurried across before the light turned red so we wouldn't get stuck with the heroin addicts nodding off on the island in the middle of the boulevard.

Sometimes Nina and I ran into Ernest, a skinny, short Black boy with mischievous eyes who lived in the Frederick Douglass Houses, a mammoth public housing development run by the New York City Housing Authority (NYCHA), spanning 100th to 104th Street between Columbus and Manhattan Avenue, just four blocks north of RNA House. He carried a book of matches, which he struck and thrust at our faces. We weren't afraid of him because the flames flickered out before they reached us, and his taunting seemed more like a cry for attention than a threat.

"Can I try?" I asked Ernest.

Surprised, he handed the matches over to me. I struggled over and over again to light it.

"Let me show you," Ernest said.

He patiently demonstrated. After that, he became our friend, and we finished the last leg of our journey down the hill to school together.

Much scarier than Ernest were the tough girls who tried to mug us at lunch.

With fifty cents in our pockets, Nina and I walked up the hill to get pizza at Sal's. As we turned onto Broadway, we saw two big Black girls approaching. "Yo, White bitch," one of them yelled at us. "Give me your money."

"C'mon," Nina cried, and we ran across the street. Cars braked and horns honked, but we made it. So did the girls who were chasing us. Terrified, we escaped into FOWAD, a discount clothing store with a Peter Max balloon-style sign in front.

"What's the matter?" the salesperson, a tall skinny guy in brown polyester pants and a beige dress shirt, asked in a Puerto Rican accent.

Nina pointed at the door. "These girls want to mug us."

"Lemme go see."

We hid among the seconds hanging from racks taller than I was, clutching the fabric, covering our faces, while the guy watched from the glass door.

Finally, he turned. "The coast is clear," he said. "You can go now."

Sherée, a large Black girl with pigtails, did beat me up. At the time, being punched in the gut seemed normal, part of the landscape outside RNA House. It happened while our class was walking through the vast fluorescent-lit P.S. 75 hallways to the gym. A tiny girl, I was situated at the front of the line; Ms. Rubinger, the overwhelmed yet dedicated teacher, a bandana tied around her fly-away brown hair, was in the back, nudging the stragglers.

It was then that Sherée swaggered up to me.

I knew what was coming.

"I'm gonna hit you," she said, and belted me in the stomach.

I crumpled, gasping.

Nina ran over and lifted me up. "You okay, Jen?"

From then on, Nina left her position in line and walked by my side so Sherée wouldn't touch me. Nina was bigger, stronger, and tougher than me, but not by that much. Still, her presence was enough to dissuade Sherée.

Nina and I took guitar lessons after school and wrote a song, "Hey Little Boy," based on our lives, with the lyrics:

Hey Little Boy
Don't Go Out at Night
Ya might get into a Big Fat Fight
Your mama's a warnya
Mama's a warnya

Not to go out at night.
Get into a big fat fight

Hey Little Boy
Our papa wants you home soon
He said it at noon.
If you stay out at night, gonna get into a big fat fight

We made the song about a boy instead of a girl because we realized early on that we had to be tough like boys, that boys had the advantage, wielded power, and controlled the streets. We were tomboys, so we dressed like boys in T-shirts, patched jeans, and Keds, and even invented *The Boy Test* to turn into them. Nina changed her name to Michael after Michael Jackson, then of the Jackson Five, and I changed my name to Jerry, after Nina's brother and because it only required replacing two letters.

Unattended, we trained after school at Riverside Park, a skinny strip of landscaped trees and grass running north-south along Riverside Drive, adjacent to the West Side Highway and the Hudson River. To get to the greenery, Nina and I navigated through the reeking underpass at 96th Street, where drunken bums slept and defecated. Avoiding dog shit, tying our long brown hair, Nina's darker and thicker than mine, into ponytails, we timed our sprints with Snoopy watches as we ran faster and faster, jumping over a black wrought-iron fence leading into the playground.

We practiced in each other's apartment to Helen Reddy's hit song "I am Woman" and Marlo Thomas's *Free to Be . . . You and Me* album, the soundtrack to our regime.

I timed Nina as she did push-ups, with "Parents Are People" playing in the background:

Some mommies are ranchers, or poetry makers
Or doctors or teachers, or cleaners or bakers
Some mommies drive taxis, or sing on TV
Yeah, mommies can be almost anything they want to be

When we felt ready to take *The Boy Test*, we climbed up the cement wall in our building's backyard, walked across the ledge and climbed down, did ten push-ups and ten sit-ups, and leaped from one concrete barrier to another, all within a certain time limit, like a triathlon, as the RNA girl gang—Emily, Julie, Elizabeth, Gina, Angela, and Debbie—cheered us on.

We both passed and felt ready to take on the world—at least momentarily.

It was the '70s, and we grew up in a milieu that empowered women and girls. At the time, Kaila attended consciousness-raising groups; around the corner on Amsterdam Avenue, bookstores *Woman Books* and *Black Books* both opened.

Still, we realized it wasn't enough to be a girl with power. We needed to *be* boys.

At P.S. 75, I became friends with Gwendolyn, a Black girl who was small like me, who lived in a nine-story, redbrick NYCHA building on West 94th between Columbus and Amsterdam. Its lobby's institutional tawny-beige tiles and tiny barred window were like a mini version of our school. One day, Gwen came over to my house, and we wandered the neighborhood, past the 96th Street methadone clinic and into an old-fashioned candy store housed in a not yet bulldozed tenement on Columbus Avenue. A lunch counter with green stools and a soda fountain featured egg creams. Hair and body potions, along with hard candies, were displayed in rows of glass bottles. Gwen and I handed the clerk ten cents for a paper bag, each full of candy.

From there, we milled about inside *The Storefront*, the political action co-op in the storefront of an abandoned building on the corner of 95th and Columbus, started by a local activist group committed to social justice and against "the establishment." The activists broke in, painted the walls, brought in old couches, hacked into ConEd and Ma Bell to get power and phone service, and squatted there. They sold fresh fruit and vegetables, printed a newspaper, wore "Free the Panthers" buttons, did guerilla theater on the street, acted out political plays, marched against the Vietnam War, and organized bus trips to DC to join anti-war protests.[1]

A tie-dyed squatter in patched jeans, hairband taming her long brown tresses, handed us anti-war flyers, directing, "Give this to your parents."

Just as we were walking out, we were spotted by Gwen's mother sporting a double-breasted brown trench coat, kinky hair ironed straight.

"What are you doing out here?" she said to Gwen. "Never, *ever* go out on these streets alone. You hear me?"

Gwen looked down and nodded.

Her mother turned to me. "Where's your mother?"

"Home."

"Let's go talk to her." She grabbed Gwen's arm and yanked her around the corner as I ran to catch up. When we got upstairs, my mother invited them in, but Gwen's mother refused, only asking that I find Gwen's back-pack and bring it to her, announcing, "I don't approve of my daughter walking these streets alone."

"I respect that," my mother said, straightening her dashiki.

"If the girls play again, it'll be at my house."

After they left, my mother hugged me. "I can understand why Gwen's mom is extra protective. She probably has more experience with violence than we do. She feels Gwen is more vulnerable because she's Black."

I sort of understood what my mother was saying. I thought of the angry girls who tried to mug us. I didn't feel particularly safe either.

"I think it's fine for you to go out alone, honey." She kissed me, adding, "As long as you don't wander too far."

Looking back, I often wonder about my parents' laissez-faire attitude toward their kids roaming the streets. I guess they felt we were part of the fabric of the city, owned the streets as much as anyone else, and saw little reason to inhibit our behavior. We never got hurt, though we certainly brushed up against danger. We learned to be street smart, becoming ex-posed to all kinds of things—like the time I found out about Holocaust tattoos.

I walked into a cramped, dusty shoe repair store on Amsterdam Avenue somewhere in the nineties to pick up shoes for my father. A small, bald cobbler, his wire-framed glasses emphasizing the bags under his tired eyes, hobbled over. "How may I help you?" he asked in thickly accented English.

I handed him a ticket. Searching the shelves, he returned with black leather penny loafers, placing them tips forward on the counter, carefully shining them one last time. It was then that I noticed the serial numbers tattooed in thick black ink on the underside of his spotted, wrinkly left forearm. He caught me staring and pointed. "Do you know what this is?"

I shook my head.

He moved his arm closer. "From Auschwitz. I was a prisoner. To keep track of us."

I remained silent, unsure what to say, not completely understanding. I knew what the Holocaust was. How could I not? In the 1970s, the subject was a constant backdrop on the Upper West Side of Manhattan, home to a large Jewish survivor community, like Nina's father's family, as well as earlier waves of Jewish émigrés, like my own. Survivors were visible on the street, sitting together on the benches on the Broadway island, kibitzing, reading the *Times* or the *Forward*, or just alone with their thoughts.

He slid the shoes forward to me. "Your father should wear them well."

I handed him some money, grabbed the loafers, pushed through the heavy glass door, and ran home.

A few days later, my friends and I chewed bubblegum in the backyard. We unwrapped *Magoo Tattoos*, licked them, and pressed them onto the top of our hands so they would stick.

Upstairs, showing off my design, I asked my mother what she thought of real tattoos. Not a good idea, she said, because it wasn't removable. "What if you choose something you like now, but change your mind? You're stuck with it forever."

I thought of how the Holocaust survivor in the shoe store was stuck with his numbers forever. From then on, I never wanted a real tattoo.

Only after leaving New York did I realize how lucky I was to have such rich, meaningful encounters growing up. Not that no one has a story in Phoenix, a city of refugees, immigrants, brave border-crossing children, and myriad other varieties of humanity. It's the suburban sprawl. Isolation of identical single-family homes. Strip-mall soullessness. Wide streets made for cars not people. No spontaneous exchange.

In the 1970s, New York City's overall financial health deteriorated. The city no longer provided adequate services and lost population, with large numbers of Whites escaping to the suburbs. Cracked pavement riddled with potholes defined streets lined with derelict boarded-up buildings. Arson fires burned throughout the South Bronx. Crime was endemic, and public schools were underfunded, overcrowded, and dangerous. The poorly maintained subways became scary and unsafe. Colorful graffiti on the outside of the cars turned menacing on the inside, with black tags and scratches defacing grimy walls, windows, and doors. Violent crime grew so prevalent that transit police barred passengers from riding in the back cars at night. This didn't stop ordinary New Yorkers like us from taking the subway. In fact, as a rite of passage, for the first time, at age nine, Nina and I took the 2 train at 96th Street and Broadway unchaperoned to Macy's and back.

The neighborhood was so blighted back then that when the first Manhattan McDonald's opened in 1972, two blocks away from RNA on Broadway between 95th and 96th Street near Off Track Betting (OTB), the event was cause for celebration. Even though it drizzled, we lined up to get in; festive salsa music blasting from cheap transistor radios clutched by people in line entertained us as we waited. For the Upper West Side, known for its Cuban-Chinese, Kosher, Middle Eastern, Italian, Greek, and Irish restaurants, Jewish refugees who'd escaped Hitler and pogroms, stoned junkies, muggings, the deinstitutionalized mentally ill living in single-room occupancy hotels (SROs), art film aficionados at the Thalia, Cuban musicians, artists, actors, crooks, prostitutes, political activists, grape boycotters, alcoholics, eccentrics, graffiti, sidewalks carpeted with broken glass, dog shit, and litter, McDonald's was the neighborhood's first taste of Americana.[2]

We couldn't wait to eat a hamburger, fries, and milkshake on "tables sprayed with ammonia by brown-uniformed employees,"[3] wearing triangle-shaped hats atop their heads. "Don't you see," *New York Times* reporter John Darnton wrote, quoting a resident about McDonald's opening, "for us, this is exotic!"[4]

Fellow RNA resident Betty, with whose children, Emily and George, we played, said, "That year for Hanukah, I gave the kids McDonald's coupons for one of those endless eight nights!"

Nina and I often went there during our P.S. 75 lunch break. Weight-conscious from an early age, I ordered a plain hamburger, forgoing the bun, and ate only the meat. When I was two, I was so chubby that my pediatrician put me on a skim milk diet. By nine years old, I'd slimmed down, but I still monitored my weight. It's hard to believe I considered a plain McDonald's hamburger a special treat.

Two years later, after my father died suddenly and my mother went back to school, then work, she devoted much less time to cooking. Often, we ate Chinese takeout, but occasionally she brought home McDonald's for dinner. No one I knew conceived back then that fast food was unhealthy. According to the 1972 *Times* article, McDonald's served "100 percent prime beef."[5] Today, seeing a McDonald's in a neighborhood does not signal wealth, much less health. Likewise, no one conceived that McDonald's would be a sign of things to come on the Upper West Side, where much of what made the neighborhood vibrant is now gone, replaced by chain stores and banks. It was an odd mix of sanitation, Americana, and fast food translating into gentrification.

When RNA House first opened, it was unprotected. We roller-skated and bicycled around the building, circling the front, sides, and backyard.

Next door, 733 Amsterdam Avenue, a moderate-rent twenty-eight-story Mitchell-Lama tower built in 1971, also known as New Amsterdam, loomed over RNA House's backyard on the 160 side, with a concrete wall separating our building from theirs. The kids in this tower threw stones at us from their second-floor plaza.

"Do you have any memory of kids from your building hurling rocks from your backyard onto ours?" I asked Yvette Marsh, a Facebook group member who grew up at 733.

"No, but I do remember the eggs. Kids tossed them into your yard and onto the street."

"Oh yeah, the eggs." I laughed.

"Did we know each other?" Yvette said.

"Maybe. When did you move in?"

"In 1972 when I was twelve, with my mother. Before we lived in a tenement on 89th Street. We couldn't believe how lucky we were to live at 733. We could see the Hudson River from our terrace. Just amazing. We felt rich. LOL. My mother left Puerto Rico for Florida, and then, at eighteen, moved to New York City to work in a zipper-making factory. She fell sick young and had to go on welfare. We thought we were middle-class. We never wanted for anything. Back then the government really helped a lot."

"It was a different world," I said.

Rust Brown, a jazz club at 733 Amsterdam Avenue, was popular with Knicks stars. At night, when we played in front, we saw Walt Frazier, Willis Reed, and Earl "The Pearl" Monroe hanging out smoking and drinking on RNA's west side steps in their fancy velvet, wide-lapel suits. We inched closer, stealing glances, gaping in awe at their greatness and "The Pearl's" two-toned blue Rolls Royce. They nodded and smiled back in acknowledgment.

"Whatcha doing up so late? It's dangerous out here!"

We laughed, ran away, and dared each other to go back. Julie had the guts. "Whatcha doing smoking cigarettes?" she blurted.

They chuckled and shook their heads.

Eventually, a fence strung with razor wire was constructed for security. "Some of us are turned off by the word 'fence.' But most often a fence is used as an enclosure of a beautiful garden or around a beautiful house," stated an RNA newsletter, justifying the barrier's exclusivity. The newsletter also reminded cooperators "to close the lobby door as you enter or leave the building and not to answer the buzzer indiscriminately," perhaps partially due to Nina, Angela, and me tormenting our neighbors by buzzing them over and over again. This was before RNA House had 24-hour guard protection. (The newsletter also mentioned that it was now illegal to smoke cigarettes in New York City elevators.)

The neighborhood hadn't gotten more dangerous; our apartment had already been broken into twice, the building vandalized, and litter strewn about the premises. Rather, RNA House cooperators finally acted upon the city's perils. The building became safer but more fortress-like, and the tenement kids could no longer access the backyard.

One spring evening, when the light in the sky lingered late, I helped my father carry his homemade turquoise telescope—bigger than me and almost as large as he was—downstairs. My father was physically weak, born with a congenital heart defect in 1928, way before there were advances in open-heart surgery. Growing up, he was badly advised not to exert himself. Subsequently, he was unable to strengthen his body and was frailer than other adults. He warned my mother that most of the men in his family died young from heart problems, and he expected to suffer the same fate, thus preparing her for the inevitable. She did her best to ignore his grim prediction.

Told not to build muscle, his strength resided in his brain. He was a brilliant mathematician, mechanical engineer, and astrophysicist, his shelves crammed with hardcover books, all inscribed with his name and date, such as *Why Smash Atoms?* by Arthur K. Solomon, with a black-and-white photograph of a mushroom cloud adorning the cover, and *Aerodynamics*, by F.W. Lanchester, with chapters entitled "Wing Form and Motion in the Periphery" and "The Hydrodynamics of Analytical Theory." Another book in his collection, *Two or Three Lines from Sketch Books of Chen Chi*, he inscribed to my mother, *For Judy, Just because, Love, Charles, April 1970.*

We lugged the telescope out of the elevator into the lobby and saw dark short-haired Frederico, who lived in a tenement across the street, telling the guard. "I want to play in the back."

"You don't live here."

He fidgeted, twisting his Mets cap. "Julie invited me."

"That so? Where is she?"

Frederico started to walk toward the back door.

"Where you going, man? You gotta leave."

My dad stepped in. "It's okay. He's with us." He motioned for Frederico to follow and the three of us moved to the front of the building. My dad found a good spot. He set up the lens and showed us how to focus it. The wind swept the smog away, the night was clear, and the full moon rose. A sea of kids from RNA House and the neighborhood gathered and formed a line. One by one we gazed at the stars, urban children in our concrete sidewalk wilderness.

Chapter 4

Breathing Life into the Sanitized Columbus Avenue Strip

AFTER ELEMENTARY SCHOOL, our cohesive RNA House gang broke up because our local junior high, Joan of Arc, was notoriously dangerous. Kids had knives, and one time someone threw a file cabinet out the window. A neighborhood friend heard that some girls came to Joan of Arc with a bullwhip and attacked a teacher. "I have no idea whether that story was true or apocryphal," she said. "But it was enough to scare those who had other options." Many RNA kids like Emily, Julie, Dore, and Robbie took the subway to public schools around Manhattan. Angela moved out, and we lost touch. Parents like my own, who'd become prosperous—my dad changing from professor to mechanical engineer—sent their kids to private school, though my mother was reluctant.

A firm believer in public education, and later a renowned New York City public education advocate, my mother would've preferred we stay in the public school system, but my father convinced her otherwise. She succumbed to the temptation because she could afford to and didn't want my sister and me to pay for the chaotic conditions prevailing at cash-starved public schools. In the 1970s, "the city laid off 11,000 teachers, or one fifth of the workforce. . . . The school week was shortened by 90 minutes, class sizes grew, sports and after-school programs were eliminated, and school-based dental and medical clinics closed. Art and music teachers, guidance counselors, and school librarians were let go."[1] Private school was a form of White flight for those remaining within city limits, driven by both fear and necessity.

We weren't kicked out from RNA House for becoming well-off, but we were required to pay a surcharge on our maintenance. This was a good deal for everyone, as the extra money helped finance the upkeep of the building and preserve the skewed maintenance for low-income cooperators.

In 1971, before the competition to get into private school during junior high became fierce, my sister enrolled in fifth grade at Columbia Grammar and Preparatory School (CGPS). Two years later, Nina and I started fifth grade there. Other RNA kids went, too: Nina's brother, Jerry, and Gina and her brother, Peter.

My parents chose the school because of its proximity. Nestled between two connected buildings off Central Park West between 93rd and 94th Street, the lower school in a beautiful brownstone, the upper in a nondescript low-rise, the walk was quick and easy. Another reason was its progressive philosophy. Established by Columbia University in 1764 and independent by 1865, the school had distinguished alumni. *Moby-Dick* author Herman Melville had attended, as did Felix Adler, an affluent German Jewish émigré who founded the Society for Ethical Culture in 1876 to promote ethical humanism, integration, universality, and social justice. Adler had also sat on the New York City Tenement House Committee to improve housing conditions for New York's poorest residents. In 1956, CGPS became coed, the first of the elite New York City prep schools to do so. In the 1950s, as the Upper West Side deteriorated and Whites—thanks to low-cost Whites-only government-backed mortgages—moved to the suburbs, the school considered relocating to the Upper East Side. Instead, it committed to the West Side Urban Renewal Area plan and stayed in the neighborhood.[2]

My route to Columbia Grammar was safer and cleaner than my old path to P.S. 75, dominated as it was by the Mitchell-Lama towers that had sprung up along Columbus Avenue between 96th and 91st Street. Though optimistically labeled "The Avenue of Tomorrow"[3] by urban renewal planners, this monotonous row of massive, angular buildings stripped the neighborhood of its former vibrancy.

It felt like a dead zone, a place to pass through quickly until life began to throb again. True, the super-slabs replaced many of the burnt-out buildings in the area, and more people lived in serviceable apartments, but lost was the spontaneity and rhythm of urban life a few blocks south with smaller brick buildings of variegated size, shape and vintage, sporting fire escapes, storefronts, and stoops, where people gossiped, debated politics, ate delicious food, and kept an eye out for their neighbors.

As urbanist Jane Jacobs said about engineered cities:

To approach a city, or even a neighborhood, as if it were a larger architectural problem, capable of being given order by converting it into a disciplined work of art, is to make the mistake of attempting to substitute art for life. The results of such profound confusion between art and life are neither life nor art. They are taxidermy . . . dead, stuffed cities.[4]

My own block, on 96th Street between Columbus and Amsterdam, didn't suffer the same deadening fate as Columbus Avenue, since it was architecturally diverse, with pre- and postwar buildings. My mother told us that our building, scaled down to fifteen stories, set back from the street with a garden, portico, and beehive window facades, was somehow better designed than the other concrete super-slabs flanking Columbus Avenue. I didn't appreciate her claim until I was well into my thirties, having gained a broader perspective. What saved the neighborhood's vitality were the collectivist activities of Mitchell-Lama folks, who, despite their brutalist environment, filled the streets with life. Kids whacked pink Spalding handballs on the outer concrete wall of Food City, and adults brought out folding chairs to play dominos, cards, and chess.

I wondered whether other people in those Columbus Avenue superslabs felt the same way. Did they also experience a sense of collectivist energy and vibrant social life? Once again, I reached out to friends I'd made on social media. How many who grew up hitting handballs, playing in their cement backyards, and hearing the Jazzmobile could I find? How many would be yearning, as I was, to ruminate about our collective past? A multitude, I happily discovered.

Like the 711 cohort, many of the kids who grew up in Columbus Avenue Mitchell-Lamas came from politicized families who sought integrated housing on the Upper West Side, valued diversity and community, went to local public schools until they were no longer viable, and relished the neighborhood. Bobby Broom grew up in my grandmother's building at Jefferson Towers, a concrete middle-income co-op constructed in 1968 on Columbus Avenue between 94th and 95th Street, with terraces stacked like subway tiles:

> Both of my parents were Black and moved to New York City in the early 1950s as part of the Great Migration. My dad, especially, was escaping the systemic codes that resulted in discrimination, poverty, and limited opportunities of America's Deep South. Dad was a US Government shipping clerk in Bayonne, New Jersey. He "retired" from that job and then was the maintenance man for the Kayser-Roth

Corporation until his actual retirement in 1978, when I graduated high school. My mom taught in Harlem at Wadleigh Junior High School.

We lived in Harlem from the time I was born (1961) at Lenox Terrace on West 135th Street. It was a really well-maintained building with terraces, doormen and gardens, and a mostly Black population. Six months after the assassination of Dr. Martin Luther King, Jr., we moved to the Upper West Side. The Harlem race riots (1964, 1967, and 1968), the gradual yet increasing deterioration of Harlem communities due to the infiltration of drugs into its neighborhoods, and my parents' desire to expose me to more diversity and opportunity prompted my dad to find a more appropriate community for us to fulfill those desires. In 1968, we moved to Jefferson Towers, and I stayed until 1984.

Curious about Lenox Terrace, I researched its history and discovered it was built with Title I funding from the 1949 Housing Act, which provided federal subsidies for slum clearance. Robert Moses, master builder and Chairman of the Mayor's Committee on Slum Clearance from 1949 to 1960, advocated for middle-income housing like Lenox Terrace in Harlem for Blacks, using Title I to advance this cause. Though opposed to integrated housing, Moses nonetheless believed Blacks should live well, albeit separately, and "reinforced the color line."[5]

Bobby continued:

There were at least ten boys my age in Jefferson Towers and then even more who were older and younger within five years. The same for the girls. Our building's yard was a neighborhood attraction. Perhaps it was the basketball hoop or just us cool kids! So, in addition to our building's inherent kid population, there were handfuls of neighborhood friends of various age ranges who were always over. We played together both outside and at each other's houses, eating and sleeping over all the time. We all spent our whole childhood right there, behind and in front of 700 Columbus Avenue.

I remember my introduction to racism. I was in around the fourth grade, and I used to walk home from P.S. 84 with a friend/schoolmate who lived in the Mitchell-Lama building directly across the street from 700. For a while, we had a little ritual where I would play with him in the courtyard of his building next to Food City. One day he reluctantly informed me that he could no longer play with me. When I asked why, he told me that his mother forbade it because I was

Black. At the time, I didn't understand why that mattered. I suspect he didn't, either. I'm sure that I asked my parents about it, and I wish I could remember what they said. I'm sorry that they had to address it at all.

Mostly, there were never any serious racial issues among neighborhood kids. Of course, these isolated incidents involving race paled in comparison to the overall feeling of community and harmony. One of my fondest memories was the neighborhood's diversity. In my building alone were Blacks of Southern US and Caribbean descent, Whites of diverse European descent, Puerto Ricans, Asians. I was brought up with a realization of commonality instilled and fostered by my formative years on the Upper West Side.

"What did you do for Junior High? Did you go to private school to avoid Joan of Arc? That's what I did," I asked.

"Yep. To Calhoun. There were around three of us from the building who went to Calhoun and others from nearby blocks, too. I'm thinking the reason Joan of Arc was so bad was probably because the kids from the Frederick Douglass Projects went there."

"Did people tell you this or are you speculating? I hate to blame the projects. They have such a bad reputation to begin with."

"Not sure, but where did all those bad kids come from? I KNEW I wasn't going to go there! All of my friends dreaded the thought, and only one who I know went. Anyone who could afford to didn't go."

"Same with us. Most RNA kids went to P.S. 75, then split up for various Junior High options throughout the city," I said.

Interested to learn why Joan of Arc was so dangerous, I consulted my mother's former colleague at Advocates for Children and author of *A Brighter Choice: Building a Just School in an Unequal City*, Clara Hemphill:

I think all the schools were in pretty bad shape in the 1970s, as was the city as a whole. White flight to the suburbs left the city without a tax base. Tons of teachers were laid off in the fiscal crisis. Budgets cut to the bone. Crime was rising not just in the schools, but throughout the city. I don't know specifically about Joan of Arc in the '70s, but my guess is there was rigid tracking and kids in the bottom tracks were pretty much abandoned—given unqualified teachers, out of date textbooks, and generally horrible conditions. Kids in the bottom tracks got angry and acted out. Teachers called kids "animals." Kids in the bottom track were denied remedial reading classes because it was assumed their IQ was so low, they were incapable of learning to read.

Later, I relayed this information to Bobby.

"Yeah, this makes more sense than blaming the Project kids," he said.

I told Bobby I could see his building from my terrace. "When I was little, I used to wave to my grandmother from there. I would pick up the receiver of the white rotary phone on the kitchen wall and dial. *Grandma, stand by the window.*

Give me a minute, Sweetheart.

"I would slide open the screen door, walk onto the terrace, and wait. Moments later my grandmother would appear, a tiny speck. I could barely see her except for her big black beauty parlor bouffant contrasted against her pale skin. I would lean over the railing as far as I safely could while we waved at each other, until satisfied, I went back inside."

"That's such a distinctive New York City memory, tucked among those Upper West Side high-rises and sensing some kind of safety in the midst of all the people and families. I remember looking out of my bedroom window and feeling connected in some indistinguishable way to all of the lights coming from the other apartments. It's kind of weird to think how that gave me a sense of peace and comfort. It's like what some people get from being in nature."

In summary, Bobby said:

I can't emphasize enough the rainbow-like feeling that it instilled. Everyone living relatively peacefully with one another. Again, youthfulness plays a part because of the inherent innocence. But to some degree, that melting pot vibe was a decision that our parents made for one reason or another. I am a product of that. It's what has shaped and determined so many of my life choices, from the kind of wife I chose to where I was attracted to raise our mixed-race son in urban, integrated, working-class Evanston, Illinois, the first suburb north of Chicago.

After talking with Bobby, I appreciated more than ever how social media allowed me to connect with folks from my old neighborhood. Following my husband around the world for school and work, I felt displaced, my rootlessness snowballing every time I packed another bag. The more I moved, the more I held onto my identity as a New Yorker. By the time I got to Phoenix, famous for its suburban sprawl and right-wing politics, my need to communicate with New Yorkers had become crucial to my well-being, especially after my mother died and I no longer had a cooperative apartment to return to.

I felt a particular kinship with those who grew up in Upper West Side Mitchell-Lamas. One of the most racially diverse areas in New York, the Upper West Side was a distinct cultural enclave within the borders of New York City. Activism was in our blood. We were raised with the idea of the common good and the belief that everyone had a stake in the collective. New Yorkers, in general, spoke with directness, openness, warmth, resilience, honesty, and transparency. We were equals because we were in this together. All classes, races, and ethnicities mingled on subways and streets, exchanging ideas, knowing where to walk and talk. Talking with Bobby reminded me how much I missed those qualities.

Liana Arboleda-Nuñez grew up at Tower West, a twenty-nine-story concrete and beige brick Mitchell-Lama rental, constructed in 1971 at Columbus Avenue and 96th Street:

My parents were one of the first residents of Tower West. My mother, the daughter of Spanish immigrants, grew up on the Lower East Side. My paternal grandparents were Spanish immigrants, moving to Colombia, where my dad was born, arriving in the US in the late 1960s. Initially, my dad lived in Queens, but was a bartender at Under the Stairs, a few blocks south, so he moved to 49 West 96th Street, a six-story building with fire escapes, to be closer to work. Since this is where my parents lived when they were newly married in 1971, they became aware of the Mitchell-Lama building because it was being built literally next door to their building. I was born there in 1977 and stayed until I was twenty-five, when I got married, so my formative years were during the late '80s, early '90s.

While I can't be certain of precise demographics, on the surface it always seemed to be diverse economically, and certainly racially, culturally, and ethnically. I recall knowing kids who went to private school, Catholic school, and public school. I knew families whose primary income came from blue-collar work, but I also recall architects, lawyers, and medical professionals. And although at the time I didn't fully appreciate it, there were numerous same-sex couples in the building, and I can't ever remember thinking that it was odd or revolutionary. It just seemed normal.

I sometimes equate Tower West to a small town in the midst of a metropolis. Everyone knew each other. People gossiped, and kids couldn't get away with much. Bad news traveled fast, but neighbors looked out for one another. Whenever I hear of small-town life, I will frequently recall life in Tower West just to get a comparison. There were annual holiday parties, Halloween parties, etc., where many gathered as tradition.

Beth Rosenblum was particularly socially concerned, having been raised by an affordable housing advocate mother, who had been the borough historian of Manhattan. Beth grew up at Strycker's Bay Apartments on West 94th off Columbus Avenue, a Mitchell-Lama co-op built in 1967 during Stage I of the West Side Urban Renewal Area plan. The apartments consisted of two redbrick buildings with 220 units, one seventeen stories, the other twenty-one:

My mom was President of Strycker's Bay Neighborhood Council, the organization formed in 1959 by St. Gregory's Church Priest Father Henry J. Browne to ensure that those dislocated by the West Side Urban Renewal Area plan were provided the means to return to the neighborhood with an affordable apartment if they so wished. There were many court battles and disagreements over the number of new units to be set aside for low-income folks. Originally, it was only going to be about 900, but they were able to raise the number to 2,500. In my building, 20–30 percent of the units were required to go to low-income, and the rest to middle-income. West 94th Street was co-named "Doris Rosenblum Way" about ten years ago in honor of my late mother.

My parents were both White, Jewish native New Yorkers; my mother was born on the Lower East Side, my father in Brooklyn. We were raised secular and never went to temple, although culturally, we identified as Jewish and celebrated Passover, Hanukah, and Rosh Hashanah. My folks saw a notice in the newspaper about the West Side Urban Renewal Area and the offer for affordable housing for families.

The building was extremely racially diverse and remains so today. I don't recall Asians living here when I was growing up; it was primarily Blacks, Hispanics (Puerto Ricans mostly), definitely a few mixed-race couples and their kids, and Whites. Some of the brownstones on the side streets were converted to low-income housing and remain so today. It was a good mix of housing types, not like the NYCHA developments; here, the affordable units were integrated with middle and sometimes upper incomes in various kinds of housing.

When we first moved in, the area was sketchy, but as I was only a child, I was not overly aware of its dangers. I recall there were streets we avoided walking down, and there was always hushed talk about area crimes. As this was one of the earliest towers built, there were a lot of empty lots and ongoing construction. Once the buildings and the retail stores were occupied, the neighborhood became a great deal safer. Many of the kids were the same age in the building, and we played together. It had much more of a community feel back then.

Antar Jones grew up in Columbus Park Towers, 100 West 94th Street, also built during Stage I of the West Side Urban Renewal Area plan in 1967, a blocky tan brick slab co-op with white concrete terraces. Like Laurie Nelson, who lived in 711, he remembers a social hierarchy in his building:

My parents were African American from Chicago. They moved from the Bronx to the Upper West Side. They learned about the building after a friend declined to live there. The story goes that the building, which had just opened, needed a Black family to live on one of the top floors, which were the largest. My family met that profile. I also suppose, honestly, we were the right kind of Black family, too.

"I hope I'm not touching on too sensitive a topic, but how do you think White people conceive the right kind of Black family? This, of course, assumes that management was White."

Antar replied:

The management—that is, the folks who were responsible for bringing the people in—were definitely White, as my mother indicated. They were being very careful who was getting those bigger apartments. The garbage collectors, New York City clerks, department of transportation folks lived in the lower floors. My father was a classical musician (flutist), who, at the time, was playing on Broadway and had probably recently played with the American Symphony, a prestigious orchestra at the time, so we fit the bill. The building was set as an 80/20 building, where 80 percent of the building was middle class and 20 percent was lower-middle to lower (working) class. The community was very mixed. Black, White, Puerto Rican, some Asians. Everything was very well maintained, but there was a lot of graffiti in the stairways. Rubble and brick abounded. The neighborhood has since been very developed, but it's less friendly now.

Local non-Mitchell-Lama kids made use of the amenities the buildings had to offer, further fostering community, and allowing for childlike traditions to emerge. Sonja Sekely, Italian and Czech on her mother's side, Hungarian Jewish on her father's side, grew up with a single mother in a tiny rent-controlled apartment in a brownstone on West 87th Street:

> I was always envious of the kids who lived in Mitchell-Lama. You guys had elevators, terraces, and big lobbies. Swoon! At P.S. 84, we always had class pets: guinea pigs, gerbils, hamster, rabbits. Whenever one of the class pets would die, we would dress it up for burial in a shoe box and head over to a classmate's house who lived in Mitchell-Lama. We would all gather around the incinerator chute in the hallway for a service. Then launch the dead pet down to the trash. We all thought this was a very proper burial. We chose Mitchell-Lama because of the incinerators and because classmates tended to live on a high floor, which made the send-off that much more exciting.

While the prevailing ethos of Upper West Side Mitchell-Lama housing was integration, landlords in private dwellings still discriminated. Rachel Christmas Derrick grew up on West 94th in a brownstone near Columbia Grammar:

> My African American parents bought the building around 1960, after having been rejected when they showed up to sign the lease for an apartment at 275 Central Park West that some White friends were leaving. The landlord was happy to let friends of the departing tenants move in—until he met them. My parents sued for racial discrimination and won. But by that time, the apartment they had wanted had been taken by someone else. Mandated to do so by the court, the landlord offered them other apartments—but, surprise, he only seemed to be able to propose units that were obviously too small.
>
> Meanwhile, my parents heard about the mixed-income urban renewal experiment slated for 94th Street. It was such a good deal that they decided to be pioneers. Some affordable housing was being developed for lower-income families, while some rentals and private homes would be for higher earners. Trees would be planted, and the street would be narrowed in certain places to slow traffic. Crime on the block was rampant. Our house was burglarized multiple times, including once when, at age twelve, I came face-to-face with a man who had broken in. However, it was a fabulous block to grow up on, with kids of all races, ethnicities, and socioeconomic backgrounds

playing together up and down the street daily, in and out of each other's houses, family parties in our homes with neighbors. We had several block-wide tag sales in front of Columbia Grammar on weekends. My brothers and I, along with other kids from the block, had "carnivals" in the Columbia Grammar stoop—lots of games, from dodgeball to homemade spin the wheel, for prizes.

I recognized that characteristics of my childhood—affordable cooperative living, exposure, street life, progressive politics, and integration—were not common features of American life. In fact, these characteristics are rarer today than when I was growing up. According to an examination of residential segregation by the Othering & Belonging Institute at the University of California-Berkeley, "More than 80% of large metropolitan areas in the United States were more segregated in 2019 than they were in 1990."[6] This statistic is no surprise. Though it's not based on a quantitative analysis, my own personal experience living in many different places and visiting friends and family in various cities corroborates these findings. I know that the Upper West Side and large swaths of the Manhattan of my youth have been largely eclipsed by the banal, and that socioeconomic inequality has grown. Still, I cling—as do others from my cohort—to the remnants of an old, more equitable New York.

Chapter 5

▪▪▪

Class Consciousness

HANDING OUT INVITATIONS in the yard, a fenced-in cement space tucked between the lower and upper schools, Becky warned us she'd invited a Black girl to her slumber party. She said she wanted to make sure no one acted shocked when the girl arrived. To me, she said: "You're coming from public school. You're used to being around Blacks. We're not. I'm doing this to protect my Black friend."

There were twenty-four kids in fifth grade at Columbia Grammar and Preparatory School (CGPS), none of them African American.

I knew Becky's intentions were good, but her warning disturbed me and highlighted what a foreign environment I'd entered in private school. I was insecure at Columbia Grammar, wondering if I was worthy enough, sensing I was an outsider. Besides Nina and me, only one other kid in our class, the daughter of a CGPS employee, lived in a neighborhood Mitchell-Lama. In my mind, we were pegged the poor kids, and I was embarrassed. I hadn't yet appreciated how ideal it was to grow up in Mitchell-Lama housing.

To be fair, back in the '70s, CGPS was intellectual, welcoming, and laid back. We had a radical curriculum, studying Communism, socialism, utopian movements, and the American labor movement. Many of the kids who attended were from Upper West Side Jewish, left-leaning intellectual and artistic families, some richer than others. Often, parents like mine encouraged open discussion about these subjects, grateful their kids weren't being fed mainstream conservative American narratives. Still, the

46

dichotomy between public school disadvantage and private school wealth and privilege was evident.

At ten years old, I felt nothing but shame for RNA House. I don't know if Nina shared these feelings with me, but it didn't matter. She was a refuge once we left school and returned to 96th Street. We were on equal footing there, where life was normal, and I was acceptable.

The first semester at Columbia Grammar, Nina and I, along with a few other private school rookies, stayed after school to do Science Research Associates (SRA) workbooks to improve our reading and math proficiencies. I was humiliated. It never occurred to me that I had fallen behind because of an uneven P.S. 75 education, which stressed creativity over basic skills. I finally learned long division and realized I'd been tutoring kids at P.S. 75 incorrectly. I worried for months afterward how the kids remaining at public school fared and thought about returning to teach them.

At the beginning of fifth grade, I spotted Rachel—super-smart, lively, funny, pretty—as someone I wanted to be friends with. Luckily, she welcomed me into her tightly knit group of popular girls, who'd known each other since first grade, and we became instant companions. Rachel lived in the prewar San Remo, a luxury building on Central Park West at 74th Street, where the opening credits for the television show *The Odd Couple* had been filmed. Tony Randall, the co-star of the show, as well as Dustin Hoffman and other luminaries, lived in the building. The San Remo was only two blocks away from the Dakota, John Lennon's famous abode.

The architect Emery Roth, a Jewish emigrant from the Austro-Hungarian Empire denied commissions on the Upper East Side because of anti-Semitism, designed the building. With cartouches above the entrances of the two-tiered limestone towers and choragic temples at the very top, the San Remo stood out as one of the Upper West Side's greatest architectural achievements.[1]

Matisses and Picassos adorned the walls of Rachel's grand, ornamented, eleven-foot-high-ceiling apartment. A buzzer underneath her dining room table summoned the maid to serve dinner, and each bedroom, including the maid's room, had a private bathroom. Rachel's mother, Joan, was a Jewish Jacqueline Onassis—statuesque, glamorous, and elegant. She held court in the living room, sipping tea and socializing with her fashionable friends, while Rachel's father, a quiet, refined man, sat in the library smoking a cigarette and reading the *Wall Street Journal*. Rachel and I spread out her gymnastics mat in a hallway as big as my apartment and tumbled down the corridor. It was exciting to be there but also disheartening to see the contrast between our surroundings. At public school, I'd felt like everyone else. At private school, I instantly realized how I was different. I wanted to be moneyed and glamorous. I saw little value in the egalitarian philosophy behind subsidized housing. Why couldn't my parents care more about making money, investing in real estate, and moving up in the world? Why couldn't they be beautiful, elegant, and tall rather than short, *haimish* intellectuals? I wanted the rules for the rich to apply to me.

Before I left, Rachel's mother offered me taxi money, which I declined. The only times I'd interacted with taxis were when I was sick, and my mother let me take one to the doctor. Descending in the carpeted, oak-paneled elevator, I chatted with the elevator operator, who wore a formal navy uniform with lapels and yellow trimmings. He escorted me through the marble-walled lobby to the doorman, who wanted to call me a cab. I demurred. Though there was a security guard in my building, he wasn't there 24/7 and didn't wear a formal uniform or hail taxis.

Feeling low, I crossed the street and waited for the number #10 bus to take me uptown, longing for what Rachel had. When it stopped, I hopped on, found an empty seat at the back, and stared out the window. I spotted a tall, skinny guy wearing round wire-framed sunglasses, a T-shirt, jeans, and a Greek fisherman's cap, walking along Central Park West, grinning. I couldn't believe it and squinted to make sure. Yep, it was him—John Lennon! I instantly cheered up. As the bus sped off, I stuck my head out the window to catch a last glimpse.

A week later, Rachel came to visit my apartment. We squeezed my gymnastics mat into the living room, wedged up against the furniture, covering all available floor space, and we tumbled until it was time for her to leave. Curling her hair around her finger, she asked me to accompany her downstairs in the elevator, which seemed unnecessary, but I agreed. After waiting interminably for it to come, we gave up and took the stairs.

I was set to say goodbye in the lobby, but she asked me to go outside, so I followed her onto the street. She lifted her arm, waved, and looked up and down the block, scanning the street for a cab.

"Just take the bus," I said.

"It's too dangerous. My mother said I should take a taxi."

A Checker cab came, and she jumped in. After that evening, I begged my mother to take taxis wherever we were going, but she refused.

Rachel wasn't the only one afraid of my neighborhood. In the '60s and '70s, many Upper West Side kids weren't allowed to venture north to 96th Street. John Spiering from my *Growing Up on the Old Upper West Side* Facebook group wrote: "I was too scared to go near that block. I grew up on West 82nd and avoided going north of 87th Street, especially past the projects on 93rd and Amsterdam. There were gangs hanging on corners, I was followed by hoodlums. I'd sneak into the subway and run out the other side."

In those days, West 96th was a borderline (both real and imagined) between safe and unsafe. My congressional district ran from 96th Street up through Harlem. Charlie Rangel, a founding member of the Congressional Black Caucus, was our congressman. Across the park, the division was more pronounced where the Metro North train tracks, originating at Grand Central Station, surfaced at 97th and Park Avenue. Suddenly, the exclusive Upper East Side became East Harlem, a.k.a. El Barrio—in the popular imagination, a neighborhood riddled with crime and dangerous projects.

My short, eccentric father, with bushy hair, protruding ears, and tortoise-shell glasses, escorted me to Sutton Place Gymnastics near the East River in the fifties. This morning was a special occasion. We were showing off our newly acquired tricks to our families. I held his hand as we navigated the 96th Street crosstown bus, the Lexington Avenue subway, and the walk to the studio, enjoying the adventure until we saw Rachel and her model-of-a-mother, dazzling in the latest haute couture wardrobe, with long polished nails, a Gucci bag, and high heels, emerge from a cab. Acutely embarrassed by my father, I dropped his hand.

I felt even more mortified when he attended a Sunday volleyball game for parents and kids at school. Wearing a yellow smiley-face sweatshirt with *Good Guy* etched in black, brown trousers, and penny loafers, he was ill-equipped to play. A tall, muscular father in a red tank top, shorts with white trim, knee-high white socks, and Adidas sneakers served the ball with aplomb. My father lunged for it and missed, and the other team scored a point. The muscular father served the ball and, again, my father missed. He laughed and smiled, remaining cheerful and happy, unperturbed at his lack of athleticism. Neither of my parents was sporty. They didn't ice skate, ski in the Swiss Alps, or ride bicycles and horses, standard activities for some CGPS families. I covered my face with my hands and cringed.

On March 13, 1974, during my first year at CGPS, my father came to fifth grade Father's Visiting Day. I watched him walk up the last step of the staircase and enter the music room, dressed for work in a black suit and tie. At that moment, I didn't care if he was offbeat or non-athletic. I was no longer ashamed of him. He came because he loved me, and that was all that mattered. We waved hello, he took a seat next to the other fathers, and the class began. In public school, there was no special day designated for fathers.

I played the xylophone in the corner with some other students. Minutes later, my friend Susie gestured me over, and I saw my father lying on the floor, knees bent, breathing heavily. My friend Adina's father, who was a doctor, pumped his chest.

Ms. Macklin, the headmistress, took me to her office, and one of the fathers kept me company until someone brought in my sister, who was attending seventh grade in the Upper School. Elizabeth and I waited, crying and shaking, until our mother, who'd been volunteering in the P.S. 75 library, arrived, breathless, and told us our father had died. He was forty-six years old.

We took a taxi home, even though we lived four blocks away.

This time I didn't have to beg my mother for the ride.

For years, I tried to figure out—why had my father died in front of me and no one else in the family. What was the reason? Was I special somehow? What was the point? But, of course, I could come up with nothing. There *was* no reason. What reason could there possibly be?

I made a film about my dad's death, and now, in this memoir, his death plays a major role. Maybe the purpose of seeing him die was to give me material to turn into art. If I don't make art, I feel dead, crippled, worthless. If I reflect and create, I am exhilarated. There is meaning. There is happiness. There is a sense of purpose.

What would my life have been like if my father had lived? If we'd remained the happy, undamaged family we'd been? To have him wait up at night until I returned home? To see him grow old? To be a grandfather? Would I still have been an artist? Would I be better at math? Would my self-esteem be strong? There is no answer, of course. There are no answers.

After witnessing my dad's death, I felt more alienated at private school than before. My grief consumed me, crippled me, set me apart, marked my difference. I stopped trying to conform, stepped away, and observed, quietly chronicling personal changes in my family and public transformations in the neighborhood, city, and country.

I began to see myself as an outsider, creating a role for myself as an artist documenting those changes. Documenting was a way to alleviate my trauma, to make sense of what was happening around me, and to share my interpretation with others.

In 1974, I witnessed Nixon's resignation, a collective trauma threatening America's stability. That summer after my father died, my mother, sister, and I flew to Florida to visit my father's Uncle Sidney and Aunt Molly, my paternal grandmother's brother and sister. When my dad was growing up fatherless, Sidney and Molly played important roles in his life, Sidney even moving in to help raise him. Once my dad married, Sidney and Molly each got apartments in a Mitchell-Lama development near Lincoln Center. Unlike my parents, who adhered to the egalitarian dream of modernist architecture and consciously chose Mitchell-Lama living, Sidney and Molly, as well as Grandma Helen, moved into Mitchell-Lamas only out of necessity. A few years before my father's death, Sidney and Molly retired to market-rate condominiums near Miami Beach.

My mother didn't like these relatives. Sidney was bigoted, referring to African Americans as *schvartzes*, Yiddish for "Blacks." Aunt Molly was tolerant but had annoying habits my mother couldn't stand, like putting garbage in the "Frigidaire" so as not to attract bugs. My mother felt obligated to go. My sister and I were happy to see our great aunt and uncle, who reminded us of our father.

On August 8th, we gathered in Uncle Sidney's carpeted living room, turned on his black-and-white TV, and watched Walter Cronkite report to the nation about "Nixon's failed leadership" and the smooth transition of power to Gerald Ford. Then Nixon gave his resignation speech:

> To continue to fight through the months ahead for my personal vindication would almost totally absorb the time and attention of both the president and the congress. . . . Therefore, I shall resign the presidency effective at noon tomorrow . . .

Uncle Sidney disliked Nixon because he was an anti-Semite. He shook his head over and over again, while Aunt Molly muttered, "That crook."

My mother turned to us girls and said, "I just wish Daddy had lived long enough to see Nixon resign."

The country collectively bore witness to Nixon's resignation. My mother had wanted my father to bear witness, too.

In sixth grade, two Black boys, Mondello and Bernard, joined our class, now comprising thirty kids. Mondello, smiley yet shy and weary-eyed, was brave enough to invite a bunch of us to his birthday party. Brave, I imagined, because he must've felt much more like a stranger at private school than I did. Mondello lived in Esplanade Gardens, a massive middle-income Mitchell-Lama cooperative in Harlem, constructed in 1967, the same year as RNA House.

I'd visited East Harlem often with my father, who took me for long walks across Central Park to the East Side. We usually meandered along 97th Street past Madison toward Park Avenue, stopping to watch the Metro-North trains. Once the railroad tracks climbed above ground north of the 96th Street redline, Park Avenue was no longer a fancy address. A tall stone wall divided the avenue, partitioning Whites commuting on trains to the suburbs. We went north, following the tracks past blocks and blocks of bland brownish-red, cruciform brick NYCHA projects with small windows and water towers on rooftops, arranged in tower-in-the-park settings amidst grass, trees, landscaped pathways, and playgrounds. Sometimes, we saw graffiti tags on a maintenance door, litter overflowing from garbage cans, and still-standing derelict tenements, but, mostly, the NYCHA projects seemed lush with green space, well-kept, and quiet, though isolated, with few people on the streets. At 110th, we circled around, stopping in at a diner in the neighborhood for hot chocolate or lemonade, depending on the season.

The jaunt to Harlem for Mondello's birthday party stood out, though. As city kids, we were used to navigating the terrain solo; no one chauffeured us to and from school, friend's apartments, dance, music, and art classes, to buy candy, eat Chinese food and pizza, or see a movie. But for Mondello's party, we piled into a rental car and drove uptown. My mother told me to take the subway. "It's not far. What's the problem?" Other parents, however, insisted we be escorted, so Rachel's mother volunteered. I wanted to be like others, so I joined my friends in the car.

Mondello's Mitchell-Lama consisted of 1,872 apartments, many with terraces, in six 27-story redbrick buildings, spanning Adam Clayton

Powell Jr. Boulevard to the East River, between 145th and 148th Street. The development, along with six others in the neighborhood, comprised 6,502 apartments, "the largest concentration of middle-income Black families in the city."[2] Another one of these developments was Lenox Terrace, where Bobby Broom resided until 1968 when his family moved into the same Upper West Side Mitchell-Lama building my grandmother lived in around the corner from RNA House. After East Harlem's far-reaching transformation into a public housing enclave, these towers were constructed to attract middle-class African Americans.

During the Depression, the Federal Housing Administration created residential security maps to establish which neighborhoods were considered safe to invest in. Neighborhoods were rated: "A" for "Best," "B" for "Still Desirable," "C" for Definitely Declining," and "D" for "Hazardous."[3] Poor areas populated by Blacks were disqualified for FHA-insured mortgages, thus beginning the practice of "redlining" and the American Capitalist Dream of suburban homeownership for White citizens only.[4] Even back in the 1930s, my Upper West Side neighborhood, from 88th Street to 110th Street, was given a "C." Mondello's district—a vast area stretching from East 96th Street north to 155th Street, and west through Morningside Heights—was designated a "D."

Using money from Title I of the 1949 Housing Act, which provided federal subsidies for slum clearance, Robert Moses, Chairman of the Mayor's Committee on Slum Clearance, oversaw an enormous and quick transformation of the East Harlem tenement-lined grid. The area metamorphosized into "a new superblocked landscape of 141 modern housing towers with parks, playgrounds, parking lots, and open spaces, built with a combination of federal, state, and city funds."[5] Covering 164 acres, with a total of twenty-four developments modeled after Le Corbusier's *Ville Radieuse*, this became the largest cluster of public housing in the city.[6] Though the 1949 Housing Act maintained segregation nationally, a provision of the bill integrated public housing in New York.

Le Corbusier's conceptual utopian *Ville Radieuse*—identical vertical, cruciform-shaped towers, free of ornamentation, with sleek, clean lines and angles, set amidst recreational parkland—was meant to liberate the individual and transform society. He declared, "Architecture must make use of modern technical processes . . . Nothing of tradition will remain. Everything will be new. There will be a new organization of the human race and a brand-new stage-set . . . Knowledge, ethics, and esthetics, all are one, expressed in architecture; a new unity."[7] Moses had no grandiose plans to free the individual à la Le Corbusier. Rather, he recognized that Le Corbusier's tower-in-the-park model was inexpensive to construct and would provide decent housing to the masses. Architectural historian Hilary Ballon wrote, "For Moses, the slums were like war-torn Dresden— dead structures to be demolished before new life could flourish. They were a physical, not a social problem, to be cured by replanning and new building."[8]

There were pros and cons to this massive bulldozing fait accompli. Slums were cleared, and decent housing was constructed. But thriving neighborhoods were destroyed in the process, dislocating residents and businesses—of little concern to Moses, whose faith lay in rebuilding. Before huge swaths of East Harlem, a.k.a. El Barrio, were bulldozed to build this vast engineered landscape, the neighborhood was seedy and rat-infested but lively and heterogeneous. Puerto Ricans migrating from the Island were the dominant inhabitants, along with a smattering of Dominicans and Cubans. Italians, as well as Jews and Irish, also lived in East Harlem. In the '30s, half-Italian/half-Jewish Fiorello La Guardia represented the district in Congress before becoming mayor.

In addition, a sizeable African American population that had escaped the Jim Crow South looking for opportunity in the industrialized North crossed into El Barrio after initially settling in Harlem. My family's favorite artist, Jacob Lawrence, documented the great migration from the South to the North in *The Migration Series*—sixty paintings narrating the exodus in an abstract, expressive, cubist style. Lawrence also illustrated African American life in Harlem, creating the *Harlem Series*, where he portrayed vibrant cityscapes with street activity, beauty shops, churches, dance halls, bars, and diners set amidst low-rise fire-escaped brownstones, painted in deep bold reds, oranges, blues, blacks, and browns. Notably, in this same Harlem, he painted *Slums, 1950*, where he departed from his usual vibrant palette. Framed through a gray tenement window with cockroaches crawling around the edges and a dead rodent ambushed in a mouse trap, he depicted a jumble of tenement windows and fire escapes in more somber yellow and reddish-peach colors.

The widespread demolition transformed East Harlem into an urban renewal "laboratory" that was watched closely by politicians, city planners, and architects in New York City and throughout the country "for the effects that the benign intervention of public housing would have on the area."[9] Initially, few understood the consequences of stripping away the basic fabric of the city block filled with schools, bars, nightclubs, bodegas, botanicas, Italian delis, Cuban restaurants, barbershops, candy stores, bakeries, shoe repair stores, hardware stores, and laundromats in human-scale buildings promoting neighborly interactions and block parties and replacing it with utilitarian, monolithic low-budget slab towers devoid of neighborhood businesses.

Problems soon arose. The Housing Act mandated that projects had to be constructed where slums were bulldozed. It was illegal to clear a slum and relocate former tenants to other neighborhoods or to the suburbs. Priority was given to displaced people. "The effect was a policy that ensured one ghetto was replaced by another."[10] The poor found themselves segregated into newly engineered ghettos, rootless and estranged from their former cohesive neighborhoods. Income limits were implemented, deterring residents from earning more money, which could lead to eviction.

Whites didn't want to live in the projects under these circumstances. Taking advantage of the Housing Act low mortgage loans only for White people, Italians, Jews, and other Caucasians fled to the suburbs in newly purchased cars on freeways Moses built to access them. In the 1950s, for the first time, "New York's suburban population increased by 2,180,492, while the urban population decreased by 109,973."[11] In the East Harlem projects, African American and Puerto Rican segregation became entrenched. In *Down These Mean Streets*, the classic 1967 novel about growing up in El Barrio by Piri Thomas (required reading in public school when I was a kid), Thomas wrote how "Big brick housing projects were all over the place, big alien intruders. They had been mutilating my turf . . ."[12]

Social workers and urbanists like Jane Jacobs rallied to the cause of humanizing socially engineered East Harlem projects. After participating in neighborhood walking tours where she talked to residents about desired improvements, Jacobs called for a reinstatement of smaller-scale buildings and class diversity. Her experiences in helping to remake East Harlem influenced her seminal book, *The Death and Life of Great American Cities*, completed in 1961, where she attacked the dominant urban planning innovations of the day as totalitarian, enraging Moses and inspiring community activism.[13]

NYCHA and city planners acted by adding features like vest-pocket parks, varying building façade colors, raising income limits, offering more social services, and rehabilitating tenements rather than tearing them down.[14] The fact that NYCHA responded at all to tenant troubles and tried to improve the quality of life speaks volumes about New York City's commitment to housing the poor. In the '60s, for the first time in East Harlem, middle-income Mitchell-Lama developments were built. One such example was Riverbend, constructed in 1967, the same year my building was built. Located between Fifth Avenue and the Harlem River Drive, from

138th to 142nd Street, Riverbend contains vast connected slab towers of varying heights and apartments of various sizes, including duplexes, surrounded by plazas.[15] In 1969, Riverbend won the Bard Award "for excellence in civic architecture and urban design."[16] Another example was 1199 Plaza, sponsored by the Drug and Hospital Workers Union, built in 1974, along the Harlem River Drive above 107th Street, encompassing high- and low-rise towers in a U-shape over twelve acres.[17]

In Central Harlem, Esplanade Gardens, where Mondello lived, was not particularly innovative architecturally, but it had added amenities like terraces that public housing lacked. His was Building 3, at 129–133 West 147th Street, near the Harlem River Drive; just outside his complex, derelict warehouses abutted the East River. The tall redbrick towers were of uniform height, and the grounds were well-kept, had trees, landscaped green space, benches, cement playgrounds, basketball courts, a parking garage, and a pool, the only Mitchell-Lama in the city to offer such a luxury, not that I spotted this perk at the time. As I got out of the car, I noticed a lot of kids playing basketball on the cement courts, reminding me of RNA House.

We didn't wait long for the elevator, which plodded along without incident to the eighth floor, just like at RNA—plain, slow, functional, and mostly reliable. It was a huge contrast from the fancy Central Park elevators revealed to me through private school, or the rickety old West End Avenue and Riverside Drive lifts with an operator manually opening and closing an accordion gate door.

"Come on in. So glad you made it," Mondello's mother greeted us warmly. She was soft-spoken, southern, and casual. Rachel's five-foot-ten mother, glamorous in a long-sleeved pale pink blouse, navy wool skirt, and high heels, towered over her. The living room was simply furnished with a couch, two big armchairs, a coffee table, and a throw rug. We sang happy birthday, ate cake in the adjoining dining room, and watched Mondello open his presents while Rachel's mother made small talk with his mom. After an hour or so, we departed as if we'd been doing our duty by venturing up to Harlem to attend his party and now our time was up. Subsequently, he never invited us over again.

I wanted to ask Mondello about being raised in Mitchell-Lama housing, his impressions of private school, if he remembered the birthday party, and if he felt, as one of the few African American kids at CGPS, even more like an outsider than I did. He and I had remained friendly at school, but we weren't close pals and hadn't spoken since graduation. I didn't know if he'd be receptive to my questions or interested in affordable housing issues, and I wasn't sure how to track him down. Then, I spotted his smiling face in a screenshot of a COVID-induced CGPS Zoom reunion posted on Facebook. I learned serendipitously via LinkedIn that he worked at the New York City Department of Housing Preservation and Development (HPD) as a Geographic Information System (GIS) analyst, analyzing data about affordable housing, worked with urban planners and real estate underwriters, and was creating a GIS database of historic and urban renewal project boundaries. I immediately emailed him. "It's good to be in touch. Do you remember how you first heard about Mitchell-Lama housing?"

"It's good to be in touch with you, too. One main reason why Mom and I ended up at Esplanade Gardens was due to housing discrimination and redlining. Mom had tried to buy a small house somewhere in the Bronx but wasn't allowed to because she was considered a single Black woman. She had sufficient funds but was shut out. Mom learned about E.G. during her very long maternity leave, when I was a baby. Getting ready to return to teaching, she attended an orientation event where her prospective boss suggested she move from Long Island to Harlem and check out Esplanade Gardens. In 1968, when we moved in, I was four years old."

"You were the same age as me when my family moved to RNA. Are your parents New York City people?"

"Both of my parents were from the South—Virginia and the Carolinas. Dad was a ship-builder handyman who later worked for the Post Office, Mom a public school teacher. She and I moved to E.G. when my parents unofficially separated, as the Brooklyn Naval Yard closed down and Dad went to Philly to work at that city's shipyard. He was a hermit, not strongly involved in the lives of any of his four children."

"RNA House had a big mix of people—Latinos, Jews, Whites, Blacks, interracial families. Was your building integrated?" I asked.

"E.G. was then probably made up of 95 percent African American residents. In the early 2000s, a noticeable number of Latinos started moving into the complex. Maybe there were a few Latino families who moved in about the same time before they melted into the complex's bricks—I literally never saw them. Everyone I knew at E.G., and knew about, had roots either from the South or from the Caribbean (mainly Jamaica), or a mix of those. My mom and my Aunt Celia still live there."

"I know you were young when you moved in, but what can you recall? What did it look like?"

"Mom and other folks were excited to be in then new co-op housing. Each E.G. building had tall, lobby-wide windows, and a guard stationed at the entrance. Parts of the main campus, between Buildings 1, 2, and 3, had clumps of decently maintained trees. There was a pool, too. Services were well-maintained."

"Did you play outside with kids from the complex?"

"I wasn't often a part of the small groups of kids around the building grounds playing. When I was eight to ten years old, I remember learning to play football and getting a little hurt; I went home annoyed at such an unforgiving concrete-prevalent 'field.' Unlike some of the playgrounds in Central Park, the playground area in the main campus of E.G. wasn't very imaginative—dull as can be, partially dominated by three or four small concrete elephants."

"Can you think of a few stories from your childhood and adulthood that illustrate the community feeling of the building? My father used to bring his telescope downstairs, and the neighborhood and building kids lined up to look at the stars."

"I joined the Cub Scouts but quit after a couple of months; the troop met weekly in the South Community room. I hated Scouts because of the lack of order—a bunch of boys playing tag, which I wasn't fast enough for, and bopping each other's heads in response to overly flexible *rules*. We celebrated Kwanzaa with Aunt Celia and her real family and with a mix of neighbors who had kids. Once a week, I rode the elevator upstairs, where a strongly accented Caribbean neighbor gave me dreaded piano lessons that I rarely practiced for. Years later, when I was maybe fourteen, I nearly walked out immediately upon entering my building's South Community room, where the complex hosted a party for teenagers. I struggled to stay twenty to thirty minutes—it wasn't my scene. The lights were already turned low and there were a bunch of kids I didn't know; a minute later a slow song came on, and I was in the middle of what seemed to me back then like a huge room full of strangers coupled up, rhythmically hugging and grinding.

"I suspect the Black kids of E.G. didn't have much freedom to play independently. Atari became a hit when I was ten to twelve years old. When I was about twelve, in the mid-'70s, I had a conversation with Mom about the new concept of latchkey kids. I think it was shortly after that she gave me a key. I do think a lot of the parents were worrying, with an especially Black '70s flavor, about their kids then."

Mondello's comment about parents worrying with a Black '70s flavor reminded me of second grade when my friend Gwen's mother found Gwen and me unaccompanied in the neighborhood. She was angry and worried we'd be harmed and never let Gwen visit me again. I was flabbergasted by how strict Gwen's mom was. My mother understood Gwen's mom's reaction, though, explaining to eight-year-old me that Blacks were subjected to more violence than White people. In retrospect, I wish my mother had been more protective, especially with my dad dead. I wish she'd worried when I stayed out late and took the subway home alone at 4 a.m. after clubbing and doing drugs. But she was often out herself and oblivious. What she didn't know didn't worry her.

"When I was in fifth grade, the year I transferred into CGPS, during Father's Visiting Day at school, my dad had a heart attack and dropped dead in front of me. I'd already felt like an outsider at private school coming from Mitchell-Lama housing. After my dad died, my isolation magnified. When you entered sixth grade, I imagined you felt, as an African American kid, even more alienated than I did."

"Jenny, I'm so sorry—wow, I feel for you. In addition to being demographically pretty much on my own, I was, for the most part, shy. So, I was in a bubble that isolated me, that blocked out a bunch of social histories and even rumors. I started to come out of my shell during college; had I done so during my CGPS years, we probably would've been hanging buddies."

"It's too bad neither of us was in emotional shape to hang out. Do you remember the birthday party you had in sixth grade? You invited a bunch of us, maybe the whole class, and we came to your house to celebrate. Did you have a good time?"

"I remember the birthday party. Totally Mom's doing. Already shy, I was nervous about the mixing of cultures, groups. I do remember being frustrated that none of my schoolmates would dance. After it ended, I felt relief."

"I was mortified I didn't have a fancy apartment. Did you feel the same?"

"The one time I was in awe visiting a classmate's huge apartment was probably ninth or tenth grade. Of all things, what truly impressed me was a huge room of floor-to-ceiling storage. But my state of housing felt very normal—no matter who was visiting. Maybe I would've felt embarrassed had I been mingling with a bunch of affluent Blacks, like you were mingling with affluent Jews. I always admired and was a little jealous of many of our classmates' Hebrew School attendance and obligations. From my offshoot Christian eyes, I saw Bar and Bat Mitzvahs as beautiful ceremonies that strengthened both individual participants and encouraged community longevity. My family has done various versions of rites of passage, but what's beautiful about what I observed of Jewish CGPS is normalness of efforts to bolster Jewish heritage."

"My dad was the moderately observant one, and after he passed away, my mother kept celebrating Passover and the high holidays in his name. She was fiercely secular. For me, Judaism is laced with sadness because it reminds me of my dad. If I'd been a boy and my father had lived, I would've had a Bar Mitzvah. At the time, though, it wasn't as common for girls to go through the ritual. I did graduate from Hebrew school, a much less involved occasion. Both ceremonies were a valuable expression of community, not that I recognized this back then."

Mondello replied, "In Social Studies class—this was in seventh grade, I believe—the teacher asked the class to estimate the Jewish percentage of the New York City and US populations. Classmates gave answers like fifty percent (city) and twenty-five percent (nationwide). I said twenty or twenty-five percent, and ten percent, respectively. Later, I was embarrassed that I had been fooled by classmates' exaggerated sense of the community's size and power. The experience did make me wonder if, in spite of my family's modest finances, I already had more exposure to the rest of the country through my trips down South and throughout parts of New York City."

"Yes, I realize Jews are a minority in the city, too, but we are such a vocal cultural and political demographic that it hardly feels like we're a minority at all, as you pointed out. Outside the city, it's a different story."

Mondello asked: "Did your childhood proximity to classmates' wealth end up motivating you? Did the discrepancy somehow drive you? I stayed nonchalant about earnings until I was about thirty-five—just when I was being chosen for policy influencing roles that I had craved."

"I think my dad's death affected my life more than any proximity to wealth, or lack thereof. I was so lost and had very little confidence in myself. I became a filmmaker and escaped to Vancouver, BC, which felt like utopia—gun control, socialized medicine, clean air, communal living. I eked out a living working in the film industry and making experimental art films, running back to shoot them in New York while staying with my mother, then returning to Vancouver to edit them, until I had a baby and could no longer afford filmmaking. I watched my New York City friends moving up even more in the world, securing better, more lucrative positions, at the same time observing myself being slowly priced out of a city I now wish I could afford to move back to."

"I was isolated, too. In sixth or seventh grade, I think there was only one other fully Black (an odd, made-up term, I know) kid. There was also a Puerto Rican girl who I had a minor crush on. They stayed for only one year; I was surprised and hurt when they didn't return. For many years,

I don't recall other Black or brown kids in our grade or in the adjacent grades. I felt a dull ache most days when I left school, taking the bus uptown—alone—as I watched a gaggle of schoolmates chatting and boarding the bus downtown. My sense of geographic divide deepened after I got the hang of the Manhattan concept of East Side and West Side.

"In ninth or tenth grade a classmate visited me. He was blonde and had a slight Southern or Western accent. He arrived at the subway station a few minutes before I met him there; as I arrived, he got punched by a couple of slightly older, asinine thugs. I was probably more psychically hurt than he was physically; all I could do was apologize. I felt helpless and, for a long time, embarrassed; my sense of not belonging increased."

"Some of my CGPS school friends were afraid to visit my building on West 96th Street and were told to take taxis home."

Mondello said: "About twenty years ago, a high-ranking department official at work told me that Esplanade Gardens was referred to by many nearby Harlem residents as 'The Gold Coast.' This guy, a charismatic Black man who grew up in Washington, DC, or Baltimore, was probably onto something."

"Well, Esplanade Gardens did have a pool! It's such a contrast with how our classmates, and the general population, perceived our neighborhoods and affordable housing," I said.

People thought of our developments as monstrosities, populated by low lives and located in dangerous neighborhoods no one wanted to visit. A close CGPS friend, who'd grown up in the Beresford, a lavish 1929 Upper West Side Emery Roth Renaissance Revival masterpiece between 81st and 82nd streets, dubbed my brutalist building "ugly," like a Soviet realist cage. Another friend called it a factory. 6sqft, an online New York City real estate and architecture journal, wrote that RNA House stuck out like a "sore thumb."[18] In 2017, *Saturday Night Live* did a skit where the vastness and anonymity of RNA House was a punchline.

In reality, the circumstances were much more nuanced. While it's true Mitchell-Lamas were often built in sketchy neighborhoods, communities lived with dignity and thrived, making these areas safer and more desirable. Cooperators paid reasonable rents and maintenance, had housing security, knew their neighbors, formed committees to beautify the grounds, and organized activities for children to keep them occupied and off the streets. Clearly, Mondello and I were beneficiaries of these programs.

NYCHA public housing projects were a more complicated story, suffering over the years from grave problems like broken furnaces, mold, and lead poisoning. Still, they were built in the postwar spirit of public responsibility, investment in citizenship, and dignity in housing. Many developments, especially in East Harlem, had landscaped green spaces with trees, benches, playgrounds, and community centers. They have proven to be a godsend in today's New York City, which caters to the rich, leaving everyone else to scrape by.

Mitchell-Lamas were, in fundamental ways, nicer than NYCHA projects, with terraces, more attractive but still functional lobbies with wider windows letting in abundant light, and they came in a variety of designs, not just the dull bleak brick model. But Manhattan Mitchell-Lamas were predominantly made of cement slabs with no greenery. RNA House's narrow tree-lined garden, spanning the building's length and set back from the street, was exceptional. So was Esplanade Gardens. My grandmother's Mitchell-Lama building around the corner on Columbus had no trees or grass, nor did my Aunt Molly and Uncle Sidney's Mitchell-Lama building near Lincoln Center.

Many NYCHA buildings were part of enormous, isolated developments, with NYCHA housing police who secured the area. Mondello's was a massive development, too, but secured with private guards, not the police, while RNA House was a stand-alone structure rooted in the city block, with one security guard. All in all, middle-income Mitchell-Lamas didn't have many more amenities than public housing—the interiors contained similar narrow kitchens and an open dining room/living room layout. We had the same radiators, window frames, kitchen cabinets, linoleum floors, and 4″×4″ white bathroom wall tiles. The major distinction between NYCHA housing and mine and Mondello's was that our Mitchell-Lamas received more financial support and were thus better maintained. Maintenance workers scrubbed off graffiti and picked up trash. When asbestos was discovered in the RNA House laundry room, it was quickly removed.

In the 1970s, collectivist principles of social housing for all started to erode. Nixon, who saw public housing as "monstrous depressing places—rundown, overcrowded, crime-ridden,"[19] cut funding for public housing, ended new construction of public housing projects, and terminated federal support for the Mitchell-Lama program. In 1974, just after Nixon resigned, Ford signed the landmark Housing and Community Development Act, amending 1937 Housing legislation to create Section 8. Now, the federal government need only sign an agreement with a private developer to subsidize a tenant's rent,[20] leaving low-income tenants at the mercy of landlords, who often didn't want to accept "welfare tenants." Those landlords who did accept vouchers offered housing in crime-ridden neighborhoods with failing schools.[21]

Outside NYC, high-rise projects were blamed for all social ills and destroyed. In 1972, when the enormous Pruitt-Igoe housing project in St. Louis was razed, architectural historian Charles Jencks declared it was "the day that modern architecture died."[22] Pruitt-Igoe's demolition was depicted in *Koyaanisqatsi: Life Out of Balance,* the 1982 experimental film directed by Godfrey Reggio with music composed by Philip Glass, as a quintessential example of modern urban life's imbalance. The problem, however, was not in modernism as an architectural project, not in the towers themselves, but in ruinous government housing policy that aided Whites and discriminated against Blacks and people of color.

Thankfully, in New York, a city of high-rise dwellers, public housing and Mitchell-Lama developments have survived. But, starting in the '70s, decreased federal funding in combination with New York City's ballooning fiscal insolvency caused NYCHA projects to suffer. They became increasingly neglected and, after advocacy groups and the federal government pressured the housing authority to relax income restrictions, populated by the unemployed extremely poor, as opposed to the working poor.[23] Still, according to professor and writer of *The Last Neighborhood Cops* Gregory Umbach, in the '70s, the projects remained "anchors of stability and safety . . . places that you wanted to get into as the neighborhoods were deteriorating around you,"[24] debunking the prevailing narrative of NYCHA housing as horrific.

My dad didn't get to witness changes in housing legislation, his death marking the beginning of the end of the common good ethos that drove US policy to provide a decent home for all. Now a fatherless daughter, I had to navigate the transformations without him, somehow mustering the resources to make sense of the world, both personally and politically, without my father's guidance, wisdom, great warmth, intelligence, and concern, not just for his daughters but in service to the greater good.

So did Mondello. He had a father, but his dad was a recluse in Pennsylvania, mostly absent in Mondello's life. Mondello and I each had our own unique, differing struggles. What united our lives though, aside from being raised by strong, single, working mothers, was Mitchell-Lama housing. Our buildings provided a ballast. We both came home to stable, nurturing, subsidized cooperatives.

New York City is special because of its mix of people from diverse economic, racial, and cultural groups living together and exchanging ideas, breeding tolerance and understanding. Middle- and low-income housing, constructed because of the determined, collective effort of enlightened politicians, urban planners, and architects, as well as communities suffering from systemic housing discrimination, enables heterogeneous populations to coexist and thrive. In order to preserve the city's unique character and halt housing inequality, the city must build and maintain affordable housing on a grand scale. Today's New Yorkers, especially children, deserve the same opportunities to live with housing dignity that Mondello and I had growing up.

Chapter 6

‖‖

Grappling with Death

NINA AND I headed south on Broadway to 86th street, bundled up in beige camel hair coats with thick belts strapping us in, our progress hobbled by knee-high black patent leather platform boots. We were on our way to the east side for Rachel's Bat Mitzvah at Park Avenue Synagogue, party to follow at the Plaza Hotel. As we stood on the corner of Broadway and 86th Street waiting for the crosstown bus, our Farrah Fawcett wings whipping in the wind, rouged cheeks growing redder from the cold, we noticed a rust brown Chevy Impala creeping slowly toward us. Stopping, the driver rolled down his window, leaned over, and said, "You girls working?"

We looked quizzically at each other, eyebrows arched, then realizing his intentions, hurried further up the hill to the bus stop, laughing. How incredible. This man presumed we were hookers. How bizarre. Though made up and wearing big gold hoop earrings, we didn't think we looked suggestive. We were swaddled, every inch of our bodies covered.

The car crept up the street toward us, but we stood in a crowd, so didn't feel threatened. Finally, the bus arrived, and we sat down in the back, peering out the window at the Chevy Impala, now parked on the street, the driver staring ahead, mouth open, tongue hanging, pants down, jerking off. We were used to dodging muggers, junkies, crazed Vietnam Vets, psychiatric patients forced onto the streets by government cutbacks, ogling men hanging out on stoops, but not guys making serious propositions. We weren't scared, though. He was simply part of the landscape.

It was 1976, the year *Taxi Driver* debuted. The Martin Scorsese film

65

starred Jodie Foster, twelve years old at the time—a year younger than Nina and me—playing Iris, an underage hooker, and Robert De Niro as Travis, a psychotic Vietnam Vet who haunts Times Square X-X-X-rated porn theaters back when Times Square was seedy, and peep shows, porn shops, pimps, and prostitutes abounded. Parts of *Taxi Driver*, like Travis's famous "You talkin' to me?" scene in a building on 89th and Columbus, were filmed just blocks from where Nina and I walked on the Upper West Side. The film depicted 1970s New York as a nightmarish, violent, debauched hell—an image shared by many at the time. Of course, the reality was more nuanced than this. 1976 was also the bicentennial when we watched the parade of tall ships sail up the Hudson River.

The famous October 29, 1975, *Daily News* headline—FORD TO CITY: DROP DEAD—regarding President Ford denying funds to bail New York out, summed up the sentiments of the nation. It also reflected the federal government's shift away from liberal values. Ford's treasury secretary, William E. Simon, "warned that bailing out the city would amount to nationalizing municipal debt and rewarding local officials who lacked the will to stanch the inevitable hemorrhaging inflicted by bankrupt liberalism"[1]—a shift which Republicans continue to this day.

While emptying out a cabinet in my childhood bedroom, I found stacks of letters my mother and I exchanged over the years when I was at camp, describing New York City's declining quality of life:

July 2, 1975—Dear Jenny, The city is literally stinking . . . the sanitation persons are on strike and not picking stuff up. It's piled all over the place. I went out for a short walk doing errands and saw just piles and piles of it. However, last night the Mets didn't disappoint. I have enclosed some New York Times Mets clippings to cheer you up.

July 3, 1975—Dear Jenny, It was still raining at six, so I had to swim to the movies. I saw Prisoner of Second Avenue. It was rather funny . . . all about the tensions of living in N.Y. The protagonist, Mel, played by Jack Lemmon, lost his job and has to deal with the heat wave, the sanitation strike, and a burglary. He ultimately has a nervous breakdown!

July 9, 1975—Dear Jenny, I brought in all my plants from the terrace because they didn't look happy . . . too hot out there and also too sooty. Yours are still okay, but I will bring them in tomorrow because I think they will also get sooty if they stay any longer.

Despite these hardships, my mother never considered leaving the city. My sister and I were eternally grateful that she didn't install us in a suburban cultural wasteland. In the city we had freedom, independence, and access to artistic experimentation. We walked across the park to the Metro-politan Museum of Art, wandering its vast halls, pretending to take refuge like the runaways in *The Mixed-Up Files of Mrs. Basil E. Frankweiler*. Or we rode the subway to the Museum of Modern Art, where we had a family membership, took art classes, and participated in interactive installations. We played in the sculpture garden, jumping over the rectangular fountains and ponds and climbing on Picasso's goat, though we weren't supposed to. Afterward, we rode the #7 bus to 96th Street, and our mother taped our paintings on the wall. As teenagers, we wandered through the museum and sculpture garden with friends, or cousins, or alone, reading next to the goat sculpture or drinking coffee or wine at the cafe.

We frequented performance spaces like Symphony Space and Lincoln Center, where we heard Ella Fitzgerald scat and watched the New York City Ballet dance to Jerome Robbins's choreography, and arthouse cinemas like the Thalia, around the corner from RNA, where we could stroll in to see a Buñuel film at a moment's notice. At Madison Square Garden, we listened to Paul Simon, Jimmy Cliff, and Phoebe Snow sing a benefit concert to support New York City's Public Library system, which was ailing financially along with the rest of the city.

The main attraction, Paul Simon, was a homegrown singer/songwriter, with New York City as his backdrop, his pithy timely lyrics commenting on the existence we lived every day: "The words of the prophets are written on the subway walls, And tenement halls." A few years later, we saw Bob Marley perform at the Garden before he died too soon. We went to sem-inal Broadway theater like *Fiddler on the Roof*, *A Chorus Line*, and *Raisin*, and downtown experimental theater by The Paper Bag Players, The Wooster Group, and at La Mama. We marched for equal rights for women and demonstrated against the Vietnam War and for nuclear disarmament. John and Yoko were our neighbors, and Knicks stars Walt Frazier, Willis Reed, and Earl "The Pearl" Monroe hung out on our building steps.

We heard myriad languages, had whimsical, marvelous, spontaneous interactions, mingling with all kinds of nonconformists. The whole city was our adventure playground. We were at the center, where events hap-pened, where we fought to make the world better. We weren't segregated or shielded in a homogeneous suburb. We didn't need to drive in to expe-rience the city. We lived this reality every day, for better or worse.

As the city's fiscal health declined, so did my emotional health. While I was grieving my father's death, the onset of adolescence heightened my sorrow. At school, I felt increasingly isolated, unable to understand or articulate my feelings. Mr. Brennan was my swim teacher, from Queens, of Irish descent. He had sweet blue eyes, ruddy skin, and messy sandy hair, beard, and mustache. I told him I couldn't swim because I had cramps from my period. I never had difficult periods, but for some reason that day, I used it as an excuse. Maybe it was because I saw other girls exploiting menstruation to get out of swimming on blustery winter days, and I wanted to try it, too. Or maybe I was grieving and couldn't recognize my pain. I sat with Mr. Brennan on the ledge of the platform in my one-piece black Speedo, my legs dangling, and we watched the kids in my class doing laps. I was thirteen.

The swimming pool at CGPS took up the whole floor of a narrow brownstone. There was little walking room around the edges of the pool, and our towels hung from hooks on the wall. The school was private, but in the '70s, it wasn't renovated, spacious, or slick. In many ways, the facilities at P.S. 75, though institutional, were superior and had a large gym and a real auditorium with rows of seats and a stage. The gym and theater at CGPS were in the same small room, with a tiny podium and no seats. Folding chairs were arranged for assemblies and performances. Later, by the '80s, after a major PTA fundraiser, the CGPS interior was modernized, and the school expanded. The pocket park where we planted a garden in an empty lot originally designated for public housing was demolished in favor of a new slick building. Nowadays, it's known as Columbia Glamour. Kids are picked up in chauffeured limousines lining the side streets, unthinkable in the '70s, reflecting demographic and economic shifts. When I was growing up, my mechanical engineer father, raising us in subsidized housing, could afford to pay private school tuition. Not so today.

It was fun hanging out with Mr. Brennan. We talked about my gymnastics competitions and the upcoming Olympics in Montreal. But then he said, "I bet you have a cool dad. I bet he has a beard and mustache, too. I bet you got your great smile from him."

I nodded and looked away. I was surprised he hadn't heard my dad passed away. He died *at school*, after all. I wondered which of my teachers knew and were aware of my grief. *Maybe none of them*, I thought, my stomach aching.

Mr. Brennan was so enthusiastic and sincere. I couldn't bring myself to tell him the news. Instead, I got up and walked away.

In 1975, my mother started a master's degree program in Library Science at Columbia University, twenty blocks north of 96th Street, and she became busy and unavailable in unfamiliar ways. She wasn't home after school, so I, like Mondello, became a latchkey kid. Often, I went to Nina's house—a refuge from private school insecurity, a return to normalcy, to my pre-private school days, and especially consoling after my father's death. A discontented feminist, Nina's mother, Kaila, was still at home, growing avocado plants and cooking pot roast with onions. If my sister was around, I hung out with her. Once in a while, I ventured downstairs to the backyard. Sometimes Dore—cute, sturdy, with straight brown hair—was there shooting hoops, but I was shy, too insecure to approach him, the easy childhood interactions gone, replaced by adolescent anxiety. Mostly, the backyard was empty. Kids were growing up, their lives taking them away from RNA House.

After dinner, my mother left the dishes in the sink and studied at her upright teak desk crammed into the corner of her room, the shelves bursting with papers and books. I cracked open her door and peered in. "Will you do something with me?"

She stopped typing and swiveled in her wooden bucket office chair to face me, her wraparound jean skirt loosened, her fingers remaining on the keys. "I can't, honey. I have homework."

I crawled onto her bed and kept her company, trying not to interrupt with chitchat. She was sweet and directed about her preoccupation. She never got mad at me for disturbing her; she just did the work, popping Tums and downing Tab along the way. Years later, she told me how stressful it had been to return to school, how worried she was about doing well, about getting a job, about juggling being a mother and studying with no set schedule, and how much easier it all became once she was employed.

I wasn't angry with my mother for becoming a graduate student. She seemed engaged and content with her new project. I didn't connect her busyness with my loneliness. It was just the current state of affairs.

Doing the laundry became my chore. Every Wednesday afternoon, I descended to the basement, pushing the cart into the drab, windowless laundry room, wishing my mother was around to help. I longed for the time when I was younger, when she was a full-time mom, involved with the food co-op, and the laundry room bustled. There were still neighbors to chat with, but it wasn't the same. We RNA House kids went our own separate ways, many retreating, like me, into private suffering, struggling unsupervised with depression and drugs while parents were off finding themselves at EST self-help seminars. My mother's life didn't center on the building anymore either. She didn't need babysitting, and she was too busy to help with the food co-op.

We sat at the dining room table, still in our nightgowns, sipping instant coffee, the Sunday *New York Times* spread over the table and stacked on the kitchen stool. My sister opened the real estate section. "Here's one in a prewar building on 100th Street. Six-room West End Avenue apartment, five hundred dollars a month. We can afford that."

"Lemme see." I leaned over my sister's shoulder, studying the classified ad.

"Don't you girls get it? I don't want to move," our mother said, exasperated. "I just put your names on the wait-list here for one-bedroom apartments."

"Can't we do better than *this*?" I swept my arm around the room.

"Do you girls know the maintenance went down because we lost Daddy's income? I can afford to go back to school. You have no idea how lucky we are to live here."

She was right. We didn't appreciate how RNA House eased our financial strain. We had no sense how important Mitchell-Lama's social justice values were to our mother or that our father's spirit lived on in the building. We didn't value the friendly guards and workers who were so attentive after our father's death or realize that, although we no longer hung out with the RNA House gang, we still saw them in the hallways, elevators, laundry rooms, and lobby. We didn't understand we were part of a community.

We also didn't know—how could we—that the impending governmental shift to a free-market capitalist ideology would eventually weaken the community feeling at RNA, or that one day upscale buildings would erupt in our neighborhood like a measles outbreak, offering multimillion dollar apartments smaller than our subsidized unit.

That diminished community spirit would soon affect many areas of American society, not only in New York City, but around the country. By the late '70s, labor unions were losing power as "unionized employers, at the core of the economy, such as GM, US Steel, and Goodwrench, began to viciously fight worker efforts to unionize . . . and employers began relying heavily on union busters."[2] The Vietnam War and Nixon's corruption eroded trust in government institutions, paving the way for Reagan's anti-government agenda; in Reagan's 1981 inaugural speech, he declared, "Government is not the solution to our problem, government is our problem."[3] The backlash against the civil rights and feminist movements were gaining momentum. Affirmative action was under attack by Whites claiming reverse discrimination, and Phyllis Schlafly galvanized the right by campaigning to defeat the Equal Rights Amendment.

My mother took a job at the Public Education Association (PEA), an advocacy organization working to reform New York City public schools. PEA was located at 20 West 40th street between 5th and 6th Avenue in an ornate Flemish-style, 1907 building designed by Henry Hardenbergh, who also designed the Plaza Hotel and the Dakota apartment building.[4] Her office was the library, a grand room with high ceilings and arched windows overlooking Bryant Park and the main branch of the New York City Public Library, a Beaux-Arts masterpiece. As information director, she governed the stacks like a queen presiding over her palace. In the '70s, when my mother started working at PEA, Bryant Park was a haven for drug dealers and users. (During the Depression, it had been a refuge for drunks and hobos.) The park was dangerous, a walled-off graffiti, garbage, pimp, prostitution, and crime disaster zone. My mother warned my sister and me never to go there. So we never did. Instead, we exited the subway and raced past the park to her office.

I didn't visit her often, but when I did, I felt reassured in her presence and with the other women who ran the organization, Jeanne Frankl at the helm. It was better than going home to an empty apartment. I didn't realize until I was an adult how important the job was to my mother's mental health. Aside from the income, it gave her a place to go to every day, a purpose, a structure, and a cause—good public schools for all New York City children.

"I have bad news for you," my mother said. I sprawled on her bed, watching the Mets game, my mother at her desk cutting out education articles from the *New York Times*. "At the end of the summer, the Greens are moving to West Hartford, Connecticut. Martin got promoted. I told Kaila I'd help her pack. Nina's very upset about it. So am I. Since Daddy died, I've relied on Kaila a lot. You're losing your best friend and so am I."

At first, I didn't register what a blow losing Nina would be. There was still the whole summer to pretend she wasn't leaving. But then she did go, and over the years, each time we visited, I felt I lost more of her. She lived in a gigantic house, or so it seemed, and, at least on the surface, she'd become a conventional suburban kid, driven to and from the mall, eventually driving herself, going to football games and the prom, wearing makeup, unrelatable to me on all accounts. Perhaps our lives would've taken different directions anyway if she'd stayed in the city, since I was plunging into depression while she remained happily ensconced in a cohesive nuclear family.

Still, it was shocking to see how she'd transformed. It's not as though I'd never experienced suburbia. My cousins lived in Teaneck, New Jersey, just over the George Washington Bridge, visible from the Upper West Side. No great distance. But West Hartford, Connecticut felt worlds apart, in the middle of nowhere, disorienting for a city kid not accustomed to driving long distances. It was as if my best friend and her mother, Kaila—a second mother to me—were living in a foreign country.

Maybe it was the confusion over seeing Nina displaced. I'd only known my cousins as suburban kids. But Nina was a product of the city, my tomboy partner in crime when we hailed taxis and yelled *Fuck You* to the driver, in adventure when we rode the subway for the first time to Macy's and back, in protection when we kept each other safe on the "pervert block" and from muggers, and a refuge from private school and coming home to an empty apartment.

She'd been embedded in the city. Both of her parents were New Yorkers, Kaila from Brooklyn, and Martin from the Upper West Side since babyhood after fleeing the Nazis. Often, Nina and I visited her *oma*, with her thick accent, gray hair, and clunky shoes, in her shabby Upper West Side apartment on West 85th Street, perfectly in place within the Jewish refugee community. How could she leave me?

It was a good move for us, Kaila told me much later. By then, I could see that it had been. Martin got a better job and Kaila became director of a rape crisis center in downtown Hartford. And, despite our differences, Nina and I remained close friends. Still, their departure was devastating.

With Nina gone, sometimes instead of going home after school, I went to Bloomingdale's and shoplifted. The Bloomingdale's neighborhood was familiar terrain. Our allergist was next door. Starting when I was nine, my mother and I made the long trek there once a week by bus for our allergy shots, first east through Central Park on the 96th Street crosstown, then down Lexington Avenue to 59th Street. When my mother applied to graduate school, she took practice GRE tests on the bus to Bloomingdale's. She plunked her oversized study book on her lap, read the vocabulary and analogy questions aloud, then scribbled the answers with a pencil, me huddled next to her, thinking she was a genius for getting everything right. On the test, she received the highest possible score in English plus the bonus points, but failed math.

Once I transferred to private school and discovered Bloomingdale's was the store of choice for my new friends, I begged my mother to shop there, and—incredibly—she relented. Previously we'd gone to Macy's, the store for the masses, or we'd ride the subway to Natan Borlam, a discount clothing store in Williamsburg run by Orthodox Jews, that still exists today.

My private school friend Tammy's mother was a personal shopper at Bloomies. With big platinum blonde hair stiff from hair spray, bright blue and lavender eye shadow, and rouge painted onto her Modigliani-shaped face, Lorraine was *ungapatchka*, Yiddish for "overdone," in the words of my aunt Molly. In contrast, Tammy had boyish square features and a large Jewish nose. Tammy and I related because we both suffered self-loathing, mine precipitated by my father's death, hers from Lorraine, who criticized her looks: "If only your nose were a bit narrower . . ."

Tammy took me to visit Lorraine in her hideaway for the fabulous and well-heeled. The soft and cushiony pillows, plush wool cream carpet, silky clothes, and scarves reminded me of the bedroom inside the bottle in *I Dream of Jeannie*. Rumor was, at that time in the 1970s, Bloomingdale's was the hottest pick up joint in town. According to *60 Minutes*, the Men's department, Active Wear, and the cheese counter were the places to cruise. Who knows what went down inside that bottle.

But that's not why I went. When my mother started working, instead of going to the allergist, I shoplifted at Bloomingdale's. I didn't consciously think to myself *I'm going to Bloomingdale's today to steal*. I thought, *I'll go to Bloomingdale's to kill time before my mother comes home from work. Maybe I'll run into Tammy's mother, maybe she'll invite me into her genie's bottle. Maybe I'll drink champagne with Cher*.

I rode the escalator to the Juniors section and wandered around, dazzled by the glitz, the glass-mirrored disco balls, the child mannequins atop platforms, posing like Charlie's Angels with feathered hair, halter tops, bell bottoms, and platform shoes. When I was little, in happier times, my sister and I posed, too, staying still, trying to fool passing shoppers. Now, I held up expensive designer jeans, brushed my hand against hanging polyester blouses, tried on brown suede clogs, mouthing along to *Voulez-vous Coucher Avec Moi . . . Ce soir, Voulez-vous Coucher Avec Moi* on the sound system.

I came to the lingerie section and stopped by stacks of soft cotton, solid-colored *Bloomies* underwear, the round lettering, overlapping circles, and straight lines reminding me of posters in my parents' Bauhaus book. I looked around to see if anyone was watching. That's when I thought, *I can get away with this, can't I?* I grabbed a bunch, slipped them into my backpack, and left.

I only got caught once. A Black security guard approached, wagged his finger at me, grabbed me by the elbow, and took me to a security office on the same floor in the back, where a White man, behind bulletproof glass, admonished me for stealing through a little speaker's hole. "There'll be severe consequences if you try it again, young lady."

I never did.

Of course, it doesn't escape me now the leniency granted White teens in those hallowed halls of commerce.

Trembling, I went home. Danny, a friendly, brown-skinned mainte-nance man opened the lobby door for me. "Alright. Howya doing? Give me that gorgeous smile of yours."

Things weren't so bad. Back in the building, I felt safe and protected.

After my father died, my sister started staying out all night with a group of kids on 89th Street and West End Avenue, one of whom must've been going to CGPS. My mother was terrified, so she said to my sister, "Bring everyone to our apartment. I'd rather you be home, so I know where you are."

Suddenly people were in and out of the apartment all the time. That's when I met Elizabeth's boyfriend Arturo. Arturo's parents had kicked him out, we took him in, and he stayed with us through high school. He was handsome, with round cheeks, brown skin, a warm smile, mustache, thick eyebrows, and tightly curled dark hair clasped in a ponytail.

At one point early on in this arrangement, my mother asked if I was upset that Arturo lived with us. "I can ask him to leave," she said.

"No. It's okay. Maybe I'll get a boyfriend, too." The truth was, though, that I wasn't at all prepared to let a guy get close to me. My response to my father's death was to fear abandonment, to be defensive, not to form a close relationship with a lover as my sister and my mother later did. I needed my father back, plain and simple, or a father figure to emerge. Neither happened.

Everyday Arturo, son of legendary Cuban composer, arranger, and conductor Chico O'Farrill, and now legendary in his own right, played the dusty baby grand piano we inherited from my great-grandmother. Often, he and I would be the first ones home after school. Always sweet but never loquacious, he'd smoke a joint and practice a Thelonious Monk tune while I spread out on the living room rug, did my homework, and listened.

Hayward—gentle, handsome, dark-skinned, spacy, with a short Afro—might be there, too. He was a bass player, one of Art's many musician friends who frequented our apartment from the neighborhood and Harlem. Hayward couldn't afford a case and would carry his bass around in a sack. Mellow, when he wasn't practicing, he spent much of his time stoned, watching old black-and-white movies on our tiny dining room TV with the sound off so as not to interfere with Arturo's piano. When my sister arrived and Arturo was done practicing, they piled into her room with even more friends—Peter, Julie, Nicky, Chris, David—and shut the door, leaving me behind. I was invited to join them when Mark was around, a tall, reserved, Black upright bass player who was on his way to Yale.

"Your sister's really pretty. Ask her to come in," he said.

I did hang out, but I was always timid and quiet, sitting in the corner on the blue carpet, splattered with my sister's oils and acrylics, my T-shirt pulled over my knees bent into my chest.

As usual, I went away to summer camp, but this time my sister stayed. She had a life in the city, a live-in boyfriend. With Nina in Connecticut, Rachel traveling, and my mother working full-time, I needed a place to go. Summer in the city in the '70s was a horrendous place for kids, anyway. The smog was so bad the skyline was obscured, and since the city was nearing bankruptcy, playgrounds weren't maintained. Urine and garbage stank up the street. The summer of '77 was particularly grim. There was a blackout with terrible looting. The Mets traded away Tom Seaver, and Son of Sam was on a rampage, murdering women and terrorizing the city, finally getting caught in August.

Camp Trywoodie was like a continuation of life at RNA House—integrated, progressive, and tolerant, though in the upstate New York woods. The camp was a successor to Wo-Chi-Ca, short for "Workers' Children Camp," an interracial camp supported by the Communist Party and labor unions that Paul Robeson visited regularly. In 1954, McCarthyism, a fire, and polio forced Wo-Chi-Ca to close. Soon after, Trywoodie took its place. Inside the 1964 Trywoodie yearbook was a letter written by a group of campers to President Johnson in response to the murders of three civil rights activists—James Chaney, Andrew Goodman, and Michael Schwerner:

> We, a group of fifty-two teenagers at Camp Trywoodie, are deeply concerned with the recent events in Mississippi. If the young people of our nation feel strongly enough about civil rights to risk their lives teaching in the south, we feel it is the responsibility of the Federal government to ensure the safety of these dedicated workers.
>
> Our camp population represents varied cultures, interests, and national backgrounds. At Trywoodie one hundred fifty children from seven to fifteen have learned to live side by side with people of all races and religions. As a matter of fact, it came quite naturally! If we, as children in our community, can work, live, and play together harmoniously, is it not possible that you, as adults throughout our nation's communities, can follow the example of minds not yet blackened by the soot of bigotry?
>
> We demand immediate action for the sake not only of America's population, but its unborn citizens! We shall overcome.[5]

The Trywoodie spirit of inclusiveness and social justice continued in the mid-70s when I was there, but now with a dose of environmental activism. We sang anti–Vietnam War and pro–civil rights songs, did Israeli folk dancing, and attended Pete Seeger's Hudson River Sloop Clearwater Festival to clean up the heavily polluted Hudson River.

Though in my element, I was desperately homesick. Being away triggered my anxiety. I began to fear my mother would drop dead like my father had. Every night before bedtime, I sat on the cabin floor in the vestibule between the room where we slept and the bathroom with my best camp friend Kelly, who tried to reassure me.

"Your mother will live. I promise you. She will live."

"How do you know?"

"I just know."

I remember thinking how kind she was but, of course, she couldn't know.

In letters from that infamous summer of '77, my mother distracted me with news from work: *What excitement around here yesterday. We had Bella Abzug, Mario Cuomo, Herman Badillo, and Ed Koch talking in front of the TV cameras about education. Lots of people came and we were all very thrilled about the event. Try to enjoy yourself. You're only away for a month.*

My sister wrote: *The other night in Central Park, Arturo and I snuck into Belvedere Castle. There was a long winding staircase almost five flights. The door wasn't locked, and the windows were broken, glass scattered everywhere. It was really scary and haunted. When you come back, we can go there.*

On the Fourth of July, Arturo and I went to Riverside Park and watched the fireworks. Everyone on the West Side was there, and they all had these green, fluorescent lights that cost fifty cents, which we couldn't afford. But they were part of the force. Do you remember, may the force be with you? From Star Wars?

I did remember. That spring the movie had opened, and we couldn't wait to see it. About seven of Elizabeth's friends and I piled into a checker cab, cheaper than the subway, and went to Times Square, cracking the windows to get high along the way.

In real time my mother narrated the devastating blackout: *Guess what! The lights went out!! All over Con Edison land—the Mets game went off the air, the air conditioning is off, and I have two candles lit to finish this letter. Outside there are people milling around, setting off firecrackers and the traffic is moving slowly—I wonder exactly where Elizabeth is?? She and Arturo went to see Star Wars again. I hope they were uptown and not in a downtown theater!!*

At least I have a radio this time. Last time we didn't have a transistor so didn't know a thing. Just heard that hospitals are treating patients in parking lots.

Neighbors Ed, Paul, and Bela all checked in to see if everything was okay. Nice! I was going to pay bills tonight. Maybe I still should, to keep me from worrying until Elizabeth comes home.

It's hot.

I'm tired and want to go to sleep but best to wait up for Elizabeth. I hope she and Arturo don't get separated and that she calls to let me know she's okay, but it's probably impossible to get to a phone . . . at 11 or so she did call and said she and Arturo were at 44th street and Broadway and were okay. But now it's 12:30 and she's not home! I'm waiting up, but I fell asleep for a while.

Now it's 1:30 am and she and Arturo arrived so we're all going to sleep.

It is now 10 am—the lights went on about 12 hours after they went off and so I didn't even have to re-set the clocks!! (Actually they are 20 minutes fast). Everything is hunky-dory at RNA, but the lower part of the city is not yet restored. I just heard on the radio thousands of stores were damaged from looting and rioting, devastating fires swept through neighborhoods, hundreds of people were arrested, and the city is estimating it will cost over $300 million in repairs. Just what we need.

My sister wrote: *The blackout was scary but exciting. There was lots of looting. It was pretty bad. Arturo directed traffic at an intersection because there were no traffic lights. Try to cheer up. You're only gone a few more weeks, and then you'll be home.*

The next summer, instead of Trywoodie, I joined my New Jersey cousins at Belvoir Terrace, a snooty fine arts camp in the Berkshires, filled with the kinds of privileged Upper East Side private school girls living in Fifth Avenue duplexes I felt inferior to. Though I studied with the crème de la crème of New York City Ballet and Martha Graham dancers, I never should have attended Belvoir. Overwhelmed, out of place, and still mourning my father, I smoked a lot of pot with the kitchen crew, got caught, was almost kicked out, and threatened to run away.

My mother wrote: *Dear Jenny, You really scared me tonight on the phone—I began to worry that you would run away without coming home and then I would be frantic. This is a lecture to keep you from going off the deep end. I really hope you will be able to keep things in perspective this year. It's a difficult period in your life when you are learning all kinds of new things about yourself . . . and you are changing and growing (maturing) rapidly. Things hurt more but things are also more beautiful. It's the swing back and forth that is the hardest. Keep building your resources and try to gain inner strength—the old fashion expression is "the courage of your convictions." I'm trying to inspire. When you do get home, we'll keep on talking. Don't run from trouble. Also, I'll break your neck if you come home.*

I stuck it out at camp. When the Greyhound bus dropped us off in front of O'Neal's Baloon, a favorite neighborhood bistro next to Lincoln Center,

I relaxed. My sister, mother, and I ate lunch there, then took the #7 bus
home to 96th Street.

In ninth grade, Daphne transferred to CGPS. She looked and acted like an
Upper West Sider with her long dark hair, olive skin, dangling earrings, and
patched jeans. She was savvy and sophisticated, and her black, brooding
eyes suggested a suffering I could relate to. She became my best friend,
my desperately needed companion, filling a hole in my life made wider
with Nina gone and Rachel busy every day on the swim team. Like me, she
was a dancer. We took jazz classes at Phil Black on 50th Street and Broadway, did modern dance at the Martha Graham studio on the East Side, and
studied at the New York School of Ballet on the Upper West Side.

When she came over, we pushed back the living room furniture and
danced late into the night to the Supremes and Aretha Franklin, and we
choreographed to Oliver Lake, an avant-garde jazz alto saxophonist. We
danced because we loved to, to stay sane, with adolescent urgency, as if
our lives depended on it.

Daphne lived on 105th Street between Broadway and West End Avenue
in a large dilapidated prewar apartment far from the privilege of Central
Park West. The apartment had three large bedrooms, the master for her
parents, one for the oldest brother, and another for the library. Daphne
and her middle brother slept in two tiny maid's rooms off the kitchen
with only a single mattress thrown on the floor and a small dresser and
closet. I was shocked when I discovered this arrangement. Why didn't her
brothers share a large bedroom? Why weren't the library books stacked on
shelves throughout the enormous apartment to free up the bedroom for
Daphne?

Daphne was assigned girl's chores like washing dishes and ironing,
while her brothers did nothing. I couldn't fathom this unjust allocation
of responsibilities. With my father dead, there was no opportunity for

traditional designations. If he'd lived, maybe there would've been, but I doubt it. Would Arturo have been welcome? It's hard to say.

Daphne's father was a leading theoretician of existential psychoanalysis, but by the time I met him, he'd had a stroke and was barely functioning.

She called him *father*, which I found odd.

One time when I went to Daphne's house, she collected the mail from her lobby mailbox, brought it upstairs, and tossed it on the table where her father was sitting. "Here's some mail for you," she said casually, as we walked into the kitchen en route to her bedroom.

Her inebriated mother, standing at the sink, overheard us. She slammed her hands onto the counter, walked to the doorway, her face twisted with rage. "How dare you talk to father like that. Greet him properly, *then* give him his mail."

Without protest, Daphne returned to the dining room, her mother following, me observing in horror from the doorway. Daphne gathered the letters. "Hello, Father."

He nodded.

"Here is your mail."

He nodded again. She placed the mail in front of him.

Satisfied, Daphne's mother permitted her to go.

We hung out late into the night in her tiny room, the window cracked open, and got high. At 2 a.m., I sped home from 105th and Broadway along eerily empty streets, except for a junkie crouched between parked cars and a man peeing on a building. Freaked out, I repeated to myself, *It's okay. Chances are nothing will happen. Broadway is well lit, so is 96th Street, both main streets. I won't get mugged.*

My mother got involved with Reuben, a lawyer and divorced family friend, who had full custody over his two kids, as his ex-wife was mentally unstable. Reuben lived in suburban New Jersey, a place my mother could never imagine moving to. The city was her center. She was hip, urban, sophisticated. He was working-class gruff, with sideburns and beer belly. Son of Jewish immigrants, his first language was Yiddish. Extremely intelligent, he'd driven a city bus to support himself through Harvard Law. My mother ignored his brusqueness, focusing on his wittiness and astute progressive politics. My grandmother called him a diamond in the rough.

There was no attempt to *blend* our families. My sister and I spent more time with Reuben's kids back when he was just a married friend than when my mother and he dated. It was as if their affair was separate, a much-needed break from the strain of single parenthood.

"Reuben and I have become more than just friends," she said one day when we were sitting around the dining room table, reading the Sunday *Times*.

"Oh, Ma."

I felt even more hollowed out than before.

"I just want you to know that Reuben won't become a father figure for you."

Instead, she became a part-time mom. During the week, Reuben slept at 96th Street; on weekends, she was at his place. Every Saturday evening, I sprawled on the off-white wool bedspread covering her bed and watched her drape her wooden beaded necklace over her black Danskin turtleneck, comb her black hair cut into a pageboy, and spritz *L'Air du Temps* on her neck, prepping for a night with Reuben at the theater or the Philharmonic before sleeping at his house in Englewood. I liked this routine, the time we spent together before the loneliness set in, before I realized I wouldn't see her again until Sunday evening, that I'd be on my own to do as I pleased.

While my mother was with Reuben in New Jersey, Arturo's musician friends filled up our apartment with their drugs, chords, and cool conversation: Mark on upright bass, pony-tailed Pablo—shortish, macho, full of himself—on sax. We crowded around the dining room table, ordered Chinese food, and listened to Charlie Parker, John Coltrane, and Ornette Coleman while we ate, smoked, and snorted cocaine before they jammed in the living room, someone always jumping up to put another album on the turntable. They talked about and played jazz in a lingo all their own, like they were kings, like they owned the world, their egos as big as the Brooklyn Bridge. My sister was able to banter with them. I sat at the table, too diffident to speak much, feeling insignificant in their presence, the kid sister on the sidelines.

Daphne visited, but we never danced while the musicians were there. They took up all the space in the living room.

"Female jazz vocalists aren't real jazz musicians," I remember Pablo saying. I figured he, who was so confident, must be right, and assumed dancers weren't real artists, either.

We were cute, the backdrop, the groupies.

They were where it was at, and it was true.

But so were we. We just didn't know it. Or at least I didn't feel worthy or important.

During the day when Arturo was out, my sister was more willing to hang out with me. Often, we rode the train downtown to buy vintage dresses, wandering for hours through the East Village and Lower East Side. We lingered in small derelict storefronts, sorting through piles of clothes from the 1930s and '40s, heaps of flimsy rayon and cotton with navy and black backgrounds, vibrant floral designs, pink birds or curly abstract lines, stuffed into cardboard boxes or dumped on the floor. Our nails would snag on beads, or we'd shake out the jackets so their shoulder pads lined up. As there were no fitting rooms, we tried them on over our clothes or held them up to our bodies, conferring about suitability.

"Do you really think it looks good?" Perennially insecure, I was always asking for my sister's approval. She and I looked alike—short and slim with long chestnut wavy hair and fair skin, though I was more pinkish with hazel eyes to her olive skin and brown eyes. Neither of us ever wore makeup.

"It's fine."

"Do I look fat?"

"No." My sister rolled her eyes, sighing impatiently, shaking her head.

The saleswomen were hunched-over Jewish émigrés in the garment business with dangling necklace glasses and smoldering cigarettes, peddling discarded clothes for a nickel or dime, long before vintage was chic. We wanted to rebel against mainstream private school culture, even though our school was among the most progressive and permissive in the city. Still, there were kids with "normal" nuclear families who seemed happy and wholesome, undisturbed, unperturbed, not grappling, as we were, with misfortunes like our father's sudden death. They were on the inside of an innocence we had lost, and we were on the outside and wanted to dress the part.

"Twenty-five dresses each. That'll be five dollars total. Here, girls. Take," the lady said, handing us bags to cram them in.

On the train home, my stomach began to ache, and I clutched the mound of dresses in my lap, the familiar stabbing pain in my gut becoming more intense as the subway screeched into 96th Street and Broadway, and we made our way east toward Amsterdam.

RNA as a refuge no longer existed for me. RNA was fraught territory, a battleground. It was where my sister retreated to her room with Arturo while my mother was at work or when Reuben was over, also behind closed doors, where I ventured into my room, the agony in my stomach excruciating, got high, turned on Billie Holiday or Bob Marley, fell onto my purple shag rug and cried and cried and cried.

Chapter 7

Salvation in Socialism

WE FREEWHEELED THROUGH red lights in the South Bronx up to Yankee Stadium. The area was deserted, derelict buildings boarded up, the streets wrecked by potholes. But this trip was as smooth as a newly paved road along Park Avenue. At the helm of the shiny black Cadillac was State Supreme Court Judge Burton Roberts, a highly regarded, attention-grabbing, cantankerous man who was the model for the judge in Tom Wolfe's *Bonfire of the Vanities*. My private school friend Tammy had invited me along to the game. We sat together in the back of the sedan, her mother Lorraine upfront with Burt, whom she was dating, though not seriously. He took her around town to fashionable places for the upper classes to be seen like the 21 Club and Sardis, but Tammy said Lorraine never loved him. Roberts devised his own set of rules about New York City driving, as if he owned the road, smug like the Yankees we were about to watch play from a luxury suite equipped with couches, hors d'oeuvres, and a private bathroom, glassed off from the hoi polloi.

The Yankees were by no means my team. I went for the underdog Mets, the children of the Dodgers, the team that broke the racial divide. My mother, who was from Brooklyn near Ebbets Field and heard Jackie Robinson making history on her way home from school, instilled in me a love of baseball. My dad grew up in the South Bronx, on the Grand Concourse, near Yankee Stadium, a haven for prosperous Jews escaping the Lower East Side. He liked the Yankees, but his attachment didn't run deep.

I whispered about Roberts in Tammy's ear. "He's breaking the law."

"I know."

We were huddled together. No seatbelt wearing back then.

"Tell him to stop."

"You tell him to stop. I can't. He's my mother's boyfriend."

I didn't feel comfortable with my mother's boyfriend, Reuben, either. I leaned forward and said, "You're breaking the law."

Burt turned his head and smiled at me. "You're very observant," he boomed. "I like that."

"Can you please stop?"

"Why would I wanna do that? Don'tcha wanna get there in time?"

Gross, I thought to myself.

My parents taught me that driving through red lights was wrong, no matter where we were, even if no one could see us, even if we were in the poorest part of town. Now, here was State Supreme Court Judge Burton Roberts, lauded for his integrity, breaking the rules when no one of consequence was looking.

After the game, I came home to a living room filled with jamming jazz musicians and my sister's usual array of friends. This time her friend Howard was there, showing off his brass knuckles. About five foot five, with tousled black hair, wide clever eyes, and smooth brown skin, he split his time between his Native-American father's Harlem apartment and his frequently smashed Irish mother's East Side flat. Howard didn't seem like a tough guy. I don't know if he ever used his weapon, though he said he always carried it. He was just confused, like the rest of us.

"Can I see?" I asked.

He handed over the brass knuckles. They were loose around my skinny fingers.

"It's for when you punch. Makes it hurt more."

"Right. Got it." I gave them back and went to my room, wishing my mother was home instead of in Boston with Reuben.

I lived a divided life—at private school I was surrounded by White privilege. Sure, there were drugs, kids with absent parents, and boundaries broken, but the chaos was cloaked by entitlement. At home, the diverse Upper West Side and Harlem inhabited my apartment—more familiar terrain, but one I no longer fully occupied.

Lost in the mix, I desperately needed something to believe in. I was grappling with the meaning of life, in the throes of an existential crisis, emotionally scarred and traumatized by my father's sudden death, feeling unworthy and neglected by my mother and sister, and since transferring from public to private school, acutely aware of economic and racial injustice. Rather than turning to God, I found salvation in communist political theories and utopian socialist ideals. I put my faith in history—a continuity with the past, a connection to my father. As I became passionate about socialism, I began to learn how RNA House fit into the bigger picture of social justice.

In tenth grade my history teacher, Amelia Miller, a frail, short young woman with dark shoulder-length hair and a slight limp, taught me that Castro overthrew the corrupt capitalist Batista regime and created a just society with healthcare, education, and housing for all, as well as equal rights for women and Black Cubans. I was blind to her lessons about the problems with Castro's regime. I studied other revolutionary movements around the world including the Chinese, glossing over lessons about the brutality of the Great Leap Forward and the Cultural Revolution, focusing instead on positive aspects, such as men and women being held up as equals under Chairman Mao.

I developed a deeper interest in China from my quiet, gentle Uncle Ben, a successful textile trader who often traveled between Shanghai and Hong Kong. He came back from trips with gifts—silk pajamas, ivory and jade bracelets, freshwater pearls. If we felt sick, he laid his large warm hands over us, claiming he could heal our ailments like the Chinese did.

One evening, Uncle Ben took my family to see Peter Pan on Broadway along with some Chinese businesspeople. We stood on West 46th Street in front of the Lunt-Fontanne Theatre, the Chinese businesswomen dressed exactly like the men in gray utilitarian Mao suits, pleasing me but confounding passersby who slowed to stare. I couldn't imagine what the Chinese businesspeople thought of Peter Pan, a sexually ambiguous character who never wanted to grow up, or of Times Square, with its pimps and prostitutes, Live Nude Girls signs, and neon Triple X theaters advertising The FILTHY FIVE, SADISM GORE, EXTREME VIOLENCE, and VAIN BRUTAL EXTRAVAGANT.

After the show, we took the subway to Chinatown and sat at a large round table in a crowded restaurant, the businesspeople ordering dinner for us in Cantonese.

On his trips to China, Uncle Ben wrote me letters that further convinced me communism was a far more just system than capitalism:

Dear Jenny—The enclosed Beijing (Peking) Review should be of interest to you and your classmates. It is particularly fascinating to note that the contents include articles concerning controversial matters such as wall posters and China's Democratic Parties. A simple "cop out" would be to assert that it is done merely for show. We must then ask how much of our

information dispensed by Washington is for anything other than effect?
The facts are that you can express your opinion and belong to a political
party other than the Communist Party.

Progress, although slow and on occasion subtle, is being made. There
is more to wear and eat, wages are up, advanced study is encouraged and
rewarded. Daily observances that indicate change, yet might not be inter-
preted as progress, include more colorful clothing, willingness to commu-
nicate, superb service for tourists, friendliness, youngsters asking you to
speak English with them, and more small private enterprise.

From Shanghai I shall go to Hong Kong. That is a different world, but
for most it is not a better one. Pressure to survive in Hong Kong consumes
most of one's physical, emotional, and spiritual resources. Some become
rich, most struggle on to the end. In China, few become rich, yet most ap-
pear content, satisfied to make progress slowly. There is some impatience,
particularly among those who have visited the Western World. They want
the barriers of non-productive habit, marginal wages, old facilities, and
general poverty to come down. I see the structures weakening, but I also
feel that they will withstand some years of strain before being replaced by
more modern conditions which, when judged honestly, are barriers of an-
other kind—competition, envy, high taxes, scandals, and power structures.

In eleventh grade, I took a class on Chinese foreign policy with Mr.
Q, an athletic thirty-something man with a beard and mustache. We prepared to represent China at the Model United Nations at Harvard. We
read books on Chinese history and diplomacy, did research at Columbia
University and in the United Nations archives, and drafted resolutions for
deliberation by United Nations convention committees. I was on the population committee and brought a resolution to the floor in favor of abortion,
drawing a tie vote; half the world's countries embraced legalization, half
voted against it.

I was thrilled, though physically and emotionally spent. It took nerve for
me to speak in front of hundreds of teenagers. But I was also exhausted
from staying up late the night before doing cocaine with my classmates and
our history teacher in his hotel room. We piled in, some of us on his bed,
others on the floor or squeezed into the easy chair, smoking pot, fooling
around, the Grateful Dead blasting from a boom box.

"How can you guys afford this?" Mr. Q. asked, bending over to snort
a line.

On the bed next to me, a couple started undressing.

"Whoa, whoa. Cool it, you guys," Mr. Q said.

After a while, he told us to leave his room for the night, and we all complied except Sarah, who'd been lounging underneath the bed sheets in a frilly flannel nightgown.

"You, too." He motioned her to go. "You can't stay here."

Rumor had it they were sleeping together, though it's hard to say.

My favorite teacher was Bob Bailey, a tall, thin, soft-spoken Southern socialist with John Lennon glasses in his thirties, who taught Radical American History. In his class, I learned about turn-of-the-century labor leader Eugene Debs, founding member of the International Workers of the World, a.k.a. the Wobblies, and presidential candidate for the Socialist Party of America. We read John Dos Passos's *U.S.A.* trilogy, which included the execution of two American anarchists, Sacco and Vanzetti, and the lyrics to *The Internationale*. We studied *The Communist Manifesto* and *The Autobiography of Angela Davis*, which particularly resonated when Davis, who, like me, attended a small progressive New York City private school, describes her awakening to communism as the solution to oppression. About *The Manifesto*, she wrote: "What struck me so emphatically was the idea that once the emancipation of the proletariat became a reality, the foundation was laid for the emancipation of all the oppressed groups in the society."[1] I, too, felt unequivocally the desire to free all oppressed peoples.

My friend Rachel and I dominated classroom discussions—Rachel because she was brilliant, and me, because I was galvanized by the struggle for social justice—while the other students remained silent, either intimidated or indifferent. We debated *In Dubious Battle*, John Steinbeck's Depression-era novel about striking fruit workers and their communist organizers.

"All the characters are White. In truth, the majority of workers were Mexican," Rachel said.

"That was a political decision on Steinbeck's part," I said.

"The characters aren't even psychologically complex."

"That's not the point. It's about the workers' struggle."

Rachel was the class valedictorian, and my other girlfriends and I were also top students. I never had a sense that boys were smarter than girls. Boys unsettled me emotionally, but never intellectually. I saw no need to equalize the playing field by segregating girls in institutions of learning. In my experience, girls were powerhouses.

Bailey took me and other committed students to the West Side Marxist Center in the basement of a prewar building on 107th and West End Avenue, as well as to talks by Michael Harrington, the Democratic Socialist who wrote *The Other America*, about poverty in the United States.

Bailey's roommate was Mark Morgan, a spritely, agile, gay history teacher in his thirties and a former Broadway dancer in charge of musical theater. Morgan directed elaborate productions of *Bye Bye Birdie* and *Anything Goes*, choreographing Bob Fosse–style chorus lines with kicking legs, thrusting hips, and tilting top hats that Daphne, Rachel, and I spent hours rehearsing. Bailey and Morgan had Sunday afternoon potluck parties in their spacious two-bedroom on 93rd and Amsterdam, opposite Joan of Arc, the notoriously dangerous junior high school in our district that convinced my parents we needed private school. Books were crammed into bookcases on every available wall in their apartment except where iconic political posters of Che Guevara and Mao Tse-tung hung, along with Liza Minelli squatting, leg extended, scantily clad in black shorts, halter and top hat, *Cabaret* emblazoned in pink Peter Max letters. We sat on clunky mismatched wooden chairs and couches with Indian print throw pillows, teachers and students alike smoking cigarettes and eating on paper plates. There may have been beer and wine, but no one cared. Students weren't policed.

The smoke got to me; I rubbed my eyes.

"I need to go to the allergist," I told Bailey.

"Where's your allergist?"

"59th Street and Park."

"Are all your doctors on the east side?"

"Yeah, I guess."

My eye doctor had an east side address, too.

"West side doctors aren't good enough for you?" He laughed.

Good point. I'd thought I was aware of all aspects of my socioeconomic privilege, but I'd never before questioned frequenting east side doctors.

I fell in love with Bailey and radical politics. The two were intertwined. Unlike friends at CGPS who were having sex with their teachers, I didn't want to have a romantic affair with Bailey, just to be fed mouthfuls of utopia, hope, and optimism, which radical politics could deliver. He never did anything untoward. Ours was not an emotionally intimate relationship. I never confided in him. We communicated only through politics, history, and theory. I'm sure he played a more outsized role in my life than I did in his, though years later he recounted how grateful he was his first year teaching at CGPS to have me in the classroom.

Bailey introduced me to *Looking Backward*, the nineteenth-century utopian novel by Edward Bellamy, about a socialist United States where everyone contributes what they can and is rewarded equally, and honor and nobility rather than money are incentives for working hard. The book transformed my perception of RNA House. At RNA, tenants paid maintenance adjusted to family income, were allotted apartments according to family size, and only those within a specific income bracket were eligible to move in. I took pride in my mother's public school advocacy and stopped longing for her to get rich so we could move into a more luxurious apartment.

Bellamy wrote, "People nowadays interchange gifts and favors out of friendship," allowing for the "mutual benevolence and disinterestedness, which should prevail between citizens and the sense of community of interest which supports our social system."[2] I thought about how RNA's food and babysitting co-op was like the utopian community in *Looking Backward*. I began to appreciate the building. It was a deep and important turning point in my understanding of where I'd come from. Instead of feeling ashamed, I embraced living there. I wanted a better society, a utopian society. What could be more just, right, beautiful?

I discovered that Mitchell-Lama housing philosophy stemmed from the international cooperative movement first organized in 1844 in Rochdale, England, which stated that "a cooperative association shall be operated purely for service and not at all for direct profit," and that "each apartment was worth one share, both in purchasing and selling. The owner of the share would receive the same amount of money that she/he bought the apartment for when they decide to sell it, regardless of speculative market prices. Along with the purchase of the share, when decisions are made, each shareholder also gains one vote"[3]—precisely how RNA House operated.

I learned that in Brooklyn in 1918, decades before Mitchell-Lama housing existed, the Finnish Home Building Association built the very first co-op based on the Rochdale Principles.[4] In 1926, the New York State Legislature passed the Limited Dividend Housing Companies Act, a precursor to the 1955 Limited-Profit Housing Companies Act or Mitchell-Lama Housing legislation, which "facilitated co-op development by giving tax abatements to housing developers that agreed to limit their profits to 6 percent and target low-income tenants."[5]

Jewish labor activists took advantage of the law and constructed four limited-equity garden apartment co-ops in the Bronx. One was the Amalgamated Houses, built by the Amalgamated Clothing Workers—a small-scale building surrounding a courtyard and facing Van Cortland Park, as beautiful as market-rate buildings for the wealthy. The Sholem Aleichem Houses were constructed by Yiddishists, "whose ranks were split between Socialists and Communists who refused to speak to one another."[6] There was the United Workers Cooperative Colony, by the "Communist-dominated United Workers" and the Farband Houses by the "National Jewish Workers' Alliance," a labor Zionist organization.[7] The founders of the co-ops "saw themselves as the first step in the transformation to a better world . . . They believed that the physical circumstances under which people live encourage collective action and identity."[8] *So true*, I thought. RNA House's unique circumstances had supported its cooperators' collective actions and identities.

My mother told me that our family's arrival at RNA was part of a greater narrative about housing and societal changes in New York City, beginning with the tenement reform movement, and that nowhere had the unified effort to provide a decent home for all been as comprehensive or successful as in New York City. "The family story begins with your great-grandmother Ida, my father's mother," my mother recounted. She sat at the dining room table, cutting out education articles from the *New York Times*, and sticking them in a folder, while I straddled my legs on the living room rug, stretching to one side, then the other, pointing and flexing my toes. "Ida was thirteen years old in 1886 when she fled pogroms in Lithuania and emigrated with her family to New York City. They arrived through Ellis Island and crowded into Lower East Side tenement buildings alongside thousands of immigrants seeking a better life in the new world. For ten years, Ida and her family lived on 16 Forsyth Street, in a vermin-infested tenement on the Lower East Side with only one water pump and a communal outhouse in a musty courtyard. It was around this time that the reform movement began . . ."

I wanted to investigate more about the history of social housing, so I did research at the public library on Fifth Avenue, near my mother's office. There I found an 1895 New York City Tenement House Committee report about living conditions in Lower East Side tenements, highlighting hazards such as poor air circulation and pernicious overcrowding:

It is here that large families occupy narrow quarters . . . as for instance, a family of 11 in only two rooms . . . the overcrowding of the population . . . has evil effects of various kinds; keeping children up and out of doors until midnight in the warm weather, because the rooms are almost unendurable; making cleanliness of house and street difficult; filling the air with unwholesome emanations and foul odors of every kind; producing a condition of nervous tension; interfering with the separateness and sacredness of home life; leading to the promiscuous mixing of all ages and sexes in a single room—thus breaking down the barriers of modesty and conducing to the corruption of the young . . .[9]

The report categorized the tenement population according to nationality. Interpolated among the Italians, Irish, French, and Bohemians, were the *Hebrews*. Sometimes *Hebrews* were referred to as *Russian Jews*, *Russian Hebrews*, *Polish Jews*, *German Jews* and *Hungarian Jews*, and collectively as a 'race,' as in, "a hardy long-lived race . . ."[10]

Apparently, the *Hebrews* who lived in the tenth ward suffered from lower death rates than other groups due to the "precepts of their religion, affording one of the best sanitary codes in existence."[11]

Though the *Hebrews* were admired for their salutary sanitary habits, they were perceived as inconsiderate and stingy:

A majority of (this race of) tenants are shirt makers or tailors and much vigilance is required to prevent them from using their apartments as small sweat-shops . . . Many of them persist in throwing rubbish and garbage out of the windows, making it unsafe for children to play in the courts . . . Tenants of this class are also extraordinarily quick to take advantage of opportunities to escape payment of rent.[12]

Another section tells of the lack of *Bathing Facilities* and *Personal Cleanliness*:

PERSONAL CLEANLINESS. 18. The vast number of persons discovered by your committee's inspectors, amounting to 11,627 on the first inspection alone, who have no regard for personal cleanliness, and who permit themselves to fall into such a condition of bodily filth as to become traveling menaces to the health and comfort of the public at large, brings up the question of the advisability of empowering the board of health to force such persons to bathe and renovate their clothing. This seems like a long step away from the theory of personal liberty, yet it has been successfully applied in several foreign cities. In one European city it is the practice of the health authorities, when a house inhabited by persistently dirty people is found, to order them all to a public bathhouse, force them to remove their clothing, and then turn the hose on them.[13]

Sometimes, after I finished at the library, my mother and I rode the train home together. Waiting on the crowded, deafening 42nd Street platform for the 96th Street express, my mother shouted: "We have no idea how difficult Ida's life was."

I visited Ida's neighborhood in search of her tenement only to discover it had been razed to build the Manhattan Bridge, which began construction in 1901. The bridge's graffitied brick and steel beams imposed themselves onto the small-scale street, disrupting the grid. On what remained of Forsyth Street, rows of dilapidated tenements lined the block. Demographics had shifted. What was once a Jewish immigrant community had, since the sixties, become part of Chinatown.

Though there's no documentation, it's possible my family was forced to relocate due to bridge construction—or maybe they moved to Brooklyn of their own volition, where they opened a dry goods store selling men's haberdashery and women's underwear, bras, and stockings. They lived above their store in a row house at 4519 3rd Avenue until the thirties, when Robert Moses, at that time the city-wide Commissioner of Parks, used eminent domain to evict them and destroy the neighborhood to build the Brooklyn-Queens Expressway. Fortunately, they were able to reopen their business in another Brooklyn row house on 8th Avenue, where they lived behind the store in one big room that had a kitchen on one wall, a large round table in the middle, and a bed behind a large bookcase. The apartment opened into a small backyard filled with mint and weeds.

During the Progressive Era of agitation and reform, the New York state legislature passed The Tenement House Act of 1901, which set "the national standard for tenement legislation . . . and is still the basis for regulation of low-rise housing design in New York City."[14] Every apartment had to have a bathroom with running water, exterior windows of a specific dimension in each room, and various mandated fire prevention construction techniques. Despite the legislation and improvements, most people still lived without bathrooms or proper air circulation in rat-infested fire traps.

Around this time, my paternal grandparents were born in substandard Lower East Side tenements, Grandpa Jack in 1899, Grandma Gertie in 1905. Gertie began working in garment-industry sweat shops soon after the deadly 1911 Triangle Shirtwaist Factory fire, as a member of the Amalgamated Clothing Workers of America. Forced into the role of caregiver for her four younger siblings after their parents died early, Gertie, tiny at four foot ten, became an independent, self-assured woman who agitated for fair wages and better working conditions. Gertie felt empowered to make her own financial decisions. In the twenties, she pooled her money with others to invest in a middle-income apartment building in Queens.

"It was Grandma Gertie who lifted the family out of poverty," my mother told me proudly, cementing the matriarchal family mythology.

Her investment allowed my grandparents to escape the tenements, moving first to Williamsburg, Brooklyn, then to the Grand Concourse in the Bronx, the street of choice offering modest Art Deco buildings for Jews who'd grown prosperous. Grandpa Jack died in 1938, when my father was 10, and Grandma Gertie raised my father with the help of her siblings in the Bronx, waiting for my dad to move out before she married Isidore, who'd also fled from pogroms in Poland and lived in Lower East Side tenements.

By the time I was born, Gertie and Isidore lived in a two-bedroom on West 16th Street between 5th and 6th Avenue in a postwar luxury tower with a doorman and carpets on the lobby floor. I knew them as elegant, cultured, sophisticated people, my step-grandfather Isidore in a black suit, bowtie, fedora and with manicured clear-polished nails, davening at an Orthodox synagogue across the street that he attended out of convenience, not ultra-religiosity. For the High Holy Days, my father worshiped alongside him. So did my sister and I. The women prayed upstairs in the balcony, but as cute little girls, we were permitted to sit with my father and grandfather downstairs.

Amid an expanse of black trousers, jackets, and hats. I clutched my father's leg, my head coming up to his waist, the fringes from his *tallit* brushing against my shoulders, and never let go as the rabbi davened and my father followed, chanting, rising, swaying and sitting again. Even though I understood nothing, the prayers and melodies penetrated my soul in a way I wouldn't appreciate until years later. The cantor blasted the shofar like a wailing trumpet, marking the New Year, and my grandfather and father wished their neighbors *Gut Yontif*.

Ready to break the fast, we crossed to our grandparents' apartment where Grandma Gertie and my mother, not ones to pray, stayed behind to prepare food—homemade challah, apples, honey, salad, and chopped liver. Grandma Gertie, smartly dressed in a cashmere cardigan, pencil skirt and heels, was discussing Eleanor Roosevelt with my mother. We ate in the dining room, around a long ornate varnished oak table formally set, with a white tablecloth and matching cloth napkins, crystal wine glasses, and Wedgewood plates.

After my father and grandpa smoked pipes, Isidore grasped my sister's and my hand as we accompanied him during his constitutional around the Village, through Washington Square Park where longhaired hippies in tie-dye T-shirts, head bands and braids congregated around the fountain, getting high and strumming guitars, Hare Krishnas with pink saris and shaved heads chanted and banged tambourines, and chess pros competed on cement tables. Out of the park we strolled, circling back, first west past "Revolution" graffitied onto a brick wall, then north up 6th Avenue, where anti-war activists handed out flyers. We ended at Woolworths on 14th Street, where Grandpa bought us presents.

Grandpa was unfazed, uncritical, never commenting on the street life around him. Perhaps he'd seen it all. Perhaps this was nothing compared to Russian pogroms. Perhaps he loved America unquestionably or was simply amused by the young people, content to be with his adorable grandchildren in our A-line jumpers, white knee-socks, and patent leather shoes. It's hard to imagine Gertie and Isidore's early years in the tenements. Were they promiscuous? Did they suffer from nervous tension? Did they have bathrooms in their apartments? Were they *stingy Hebrews*? Were they so filthy they became a menace or were they *sanitary Hebrews*? How did they survive under such grueling tenement conditions? How did they maintain their dignity and optimism?

The Great Depression exacerbated the housing crisis in New York City, and throughout the country. Though my father's family was well-off, my mother's parents weren't as fortunate. Under dubious, undisclosed circumstances during the Depression, Grandpa Leon, son of Ida, lost his law license and became a traveling salesman à la *Death of a Salesman's* Willy Loman. Extended family members moved into their small two-bedroom Brooklyn apartment and stayed until after the War.

"My parents—your Grandma Helen and Grandpa Leon—moved their bed into the dining room," my mother continued, snipping away at the education articles in the *New York Times* and tucking them into their folder. "Big Grandma Esther—your great maternal grandmother—slept with

Aunt Susan and me. Aunt Syd and Cousin Alan were in the second bedroom. Sometimes, little Grandma Ida, Uncle Herbert, and Uncle Richard
were there too. With the help of relatives, we kept our apartment. Others
lost their homes."

While there had always been a homeless population, now that in the '30s
large numbers of middle and working-class Whites were living in Hoover-
villes, the government finally interceded, though imperfectly. Roosevelt's
New Deal government built segregated subsidized housing, planting the
seeds of institutionalized racism, the fallout of which we still see today.

During the Depression, New York housing advocates admired European governments' roles in clearing slums through government financed
low-cost housing. In 1934, New York passed the Municipal Housing Authority Act, allowing municipalities to form local authorities to develop
housing projects, and the New York City Housing Authority (NYCHA)
was born.[15] Whites-only First Houses was the first federally funded public
housing project in New York City completed by NYCHA. The project,
designed by architect Frederick Ackerman, who "dreamed of a society
free from privilege and of rights conferred by property . . . of a civilization
where people would work cooperatively with honesty and integrity . . .",[16]
consisted of 122 three or four-room apartments in eight small, human-
scale buildings surrounding a courtyard on the Lower East Side.[17] The
"worthy poor"—those with jobs, wedding rings, and sobriety—were "carefully selected" to live in these new apartments, which included a kitchen
with an electric refrigerator, a bathroom, a living room with oak floors,
windows in every room, steam heat, and hot water. The first tenants paid
$6.05 a month rent.[18]

On December 3, 1935, First Houses opened to great fanfare. President
Roosevelt telegrammed congratulations, and New York Governor Lehman,
Langdon W. Post, the first chairman of NYCHA, Eleanor Roosevelt, and
New York City Mayor Fiorello La Guardia gave speeches broadcast to the
entire nation. Crowds of women and children, including former inhabi-
tants of cleared slums and future tenants, gathered to celebrate. The Police
Department band and 400 schoolgirls performed the national anthem.[19]

Governor Lehman said: "The clearance of slums and the provision of
new dwellings for low-income families in our State has opened up a new
field of public responsibility. Previous to the still existing depression, it was
assumed by the majority of people in our State that the housing problem
was a personal one, a matter of individual responsibility."[20]

Eleanor Roosevelt said: "I hope the day is dawning when private capital
will devote itself to better and cheaper housing, but we know that the

government will have to continue to build for the low-income groups. That is a departure for us, but other governments have done it. Low-cost housing must go on in the United States."[21]

Chairman Post acknowledged that First Houses was expensive but necessary for the common good: "It is impossible to regard slum clearance in New York as a project which will pay for itself. It can be achieved only by subsidies from the Federal Government or the city or both . . . It must be regarded as an investment in better citizenship."[22]

Further boosting the affordable housing cause was The National Housing Act of 1937, sponsored by New York State Senator Robert Wagner, which created the United States Housing Authority (USHA), a federal agency within the Department of the Interior that loaned money directly to municipal authorities to better housing conditions for low-income families, again on a segregated basis. By the end of 1941, under the watch of fiery, outspoken, populist Fiorello La Guardia, the tenement-raised mayor of New York City, "thirteen separate public housing projects containing a total of more than 17,000 apartments had been constructed in New York, far more than any other city in America."[23]

After World War II, while the US government was rebuilding democracy in Western Europe through the Marshall Plan, there was a desperate domestic need to construct housing for low and middle-income American families. In response, the Truman administration passed the Housing Act of 1949, which declared that "the general welfare and security of the Nation requires the establishment of a national housing policy to realize, as soon as feasible, the goal of a decent home and a suitable living environment for every American family."[24] Truman asked, "How can we expect to sell democracy to Europe until we prove that within the democratic system, we can provide decent homes for our people?"[25]—a far cry from today's ethos.

I learned that in New York City, progressive government activism peaked with the 1949 Housing Act. Using Title I funding, and led by Robert Moses, politicians, urban planners, and architects combined forces to socially engineer large swaths of slums into New York City Housing Authority (NYCHA) towers for the working class, representing modernity and advancement. Le Corbusier's modernist, machine-age, low-cost, no-frills tower-in-the-park model became the design choice for New York City planners and architects implementing this new progressive agenda.

In addition, Moses took advantage of New York City's "tradition of strong union-sponsored housing dating back to 1926,"[26] the year New York State passed the Limited Dividend Housing Companies Act, and formed an alliance with Abraham Kazan, president of the United Housing Foundation (UHF), to build middle-income union-sponsored housing. Moses feared, as did many in government in the postwar period, that "New York would become a polarized city of rich and poor unless it took aggressive steps to provide for the middle class."[27] Through Title I, Moses and Kazan "launched the biggest expansion of union-backed cooperatives in the city's history."[28] Among other projects, the UHF worked with sponsoring labor unions to build Mutual Redevelopment Houses, better known as Penn South in Chelsea, East River Houses and Seward Park Houses on the Lower East Side, Co-op City in the Bronx, and Rochdale Village in Queens.[29] As author of *Freedomland: Co-op City and the Story of New York* Annemarie H. Sammartino wrote, "in the 1950s and 1960s, the UHF was responsible for more than half the publicly subsidized, limited-income housing built in New York City."[30]

Concurrently, using Title I funds, as well as private investment, New York State passed the 1955 Limited-Profit Housing Companies Act or Mitchell-Lama Housing Program, designed, as was union-sponsored housing, for moderate- and middle-income families, who were fleeing to the suburbs in large numbers. New York State Governor Nelson Rockefeller, who served from 1959 to 1973, also feared New York City was losing the middle class to the suburbs. He said: "The lack of urban housing for middle class families is a persistent municipal problem for New York City and every major city in the State and the nation. This income group from which the City largely draws its civic leadership and economic support, has been forced into the suburbs to find adequate homes."[31] By 1958, throughout the boroughs, "25 Mitchell-Lama cooperatives were either in planning or under construction."[32]

By 1960, New York City had made significant gains housing low and middle-income New Yorkers, although under Moses' watch, there were many abuses. Moses used increased eminent domain powers to ruthlessly raze cohesive New York City neighborhoods, including Manhattantown, a vibrant working class African American community two blocks north of RNA House. Far from a slum, Manhattantown was considered "a miniature Harlem with its own Renaissance."[33] Luminaries like Billie Holiday and Arthur A. Schomburg, whose art and writing became the basis for the Schomburg Center for Research in Black Culture, lived there for a time.[34] Nevertheless, Moses condemned the neighborhood "based on median income."[35] In its place rose Park West Village, seven redbrick high-rises with terraces, tennis courts, parking lots, and playgrounds. Though Park West Village rents were controlled and geared toward the middle class, hardly any of the Manhattantown residents could afford to move in and were permanently exiled from the neighborhood.

Similarly, San Juan Hill, a working class African American and Puerto Rican neighborhood extending from 59th Street up to 65th Street, between Amsterdam and West End Avenue—the setting of *West Side Story*—was demolished, with thousands dislocated, not for residential towers but to build Lincoln Center, a major international cultural center. Growing up, Lincoln Center played an enormous role in my education, cultural exposure, and enjoyment. My family frequented the place on a regular basis to see the ballet, theater, the Philharmonic, and the opera. Lincoln Center has enriched the lives of myriad New Yorkers, those throughout the New York City Metropolitan Region, and throughout the world. It's hard to imagine the Upper West Side without it. Yet it was constructed at considerable human cost.

Author of *Rochdale Village: Robert Moses, 6,000 Families, and New York City's Great Experiment in Integrated Housing* Peter Eisenstadt illuminated the paradox at the heart of Moses' slum clearance approach. "Moses was a great champion of Title I and the Mitchell-Lama housing program, which were forms of urban renewal that often involved tearing down existing structures and tenant relocation. Moreover, Moses shared with the idealistic socialists, social democrats, and labor unions, who supported limited-equity cooperative housing, the belief that tenements and similar structures were terrible housing and breeding grounds of innumerable social ills and needed to be replaced. Yes, there were great casualties, but there were also enormous benefits."[36]

By the late 1950s/early 1960s, the public perception of Moses' slum clearance tactics was that the drawbacks were outweighing the advantages, and he was forced to resign. Eisenstadt continued: "While in power, Moses accumulated a lot of enemies. After the Upper West Side Manhattantown fiasco, he definitely lost the liberals, and everyone was agreeing with Jane Jacobs. And certainly, after Robert Caro's *The Power Broker*, which became the defining tome excoriating Moses, Moses became the all-purpose explanation, as in Caro's subtitle, for the 'fall of New York.' I do not think that Robert Caro has written the last word on Moses. In my opinion, there was an overreaction; not all urban renewal was bad, and not all Jane Jacobs's style restoration was good—it certainly fostered gentrification."[37]

In reaction to Moses' across-the-board demolish and reconstruct method, the West Side Urban Renewal Area plan, stretching from 87th to 97th Street, between Amsterdam Avenue and Central Park West, took a different approach. It provided affordable apartments to ousted families by tearing down old-law tenements built between 1880 and 1900[38]—those without proper ventilation, running water, or fire escapes, replacing them with moderate and middle-income Mitchell-Lamas and low-income NYCHA rentals, and restoring decaying brownstones. Aiding the plan was the amended 1954 Housing Act, which designated federal funds to rehabilitate rather than raze existing structures.[39] The idea was to create a just, economically balanced society and retain the integrated character of the Upper West Side, populated both by wealthy White families living in luxurious buildings with doormen on Central Park West, West End Avenue, and Riverside Drive, and working-class Blacks and Puerto Ricans living along Amsterdam and Columbus Avenue in substandard housing.

Although many deteriorating structures were rehabilitated, others were bull-dozed, if not on the scale of prior slum clearance programs. Nonetheless, dislocated folks and small businesses lamented the loss of their homes and stores to make way for better, abundant affordable housing. Though the West Side Urban Renewal Area had the highest percentage of returning residents of any urban renewal area in New York City, scores didn't come back to the neighborhood. I'll never know how many people on West 96th Street displaced by RNA House actually moved into my building. Throughout my life, RNA House has had great significance for me. Upon my mother's death when I lost my childhood apartment, I was devastated. How did the people who were living on West 96th Street feel about losing *their* homes to make way for *mine*?

Maintaining an integrated socioeconomic balance on the West Side while accommodating all populations did not come without struggle. Many families who had bought and rehabilitated brownstones fought back against the construction of more low-income housing. In 1966, the New York Times reported: "The city . . . is committed to providing low-income apartments—but not so many that middle-income families will flee to the suburbs. Finding a percentage that would satisfy all groups is impossible, but the West Side has established the principle that a sizable number of poor people must be accommodated in any urban renewal project."[40]

Initially, the West Side Urban Renewal Area plan skewed toward the upper middle class. "Of 7,800 projected new units of housing, only 400 would be low-rent public while 2,400 would be moderate-income units built with public subsidy and a full 5,000 would be market rate."[41] In response, newly radicalized Black and Puerto Rican communities reeling from slum clearance in Manhattantown and San Juan Hill formed a coalition with Mayor Robert F. Wagner, son of progressive New York Senator Wagner, local Democratic clubs, and the Strycker's Bay Neighborhood Council

(SBNC)[42] to fight back. SBNC was formed in 1959 by St. Gregory's Church priest Father Browne, whose Puerto Rican worshippers were facing displacement. Due to the coalition's advocacy, particularly Father Browne's efforts, the city "increased the number of low-income units in the plan from 1,000 to 2,500 and the number of middle-income units from 4,200 to 4,900. The number of luxury units was reduced, from 2,800 to 2,000."[43] Jackie Robinson, the first Black major league baseball player, called the West Side Urban Renewal Area plan "the first truly integrated project the city ever attempted,"[44] and bought a unit in a racially mixed brownstone co-op on 93rd Street.[45]

Stage 1 of the West Side Urban Renewal Area plan included four middle-income Mitchell-Lama cooperatives with a total of 825 apartments sponsored by local civic groups: Goddard—Riverside Community Center, the Strycker's Bay Housing Corporation, the Columbus Park Apartment Association, and Riverside Neighborhood Assembly.[46] Monthly carrying charges ran from $18 to $28 a room. 15 percent of the apartments in each co-op charged $18 a room, "comparable to charges in the city's low-income public housing projects."[47]

RNA House was sponsored by Riverside Neighborhood Assembly, an association of West Side civic groups, including the American Jewish Committee, the Anti-Defamation League, the NAACP, and the Office of Labor and Migration of the Commonwealth of Puerto Rico.[48] Led by public school community coordinator Sarah Chartock and Philip Michaels, Riverside Neighborhood Assembly's mission was to "integrate a large influx of Puerto Rican residents into the life of the West Side community of New York City"[49] by organizing "'intercultural committees' to increase participation by newcomers in parent-teacher associations,"[50] to "encourage better inter-group relations . . . and understanding among various racial, religious and nationality groups . . ."[51] and to use "all the talents and knowledge which we as citizens can gather to create a sense of community on the West Side."[52]

Riverside Neighborhood Assembly believed that "schools have a stake in the community and a right to participate in community betterment."[53] As part of this agenda, RNA House was originally built for teachers and other school employees in the neighborhood. Priority was also given to approximately 100 residents displaced by the building's construction.[54] At the time Puerto Ricans and Blacks were reluctant to move into Mitchell-Lama co-ops because the concept of cooperative housing was unfamiliar. They preferred to remain in substandard yet familiar living conditions rather than move into unknown circumstances. In contrast, Jews, who had a history of advocating for and building cooperative housing dating back to the 1920s, were eagerly buying up shares of co-ops in West Side Mitchell-Lamas and throughout the city. In order for integrated cooperative housing to succeed, outreach to Puerto Ricans and Blacks was necessary.[55]

In an effort to reach these minority populations, Riverside Neighborhood Assembly and other civic groups sponsoring West Side Mitchell-Lamas created a free, bilingual English/Spanish booklet called *Home Ownership—Apartment Style*, explaining how cooperative housing worked.[56] They established sales office storefronts in the neighborhood, spoke with possible cooperators, and sought out folks who supported urban renewal and local public schools.[57] In large measure, this outreach succeeded. The New York Times declared, ". . . through the pressure of neighborhood organizations . . . the West Side shows promise of becoming what it was meant to be: an integrated community accommodating both bodegas and Gristede's, luxury apartments and public housing, matrons in slacks caring for well-trimmed poodles, and mothers in house dresses struggling with 12 hungry kids."[58]

In RNA House's 1965 groundbreaking ceremony, Mayor Wagner said:

> This project will provide a maximum opportunity for the moderate-income residents of this neighborhood to remain and enjoy the benefits of the renewed Upper West Side . . . One of the major lessons on the West Side has been the value of citizen cooperation and participation in the renewal process . . . Because of our emphasis on this theme, we have given first priority to the construction of low-rent housing in this area. Now that the public housing is well along, the neighborhood-sponsored cooperatives in Stage I are moving and will have top priority. We all have the same objective and that is the continued development here of a happy, healthy neighborhood as an integral part of our city—in which each family can live with decency, dignity and sense of human worth that is the birthright of each and every human being.[59]

This was the utopian landscape from which West Side Urban Renewal Area Mitchell-Lama housing emerged. I was proud of this history and how Mitchell-Lama housing was situated within it. I began to understand how generations of my family—Ida, Gertie, Jack, Sidney, Molly, Grandma Helen and my parents, sister and me—had all benefited from the housing reform movement. But as I adopted progressive politics, governmental policy shifted to the right. Nixon placed a moratorium on new public housing construction and terminated federal support for the

Mitchell-Lama program. These changes, coupled with resistance from many well-off brownstone homeowners who lobbied to restrict building more low-income housing in the neighborhood, essentially killed the West Side Urban Renewal Area plan. Subsidized buildings slated to go up did, but many sites remained vacant until the Reagan administration ruled that upscale towers could be constructed on all remaining vacant West Side Urban Renewal Area plan lots.[60]

In 1980, just eight years after the first McDonald's opened in Manhattan, plans were announced to build *The Columbia*, a luxury high-rise with its own health club on the northwest corner of 96th Street and Broadway. Previously occupying the location were two low-rise buildings accommodating the Riverside and the Riviera movie theaters—lavish vaudeville houses with gold leaf proscenium arches and murals on domed ceilings. When these buildings were deemed unsafe and torn down, a community garden sprouted, only to be demolished for the luxury building, a common occurrence when I was growing up. Pocket parks bloomed in vacant lots and then disappeared as quickly as they'd emerged.

People in the neighborhood came out in droves to protest. "Housing for people, not profit," they chanted. "Go back to the east side."[61] The protests ultimately proved ineffectual, and The Columbia rose. It was a pivotal moment that transformed the neighborhood and reflected the wider change in the fabric of the city.

On December 8th, 1980, my sister and I were in our separate rooms, Elizabeth painting, me reading Simone De Beauvoir, both listening to the radio. It was late, almost 11 p.m.

"John Lennon's been shot! John Lennon's been shot!"

We met halfway in the hallway.

"Did you hear what happened?" Elizabeth exclaimed.

I nodded. We stared at each other, then we went into her room and listened until the deejay announced he was dead.

The next day at The New School for Social Research, which I was attending instead of finishing my last year of high school, I couldn't focus during my Colonial Literature class. My friend Talia and I asked the teacher if we could skip out and go to the Dakota.

"I'm not going to stop you," he said.

We took the subway uptown to 72nd Street. As I stood in front of the Dakota, I pictured John Lennon walking along Central Park West, how I'd seen him from the bus, and how it had comforted me. We huddled with thousands of mourners, some weeping, some holding candles, some singing John Lennon songs.

John Lennon was murdered twenty-five blocks away from RNA House, cementing what felt like an end of an era. Ronald Reagan had just been elected president, and the first luxury building, The Columbia, was under construction at 96th Street and Broadway. Soon the ultra-rich would take over the neighborhood with a vengeance. Greed, cocaine, and crack were about to explode upon the scene. I was seventeen and my dad was dead, and now, John Lennon was, too.

Chapter 8

▦

Two Utopias

"Y'ALL SHOULD CUT ties with your families," Janet told Katherine, Eliza, and me, as we crowded into our narrow kitchen. We were roommates in a renovated fifth floor apartment in a brown brick tenement, fire escapes on the façade, not far from 96th Street. "They're not doing you any good."

In 1983, after a stint at Oberlin College and Boston, where I'd done an internship at WGBH for "The Vietnam Project: A Television History," I'd moved back to the city to study film and history at NYU. At first, I lived with my mother at RNA House. By then the state had reduced Mitchell-Lama funding, so the full board, representing the cooperators, switched to self-management to achieve more satisfying operation and cut costs. My sister had moved to Brooklyn with her boyfriend, Tim, whom she'd eventually marry. I wanted to move out, too. On the street, I ran into Janet Keegan, my favorite former seventh-grade English teacher at CGPS, training to be a computer programmer. A charming, caring, colorful woman in her forties from North Carolina with thick straight strawberry blonde hair, she'd noticed my thirteen-year-old grief and consoled me. Now she invited me to live with her, and I accepted.

She held the lease in a five-story walk-up and slept in the largest bedroom in the back. The rest of us twenty-something women alternated bedrooms. Two were tiny, with space only for a single bed, nightstand, and closet. The fourth, partitioned from the living room, was larger and overlooked 105th street, the light streaming in through big windows compensating for the rumbling trucks and blasting music. Initially, I lived in

105

a tiny room. So did Katherine, a robust, kind Black woman with a short afro, who'd moved to the city from South Carolina to study voice. In 1986, we watched her perform at Lincoln Center in the chorus of the opera *X* composed by Anthony Davis, about the life and times of Malcolm X. Eliza, a serious pale-skinned woman in her late twenties studying to be a social worker, got the room facing the street. After six months, we rotated, then rotated again.

Janet was a member of the Sullivanians, an Upper West Side cult that believed families were dysfunctional, and all contact with them must cease. Coupling was frowned upon, group life considered better, more stable, healthier. The collective should raise children. Though my relationship with my mother could be painful, she was precious to me. I had no desire to end contact and resented Janet's insistence. I lived with Janet, as did Katherine and Eliza, because we liked her, and we could afford the rent. None of us had any intention of cutting off ties with our families.

One productive idea the Sullivanians promoted was for cult members, many of whom, like Janet, were teachers and artists, to retrain in computer programming in order to remain living on the Upper West Side. They understood the neighborhood was gentrifying quickly. The remaining empty lots along Columbus and Amsterdam Avenue were bought by developers who built upscale condos. The dilapidated tenements across from RNA House were refurbished, with new track-lighting and fresh paint on the façade, now renting at market rates. The methadone clinic was long gone, converted into a dentist's office. On 96th Street between Amsterdam and Broadway, the tenements where the Puerto Rican men sat calling out *Mamacita puta, muy bonita madre, dame beso* (Mama whore, very pretty mother, give me a kiss) remained, but the men had disappeared, replaced by young White guys in suits.

Luxury buildings appeared on Broadway up to 110th Street as the 96th Street boundary tumbled. Single-room occupancy (SRO) hotels, which historically had housed immigrants, artists, single working men and women, Jewish war refugees and other displaced people, the deinstitutionalized, drug addicts, sex workers, paroled criminals, and variegated bohemians were converted into upscale co-ops. Their loss eliminated affordable housing for the neediest, exacerbating the affordable housing problem.

Once, after visiting my mother, I bumped into Dore, an RNA childhood friend. He'd just moved back to 96th Street after graduating, living with his parents for a few years before moving to California.

"Remember Freddy?" he asked.

"Sure." Frederico, who'd lived across the street in one of those tenements, used to play in the backyard, and he'd helped set up my father's telescope on the sidewalk.

"He committed suicide. He jumped out the window."

"Oh, no. What happened?"

"Don't know. I lost touch with him."

I crisscrossed bustling 96th Street, negotiating the heavy traffic, a stupid thing to do. Years ago, after leaving a school bus, an RNA House girl got hit by a car as she crossed against the light mid-street, breaking her leg. The cooperators were furious the driver didn't deliver her to her door and made sure it never happened again.

I stared at Freddy's now renovated building, thinking about him and my father. My stomach ached, like a knife stabbing my gut. Deep, sharp, ongoing pain.

I headed back to my shared 105th Street apartment.

I asked some friends from my Facebook groups about their lives in the 1980s after college. Though almost all had left the neighborhood for various reasons, including being squeezed out because of skyrocketing rents, many spoke of their old stomping grounds with affection. Only my childhood building friend Gina was back at 96th Street, sharing her three-bedroom apartment with her brother, Peter, now that their parents had retired to Florida. I couldn't imagine my mother living anywhere other than RNA House. Relaxing in a warm climate and no longer fighting the good fight to improve public education wouldn't have fulfilled her. The city was her political, emotional, cultural, and aesthetic center.

At this point, I had no desire to take over #14E, anyway. I needed distance from our concrete slab. I didn't yet realize that staying would've meant housing security for life. Instead, I was focused on figuring out what I wanted to do, while coping with my personal struggles resulting from my dad's death. I couldn't think about the larger picture of affordable housing. Nor was the problem as pressing in the early '80s.

At NYU, I double majored in history and film. I wanted to become a filmmaker because it seemed a perfect means of being political. I could visually document society around me, tell the stories of those long ignored. I took classes with legendary filmmaker George Stoney, who made over a hundred documentaries and "devoted himself to training community activists in the use of film as a tool for voiceless people."[1] It was Stoney, along with other media activists, who lobbied to require cable companies "to give citizens a share of the new cable broadcast spectrum—public access. That requirement was added to federal communications law in 1984."[2]

Identifying with the marginalized, I made *Mothers in Labor*, a short documentary video about single teenage mothers training in manual trades, which, thanks to media activists like Stoney, aired for a year on Manhattan Cable TV. After filming the young women at New York City College of Technology in downtown Brooklyn, I captured them working on site as plumbers, electricians, tilers, and carpenters. Puerto Rican Lizzette Vega, a tough, articulate mother of three, scored a plumbing job at Starrett City, a massive tower-in-the-park Mitchell-Lama development in Brooklyn, designed by architect Herman Jessor, who was instrumental in building cooperative housing in New York. The sink she fixed looked just like the ones at RNA House—functional, unembellished stainless steel.

Lizzette was proud to be a skilled worker and eager to share her accomplishments. "I believe in myself. I got what it takes and all it takes is wanting to do it. Right now, I have no benefits. I wanna get into sheet metal, got union, good pay. I didn't come from money. I didn't come from Park Avenue. I'm not knocking the Park Avenue people. I'm not knocking people with money. All you have to do is want to and the opportunity is there." Not exactly brimming with confidence at this point in my life, I felt empowered watching Lizzette fix a leaky faucet.

I made the film to combat the narrative Reagan pushed that single mothers of color were "Welfare Queens" gaming the system. Scapegoating these women, Reagan made eligibility for food stamps harder to obtain, while passing a massive tax cut for the rich. Following Nixon's lead, he cut funding for housing vouchers and for the mentally ill, worsening the housing crisis in New York and throughout the country. Reagan also slashed benefits for children of deceased parents, reducing them each year until they stopped entirely, all part of his Reaganomics trickle-down revolution to cut down on big government. I was lucky I still received survivor's benefits, but during my last year of eligibility, I received only a quarter of my original benefit. It was the beginning of the end of liberalism and the middle class, and the birth of today's enormous gap between the 1 percent and the rest of us.

███

On a trip to Oberlin to watch friends graduate, I ran into my old friend Alan, a gentle, skinny, blonde guy who looked like John-Boy from *The Waltons*. Alan was a poor scholarship student from a small mining town outside Reno, Nevada, where his brothers and stepfather mined gold. After graduation, he and I drove back to New York in his uninsured "exploding" Pinto to Staten Island, where he moved into a cockroach and mouse-infested dive with two former college friends. The four-room apartment was in New Brighton, right across the river from Bayonne, home to New Jersey's chemical and oil plants. In those days, Staten Island had the highest cancer rates of the five boroughs thanks to the carcinogens wafting from New Jersey.

After a while, Alan and I decided to live together. Janet discouraged it. "You'll break up, without any place to go."

I didn't listen. Knowing we'd be priced out of the Upper West Side, we looked for a home in still bargain-basement but trendy Lower East Side tenements, the kinds of places my grandparents lived, with a bathtub in the kitchen and a tiny window facing a brick wall. But I couldn't imagine such a life when an affordable Brooklyn brownstone apartment on a tree-lined street with a visible sky was a viable option. I'd already experienced gritty New York City living. I didn't need more of it, even to be cool. What would my grandparents have thought of my choosing a tenement when all they wanted was to escape one?

We settled into a small one-bedroom that a friend sublet to us illegally in a five-story prewar building next to Prospect Park in quieter and cheaper Windsor Terrace, Brooklyn. The landlord would try to evict us to raise the rent, she warned, but we took the flat anyway. It was inexpensive and required no deposit. The tight-knit, blue-collar Irish-Italian neighborhood bordered Park Slope, considered the Upper West Side of Brooklyn, and was not too far from my mother's childhood Crown Heights apartment. Generations of firemen, cops, and construction workers lived on the quaint, leafy, brownstone side streets. The main drag, Prospect Park West, was lined with two-story brick buildings occupied by local small businesses—a deli, pharmacy, small supermarket, hardware store, and Farrell's, an Irish bar and grill and neighborhood institution since the Depression. Holy Name of Jesus Catholic Church, a larger than life crucifix on its brick façade, was the grandest structure in the area. No synagogues were in sight.

It bothered me that Windsor Terrace was so White, that people of color were absent except delivery boys, and that I was an outsider. Paint peeled from the dirty white walls of our apartment, and the radiator hissed. What made it all worth it, though, was that our bedroom and living room windows had a view of the park. It felt like we were living in the country.

Alan scoffed at this idea. "Wait till I take you out west. Then you'll see the *real* country."

The park view was good enough for me. I began to realize how rough my 96th Street environment was on a noisy thoroughfare surrounded by cement, and a backyard secured by a fence with razor wire.

With my mother's urging, Alan became a public elementary school substitute and worked toward a teaching credential, while I finished at NYU. I also volunteered at the Collective for Living Cinema, an artist-run cooperative in Tribeca, founded in the '70s by a group of recent experimental film graduates from SUNY-Binghamton. It was a time when artists still inhabited the neighborhood and "no line separated the avant-garde from feature filmmaking."[3] I helped organize a retrospective of Dziga Vertov, a revolutionary Soviet documentary filmmaker best known for *Man with a Movie Camera* (1929), which used jump cuts, montage, and superimpositions of workers, factories, and buildings to portray a day in the life of the modern city.

Working at the Collective was cool. On Friday and Saturday nights, the place was packed, the loft buzzing with experimental filmmakers who used devices antiquated today like an optical printer to manipulate 16mm film frame by frame, and an enthusiastic audience of admirers who appreciated their efforts. It was at the Collective that I learned to approach the medium as an art form, not just a political tool. I enjoyed using the optical printer to distort images, and the tangible feel of splicing and taping film strips to craft movies.

That December, leaving a snowy Brooklyn behind, Alan and I took a three-day train trip to Nevada. At night we slept entwined in our seats; by day, in the wide-windowed dining car, I stared in awe at the remarkable Rockies. In Reno, we were met by Alan's older brother, Matthew, his baseball cap flattening his curly-red hair. In his pick-up truck, he sped us home to Hawthorne, unnerving me. Stepping out of the truck, I felt better inhaling the crisp clean air, and feeling the sun warm my body. Six thousand people lived in the small valley town, ringed with mountains. Alan's house was half mobile home, half ammunition box. For Christmas, his family set up a plastic nativity scene at the foot of a cardboard hearth.

Alan's sweet, spindly, mother, Alayna, kissed me. "I know what you're up to in New York. You can't do that here." She pointed to the cot where I'd sleep during the visit. "I don't want you setting a bad example for Lil' David."

Lil' David raced over to embrace Alan; his head reached Alan's waist. "I don't mind," he said, impish grin spreading across his face.

We visited Matthew and his wife, Sandra, in their two-room apartment in a run-down motel. Out of work at the gold mine, he and his wife were on welfare and home during the day, smoking cigarettes and drinking beer in front of their hairless twin babies. In contrast to Matthew and Sandra's dire predicament, the young single Brooklyn mothers trained in manual labor jobs had much more promising futures.

They live in New York. There's nothing here.

"Before I lost my job, I sent money to restore Lady Liberty," Matthew told me.

"Really? Wow," I said.

Starting in 1982, a federal campaign to restore the Statue of Liberty for its centennial requested donations nationwide. Parochial New Yorker that I was, I hadn't realized anyone outside the New York metropolitan area cared about the iconic statue.

The next day, we drove to Mt. Grant through old historic mining towns, stopping to hike near a pristine lake, mountains majestic in the distance. I began to understand why Alan laughed at calling Prospect Park the "country." On the way back, we ate lunch at a dive bar, the air thick with cigarette smoke and musty gray-haired ladies gambling at slot machines. Though Nevada was beautiful, I was relieved when we boarded the train home.

Alan and I lasted in our Windsor Terrace apartment for a year. One day, as I pushed open the cast iron lobby door with an armful of groceries, a stout man lurking in the shadows of the unlit foyer menaced me. "I know who you are," he said, hoisting his belt to hold up his paunch.

"Yeah," I nodded. I knew who he was too. I didn't deny living there. I understood we had no rights and didn't try to fight him.

The landlord took us to court, and we were evicted.

Around this time, Alan and I split up. Luckily, nearby on Prospect Park West, I spotted a *For Rent* sign in the window of a railroad flat above the hardware store. I signed a legitimate lease and invited a friend to move in. The place was more spacious than the other apartment, but my friend had to walk through my bedroom to access hers.

I soon graduated from NYU. At the awards ceremony, along with a fellow student director with a separate project, I received the Best Short Documentary prize for *Mothers in Labor*. It was great timing. Devastated from the breakup, I needed the boost.

▟▛

I found a job at Film/Video Arts (FVA), an independent film center on 12th and Broadway, opposite the legendary Strand bookstore, that rented film and video equipment, held screenings, and gave workshops for independent filmmakers. The place served all kinds of artists from those making educational films to those creating nonnarrative experimental videos like Irit Batsry and David Blair to names that would make it big like Jim Jarmusch working on *Stranger than Paradise* and Todd Haynes on *Superstar: The Karen Carpenter Story*. At the front desk sat warm and welcoming David, all-American but hipster edgy, with his handsome rosy-cheeked face, chiseled features, and rhinestone stud earring. I knew right away he was gay but fell in love with him anyway. We became the best of friends, working side by side, answering the phone, and scheduling filmmakers.

David had recently moved from Seattle to New York City with his Samoan boyfriend, Isaako. Equally but differently dazzling, Isaako was well-built, brown-skinned, with wavy black hair, full cheeks, and wide nose. Both were intellectual, creative, angry about the unjust state of the world, and cynical things could improve. Lacking ambition, they weren't seeking good jobs. They'd come to New York to experience it, had no intention of staying, and scraped by on very little money at a time when you still could, living first in a dive in Hoboken, New Jersey, then in downtown Brooklyn near Borough Hall before it transformed into a shopping mall. They made a striking couple and a perfect antidote to my breakup with Alan. The last thing I wanted was straight male companionship. We tooled around the city together, filming and photographing places too dangerous for me to go alone, like decaying factories and mills in darkest Brooklyn.

One day I invited them over and they suggested we get a beer at Farrell's. I'd never felt comfortable venturing into this male dominated, White working-class pub, where until the '70s, women were denied service at the bar, dependent on their male chaperones to buy them drinks. Apparently, Shirley MacLaine broke the barrier, ordering a cocktail on her own. The rule didn't officially change until 1980, only six years before David, Isaako, and I entered.[4]

David held the door open for us, the neon Farrell's sign above brightening the otherwise conservative main drag. Inside were dark wood walls, a tin ceiling, mosaic tile floor, and a loud, all-White crowd standing at tall cocktail tables, drinking, talking, and laughing. A few stared at us, gestured with their chins, some pointing, then resumed socializing. At the bar, Isaako tried to make eye contact with the bartender, who ignored him. The place was packed, lots of people vying to be served, so we thought nothing of it. David lit a cigarette, and we chatted. After twenty minutes, David ordered and got drinks instantly. Not much of a selection, we drank Budweiser's out of massive Styrofoam cups.

David wrapped his arm around Isaako. That's when the crowd quieted, and people scowled. The bartender leaned in, eyebrows raised: "Ya might wanna leave."

In 1986, racial tensions ran high. That same year, Michael Griffith, a Black man from Trinidad, was hit by a car on a highway in insular Howard Beach, Queens, after being chased by a mob of White thugs. Mayor Koch called Griffith's death a "racial lynching" and mandated city schools to "hold teach-ins to promote racial tolerance."[5] Windsor Terrace wasn't nearly as narrow-minded as Howard Beach, but tensions could easily escalate.

We plunked down our drinks and scrammed.

Later, safely ensconced at an integrated West Village gay bar, David said: "You must move back with us to Seattle, Jennifer. Try something new. The counterculture is aggressive in New York—people wear black, have mohawks, hostility is considered cool. Life is better in Seattle. It's a rainforest, the air is fresh, you can see Mt. Rainier from the city, eat fruit off the trees, live a country life in a cosmopolitan city, more cosmopolitan than New York, if you ask me."

I nodded, sipping my vodka and cranberry juice. "Sounds great."

"It's communal. Friends share houses for cheap. You'd love it. The coffee is *soooo* much better. The next time I visit, I'll bring back Starbucks. It's the best in the world."

David loaned me the book *Ecotopia* by Ernest Callenbach, a 1970s cult classic about Washington, Oregon, and Northern California seceding and forming an eco-friendly utopia. People grew organic fruits and vegetables, recycled, shopped using reusable bags, shared bicycles, and drove electric cars. Marijuana was legal, communities were built around transit hubs, so no one owned a car; homelessness was nonexistent. In *Ecotopia*, society was organized around ecological sustainability, a "revision of the Protestant work ethic . . . Mankind . . . was not meant for production, as the 19th and early 20th centuries had believed. Instead, humans were meant to take their modest place in a seamless, stable-state web of living organisms, disturbing that web as little as possible. This would mean sacrifice of present consumption but would ensure future survival"[6]—a shift in thinking we need more than ever today.

Ecotopia was similar to the social order in *Looking Backward*, where citizens did what was morally correct, not with the threat of punishment but based on beliefs. Callenbach wrote:

> . . . probably our greatest economies were obtained simply by stopping production of many processed and packaged foods. These had either been outlawed on health grounds or put on bad practice lists . . . the lists aren't enforced at all. They're a mechanism of moral persuasion, you might say . . . In Ecotopia, you will find many things happening without government authorization. But the study committees do operate with scientific advice . . . Scientists in Ecotopia are forbidden to accept payments or favors from either state or private enterprises for any consultation or advice they offer. They speak, therefore, on the same uncorrupted footing as any citizen. Thus, we avoid the unfortunate situation where all your oil experts are in the pay of the oil companies, all the agricultural experts in the pay of agribusiness, and so on.[7]

Another parallel to *Looking Backward* was that work was valued equally. During the dedication of a solar energy plant, Ecotopia's female president ceded the floor to the construction workers who "talked about the actual construction."[8] I thought of the fanfare at the triumphant opening of First Houses, NYCHA's original housing project, where progressive politicians spoke of public responsibility and the common good. The celebration could have gone further by giving voice to the actual workers who built the development.

"The Northwest is a hell of a lot closer to utopia than here." David continued with this mantra for a year until I agreed to move. But instead of following them to Seattle, I enrolled in a film program in nearby Vancouver, BC.

My alarmed mother didn't understand my need to escape and took my rejection of the city personally: "Does this mean you're renouncing New York for good?" she asked, as if the city were a political party, ideology, or religion, which in a way, for her, it was.

Leaving town wasn't a hard decision. New York in the '80s was particularly bleak. This was the Reagan era. Funding for affordable housing was slashed. The growing crack plague devoured already insufficiently subsidized NYCHA projects, where crime soared. "In the 1960s and 1970s, there was an informal economy [in the projects] for things like lunch services, baked goods, and auto repair. But in the . . . '80s this became less profitable."[9] Now, dealing drugs was more lucrative. AIDS had reached epidemic proportions, the Upper West Side among neighborhoods with the "highest concentration of AIDS cases in the city."[10] The gap between the rich and poor grew exponentially. According to the *New York Times*, wealth disparities were greater in Manhattan than in Guatemala.[11] Poor people became further cut off from the economic mainstream, and the middle class experienced more economic and social pressures.[12] A shantytown sprouted up in Alphabet City, where blocks and blocks of homeless people lived in tents. Business Improvement Districts hired "goon squads" to systematically kick homeless New Yorkers out of ATM bank lobbies.[13] Keith Haring's chalk drawings were the only things brightening up otherwise grim subway stations.

One ice-cold evening in the East Village, bundled in a brown tweed vintage coat with a fake fur collar and a black scarf wrapped around my head, I walked briskly down the street, thinking only of getting warm on the subway back home to Brooklyn. A tall, obviously homeless Black man in a jacket with one arm ripped off and shoes that didn't cover his bare feet came barreling up to me. "Hey, aren't you one of them Baum girls?"

I looked up, startled, and pulled down my scarf so we could get a better look at each other. It was Armand Argent, from private school. "I was in your big sister's class. I'm really sorry about your father, man. Hey, I don't mean to scare you, man. I'm Armand Argent. Remember me? Am I scaring you?"

Freezing, we walked down the street together at a furious pace, focused on the icy streets ahead.

"I'll leave if you want me to. I don't mean to scare you."

"It's okay. You're not scaring me."

"That was heavy shit, man. Your father dropping dead in music class. Heavy shit."

I fixed my gaze on him.

"How's your big sister? Heavy shit."

"She's good."

"I don't mean to bother you."

"You're not bothering me. How are you?"

"Heavy shit, man. I remember that day. I'll leave you alone now, man. Don't mean to scare you. Am I scaring you? What's your name?"

"Jenny."

"Hey, Jenny. Maybe we could go out sometime. Heavy shit about your father."

Armand abruptly disappeared around the corner. I hurried to the subway.

It was surreal he could think and care about us while being homeless and obviously disturbed. Where did he go? What had happened to him? Where would he sleep that night? I didn't get a chance to ask.

In 1988, I was awed upon arrival by Vancouver's beauty—its snowcapped mountains, unsullied beaches, and lush mossy rainforests—though at first, I didn't fully embrace my new environment. Vancouver felt like summer camp, not real life. Real life was New York. Real life was hardship, the grind, the subway, the homeless, the crowds, the concrete. Real life was tough, stressful, striving for social justice. Real life wasn't resort living. Politics seemed invisible. Who was the mayor? Who cared? Vancouver had the air of a town people escaped to, at the edge of the continent, as far away from New York as possible.

At night, the silent darkness scared me. Not a soul was on the street, and I had trouble sleeping. I was relieved when the sun rose and I could see outside, get my bearings.

Vancouver's demographics differed from New York. Though diverse, the city had few Blacks and Latinos. There was a very large Chinese community, the population growing when many were brought over in the nineteenth century to work building railroads or emigrated from Hong Kong. Vancouver had sizeable Japanese and South Asian communities, as well. Much to my surprise, lots of White people had British accents. David and Isaako had primed me for the Northwest, not Canada. Naively, I hadn't realized or expected it to be so culturally aligned with Great Britain, the Queen on bills and red poppy seed pins worn for Remembrance Day. Slowly, I began to realize that Vancouver was benign, a place to heal where I could fall and land on pillows. In comparison, New York's grit, clamor, and concrete seemed hellish. This was as real as New York, but in an alternate way.

I moved into a big Victorian house with a bunch of enthusiastic artists and poets who routinely said *Right On!* Together, we cooked meals, grew fruits and vegetables in our garden, ate figs and peaches off our trees, and nibbled on wild berries. As Callenbach wrote, ". . . life here seems like a throwback to a past."[14] And so it did. I found instant community with my newfound friends, dressed like hippies with peasant blouses and long flowing skirts.

"It's *sooooo* beautiful here," I repeated over and over, much to the amusement and bewilderment of my new housemates.

"What's it like where *you're* from?" they'd respond.

Though, socially, life was organized similarly to Ecotopia, environmentally, the BC government viewed its natural resources as commodities, ruthlessly depleting wild salmon and clear-cutting old-growth forests. I had friends who were tree-planters, spending summers replenishing trees decimated by the timber industry. There were other major problems, too, like the enduring mistreatment of First Nations people.

In other ways, the government was politically enlightened. One of my poet friends, impish, quirky Rutherford, sporting a signature wool ascot cap, told me he'd traveled around the world writing poetry and came home broke. "I went to the welfare office, explained my situation, and they put me on the dole." In New York, Rutherford would've been laughed out of the office. In BC, his poetry was valued as a contribution to society.

Canada was a more middle class society than the US. People didn't own guns, so gun violence was rare, the marijuana was better than anything I'd smoked on the east coast, and there was universal healthcare. One day while walking upstairs, I found myself breathless, in the midst of a major asthma attack. My housemates and I piled into a car and drove to the local hospital. Immediately, I was taken into a clean emergency room and put on a nebulizer until I could breathe again, while my friends waited outside, streaming in one by one to check on me.

"Feeling better, Jen?" sympathetic, fretting, gorgeous Luke asked.

I nodded.

"Right on," he said.

The treatment was free. No questions asked.

Though life was far from perfect in BC, I felt I'd found utopia.

Chapter 9

☰

Gentrification Turns into Revanchism

IN THE 1990S, during frequent trips home from Vancouver, I often visited my mother at work. The Public Education Association (PEA) had moved to an ugly building in the west thirties. A luxury tower replaced PEA's former ornate low-rise 1907 Flemish-style building overlooking Bryant Park. By the '90s, through a public/private partnership, Bryant Park had been restored. Gone were the drug dealers, pimps, and prostitutes barricaded from the public. Now the park resembled the Jardins des Luxembourg in Paris with privately guarded bistro tables and chairs, renovated, clean, functional public restrooms, a concert stage, and kiosks. One time, my mother and I strolled through the park up to a kiosk, bought espressos, a vast improvement over the city's ubiquitous watery, bitter diner coffee, and sat at a table to sip it. "It's a shame the park wasn't restored when I worked next door," she said.

We walked west to Times Square, also in the throes of gentrification, transitioning from peep shows and X-rated movies to something not yet defined. Along 42nd Street, the American neo-conceptual artist Jenny Holzer's truisms were on display in big, bold black letters on old, abandoned movie theater marquees before they were torn down: A MAN CAN'T KNOW WHAT IT'S LIKE TO BE A MOTHER, MOTHERS SHOULDNT MAKE TOO MANY SACRIFICES, RAISE BOYS AND GIRLS THE SAME WAY, SLIPPING INTO MADNESS IS GOOD FOR THE SAKE OF COMPARISON, ALIENATION PRODUCES ECCENTRICS OR REVOLUTIONARIES.

At that moment, I wished I lived in New York again, but by then, I'd been so indoctrinated to believe I could never be happy there that I didn't take the possibility seriously. Instead, during protracted visits over the years, I observed New York gradually revamp, not truly grasping the metamorphosis as it was happening under Mayor Giuliani's watch.

Occasionally, I invited Vancouver friends to visit. My mother welcomed all into her increasingly crowded apartment. Her books, work files, and clothes spilled into our bedrooms stuffed with things my sister and I had left behind, like a stained 1960s sleeping bag, where yet another friend could sleep. One time, I took my beautiful earthy friend Nora onto the terrace to show off the view. She noticed a charred, boarded-up brownstone on 95th Street between Amsterdam and Columbus. "There was a fire in your neighbor's building."

I laughed, perhaps too sarcastically. "I don't know them, Nora. That's a block away." I was amused she thought I'd know the inhabitants and that she assumed a recent fire caused the wreckage. In fact, the building was simply the last derelict structure on the block. "They all used to be like this," I said.

Other Canadians were in awe of the city. Mark, a clean-cut guy sporting a white T-shirt and white short shorts, said: "Oh my god, Jennifer. This is *soooooo* amazing," his reaction as fresh and green as mine was upon arriving in Vancouver, repeating: "It's *soooooo* beautiful here."

Another friend, curly-haired Stefanie, uncharacteristically blunt for a Canadian, was horrified when she saw 96th Street. "Now I understand why you wanted to escape. It's *sooooo* ugly here. The noise and traffic are unbearable. The air pollution is horrendous." Her more diplomatic boyfriend, Stan, hushed her: "Stop, Stef. You'll make Jen feel bad."

Jules, a hip touring musician, was terrified. "I'm really scared, Jen. I don't know if I can take this. I don't want to get mugged. I don't want to go out at night."

After being in New York, it took me a while to readjust to Vancouver—the rhythm, rain, rootlessness. Finally, I'd adapt, convinced Vancouver was the place for me, until I'd get pulled back home, like when my mother announced over the phone that my grandmother passed away. "Buy yourself a plane ticket," she said.

My grandmother's death wasn't a surprise. She'd been fighting colon cancer for years, becoming less self-sufficient. Only then did she feel unsafe walking the streets alone. When I visited, I'd escort her to the beauty parlor and the supermarket.

Helen was a warm, buxom woman who, as she aged, started wearing a wiglet to mask her thinning hair. More done up than her daughters, she wore makeup and high heels. In the late '60s, after robbers broke into her Mitchell-Lama apartment, stealing her valuable jewels, she wore costume jewelry. As a young woman, she'd gone to Hunter College but dropped out. She enrolled in Katherine Gibbs Secretarial School and learned shorthand and typing but postponed work outside the home until she was widowed at fifty. In the '60s, after Grandpa Leon died, she worked as a legal secretary for Perry H. Chipurnoi—a candy manufacturer in Long Island City. Every day in her pumps, she rode the subway from the Upper West Side to Queens and back, unfazed by crowds or noise or crime, bringing home Juicy Jellies treats for us girls.

Grandma was a calming influence in our lives, unruffled by stress or turbulence. "You want to worry? Go ahead, worry," was her mantra.

The youngest and only girl in a family of four boys, she was content to follow her brothers' lead and discouraged from thinking independently— at least that was my mother's explanation for her lack of intellectual curiosity. Unlike my mother, who'd earned a New York City Regents Scholarship to attend Barnard College and had a keen interest in education, politics, history, art, and literature, my grandmother was content to peruse *Reader's Digest*, play poker, and gamble in Atlantic City. "You, Elizabeth, and Mommy like to travel the world," she'd say. "I'm content to sit at home and hear your stories," and "My boss wants me to vote for Reagan, but if you tell me 'No,' I won't."

She was no dummy, though, channeling her intelligence into word mastery, completing the Sunday *Times* crossword puzzle and creaming us all in Scrabble. According to my Aunt Susan, to keep herself occupied while we struggled to form words, Grandma Helen balanced her checkbook. Once we finally finished our turn, Helen quickly devised a seven-letter word, then returned to her bookkeeping. We knew she was near death at age eighty-one when she could no longer conjure high-scoring words.

After her funeral, my mother and aunt cleaned out her one-bedroom for the next person on the Mitchell-Lama wait-list. There wasn't much to save other than the lovely wool afghans she'd crocheted. I wasn't as attached to her apartment as I was to mine, but the flat was still meaningful. At sixteen, Daphne and I stayed for a week in her apartment while Grandma wintered in Florida. Daphne's mother ridiculed us: "You're playing at being adults." But my mother was supportive. Daphne and I left a bag of pot in a living room drawer. My grandmother's friend, who had a key to the apartment, snooped around, found the bag and told my grandmother about it.

There were many positive aspects to co-op living. Nosey neighbors weren't among them.

Grandma Helen said: "It must've been a friend of theirs. My granddaughter wouldn't do such a thing." That summed up my grandma—uncritical, unsuspecting, or simply permissive, supportive, a stable force in our lives.

Now gone.

Rudy Giuliani became mayor in 1994 and for the next decade ran the city like a police state. In 1995, in an attempt to rein in crime in the perilous projects, he merged the NYC Housing Authority police, broke from years of budget cuts under Reagan and shrinking rent proceeds from unemployed tenants, with the NYPD. The MTA police also consolidated with the NYPD, though crime was already declining on the subways. Both were examples of Giuliani's strongman rule.[1]

During Giuliani's tenure, the Broken Windows theory of policing became fashionable. The city must rid itself of broken windows, graffiti, streetwalkers, pot smokers, the homeless, and even jaywalkers—surface problems that illustrated the city's neglect. Once the city was beautified, law and order would prevail, and violent crime would disappear.[2] Giuliani and police commissioner William Bratton attempted to sweep away all benign acts of lawlessness in a city known for its free spirit. Opening a beer can in public, jumping a turnstile, scribbling graffiti, sleeping on the street, possessing a joint or an expired vendor's license could land you in jail. Before Giuliani, people committing minor offenses "would have received court summonses and been sent home"[3] with a warning. Broken Windows was given credit for crime reduction in the city, but in reality, the crime rate had been falling before Giuliani was elected. Likewise, throughout America, in cities where the Broken Window theory of crime reduction hadn't been implemented, violent crime fell just the same.[4]

Under Giuliani, gentrification changed dramatically. When my family moved into RNA House in 1967, the city was in fiscal straits and the White middle class was departing in droves for the suburbs. We never heard the word "gentrification" back then; "Urban renewal" was the term we used to characterize the city's attempt to keep middle-income families like mine in New York, as well as provide decent affordable housing to low-income people and relieve the post-WWII housing shortage. The West Side Urban Renewal Area was populated by minorities, the working class, immigrants, artists, actors, writers, teachers, professors, civil servants, sex workers, drug addicts. When Ed Koch was mayor from 1978 to 1989, the term gentrification was used to describe the new moneyed class moving into economically diverse neighborhoods like the Upper West Side and changing their nature.

Giuliani turned gentrification into revanchism, "a systematic attempt to remake the central city, to take it back from the working class, from minorities, from homeless people, from immigrants who, in the minds of those who decamped to the suburbs, had stolen the city from its rightful White middle-class owners."[5] In the early '90s, rents in Tribeca became unaffordable and, much to my dismay, the Collective for Living Cinema closed. As in the art world, independent filmmaking commercialized, dominated by money and power rather than personal expression, the concept behind the Collective as obsolete as the optical printer. On the Upper West Side, chain stores, banks, and health clubs opened, and glitzy glass towers replaced rent-controlled apartments. Minorities and immigrants were pushed out in favor of rich White people. The Upper West Side still remained diverse, thanks to its mix of housing, but corporate America was clearly infringing. Meanwhile, as federal funding for public housing shrunk, life in NYCHA towers, with services declining, continued to deteriorate.

I checked in with my Facebook group friends about the state of NYCHA housing in the 1990s. Liana Arboleda-Nuñez, who grew up in the '80s and '90s at Tower West, a moderate-income Mitchell-Lama rental on West 96th Street, recalled life in the Frederick Douglass Houses, the massive NYCHA tower-in-the-park project spanning West 100th to 104th Street:

My best friend lived in Douglass, so compared to some of their conditions, I felt like I lived in a palace, and I was very grateful. NYCHA compared to Mitchell-Lama was a world of difference. Overall, individual NYCHA apartments, at least the numerous homes I visited, were pretty well kept. It was the buildings that weren't maintained. Buzzers rarely if ever worked, elevators frequently broke down, and often had urine in them. I once got stuck in one.

There was no reliable security at Douglass, making coming home late at night alone very worrisome. When we were older teens and went out to the clubs, my friends who lived in Douglass opted to come to my house to sleep since we had 24-hour security. Generally, the vast majority of people I knew in the projects were hard-working and wanted an affordable place to live. It just seemed that a few bad apples littered, vandalized, did drugs. I know so many who came out of that environment that went on to do amazing things with their lives.

David Berelson grew up in the Frederick Douglass Houses in the '50s and '60s, when the projects were new and well-funded:

I lived in Douglass from 1957 to 1970, so thirteen years. I left when I was nineteen. My parents continued to live there. The project was built in 1957, and we were one of the first families in the building. Most of the towers were seventeen to twenty stories high, but we lived in one of the two nine-story buildings on the sixth floor. My bedroom had a southern exposure, and I could see the Empire State Building until the Mitchell-Lama buildings went up on Columbus Avenue, which blocked my view.

There were areas with monkey bars and where we played ball, hopscotch, jump rope, marbles, and chalk games on the ground. We bicycled and roller-skated around the development. There were grassy areas, but you weren't allowed on them. People went anyway. If the housing police caught you, you got in trouble.

There were White, Black, and Puerto Rican families. Not so much Black in my building; more so in other buildings. It was fairly well integrated in the 1950s and 1960s. Most of the White families were Irish Catholic, and I had to put up with a lot of crap from the Irish Catholic kids for being a Jew. I got more grief from them than from the Blacks and Puerto Ricans. Still, I played with them because that's all I had to play with, and I remember just wanting to be accepted by them. There was one other Jewish family in the building, but they were Orthodox and ostracized my family because we weren't Shabbos observant.

We had three bedrooms, because I have a brother and sister (twins) four years younger than me, a kitchen (not an eat-in kitchen), and a living room/dining area combo. There was no intercom/buzzer system in the lobby when I lived there. I seem to remember one being installed after I moved out. The elevators worked most of the time. Sometimes they smelled like urine, but most of the time they were ok. Later on came the graffiti, but that was much later.

We had a porter who was always mopping the floors. I don't recall any leaks or mold problems. But again, the buildings were brand new when we moved in. After a number of years, I still don't remember issues with leaks or mold. Every three years, the apartment was painted.

There were no gangs. I felt safe. Once, someone tried to mug my father, but he didn't want to give up his money, so he started yelling at the mugger who got scared and ran away. Even when I was in high school and started coming home late on weekends, I didn't feel unsafe.

Today, the Frederick Douglass Houses is considered one of the most dangerous projects in the city. NYCHA housing was not inherently dysfunctional. With proper government funding, project dwellers flourished. The lack of financial support, as well as other systemic causes, weakened the projects; it was not the fault of the residents.

With the return of the moneyed class, property values skyrocketed, and new condos rose. Dozens of Mitchell-Lama landlords of low- and moderate-income rental buildings, permitted under law, opted out of the Mitchell-Lama program. In co-ops like mine, it was harder to withdraw as this required a two-thirds majority vote of shareholders. Nonetheless, some co-ops privatized, meaning once cooperators bought their apartments at an "insider's price," they could flip their flats and make a fortune. However, RNA House didn't betray the affordable housing cause as two votes for privatization—one in the '80s and another in the '90s—failed by big margins.

In 1992, the 25th anniversary of RNA House, the Department of Housing Preservation and Development (HPD) declared it one of the best-run self-managed Mitchell-Lama cooperatives in the city. Charles Rangel, our congressional representative at the time, issued a proclamation, celebrating RNA House's contributions to the community, and the board published a booklet:

> We acknowledge the hardworking cooperators who beautified the backyard by adding benches, chairs and plants and the lobby with tile walks, plants, art, blinds, made possible by fundraising efforts.
>
> The social aspects of our cooperative are enhanced by the existence of the "Neighbor Help Neighbor" committee and the real concern neighbors have shown for each other. The atmosphere of

cooperation and friendliness which characterizes RNA is a pleasing fact of daily life. It is underlined by our celebrations of Christmas and Hanukah, New Year's, children's parties, anniversary parties, and now this special 25th anniversary party.

We have good reason to celebrate 25 years of living together, 25 years of unceasing effort to maintain the goals of the founders of RNA. The goal of maintaining and achieving a viable cooperative and a satisfying quality of life is the continuing responsibility of all of us as we begin together our second quarter century.

Lafayette Quarterman
President, Board of Directors
RNA House, Inc.

This sentiment wouldn't last. As Upper West Side property values soared, the temptation to privatize grew, eating away at RNA House's harmony.

In 1995, when Giuliani ordered hundreds of police, using tanks, snipers, and helicopters to clear out a squatter's community in the East Village comprising people who'd occupied and were rehabilitating an abandoned building, it was his "revenge against the street—the public, cultural lever that wedged the systemic class retake of the city,"[6] wrote *Vanishing New York* author Jeremiah Moss. The 1990s were the last hurrah of funky New York before Times Square turned into Disneyland and Manhattan became a playground for the rich. Sure, there was crime, crack, and the harsh Giuliani administration, but the city retained its cool and the middle-class could still afford Manhattan.

Chapter 10

Could I Ever Return to Utopia?

I SAT IN A folding chair at the laundry room table across from Beverly, a no-nonsense Black woman in her seventies and scanned the room—the walls painted the same dreary gray, fluorescent lights tinting tables green, the lending library in the alcove stuffed with books, the dusty round security mirror suspended in the corner, the droning laundry machines I'd climbed on as a child. Beverly sorted through my paperwork. It was 2000 now, and I was thirty-seven. After twenty-four years, my name had finally come up on the RNA House wait-list and I was awarded a one-bedroom apartment. Although I was living in Vancouver, I was eligible because I had New York City residency.

Studying my tax return, Beverly said, "Yup. You qualify. Now you can move to New York for good, make some real money."

For over ten years, I'd bounced back and forth between Vancouver and New York. While in the city, I'd stay at #14E, shoot films, and work at Film/Video Arts. Then, I'd return to Vancouver on various visas to edit my footage and work in the film industry. My favorite film, *The Boy Test*, set in 1977, was a short, semi-autobiographical experimental piece about a tomboy, Jackie Rosen, named after Jackie Robinson, who witnesses the death of her father and transfers her love to Mets pitcher Tom Seaver, writing him letters about her quest to become a boy and play in the major leagues. Woven through the film is documentary footage of the Seaver trade, a.k.a. the midnight massacre, and a tearful Seaver writing a letter to his fans thanking them for their support.

I filmed *The Boy Test* in my mother's apartment, RNA House's back-yard and rooftop, around the neighborhood, in Central Park, and at Shea Stadium. The film crew was fantastic. Normally notorious for wrecking locations, they repaired broken furniture and appliances for my overworked mother. In the film, based on memories of grieving my father, I staged a shiva, an ancient Jewish tradition where mourners sit for seven days, shiva meaning seven in Hebrew. The cast crowded into our living room, the main Rosen family characters seated on cardboard boxes close to the ground, symbolizing proximity to the dead and the lowering of the body to express grief. Little did I realize that fifteen years later, my sister and I would conduct a genuine shiva for my mother.

Three shivas transpired at #14E—two real, one imagined.

"I remember your father," Beverly said. "We were on the board together. He was a good man." I calculated my dad's age. If he'd lived, he'd only be 72.

Still young, I thought.

My soon-to-be husband, Jacob, and I bought the apartment for $6,000 and paid $500 per month in maintenance. The place was in terrible condition—chipped linoleum, the white walls smudged gray; cockroaches abounded. What's more, unlike #14E, this one-bedroom faced 96th Street and was so noisy that even on the twelfth floor, we had to keep the windows closed at all times. Jacob wasn't impressed. Swarthy, English/French-speaking, half-Sephardic, half-Ashkenazi Jewish, he was raised in a quiet, leafy affluent Montreal neighborhood and saw little appeal. But I didn't mind. I was thrilled to have my own RNA House apartment.

I'd come full circle. I longed for the city, at least part-time, even if it meant living amid clamor, concrete, and razor-wire. Vancouver was healthy, wholesome, and relaxed, but I yearned for gritty New York. I appreciated RNA's Modernist uniqueness, its clean lines, angles, and geometric grid. I applauded brutalist buildings for the political era they represented—a time when governments, architects, and city planners were committed to the common good. Most importantly, I realized that as an independent filmmaker with a student boyfriend, I needed subsidized housing more now than ever, especially under current housing crisis conditions.

Moreover, though I loved Vancouver, I didn't fully fit in. My films, steeped in New York City identity and culture, were not always welcome in Canada, a nascent society living in Hollywood's shadows. In 1988, upon arrival at Simon Fraser University's film program, I was shocked students had to be encouraged to tell their own stories. "Examine your street corner. Study the people, the architecture, the lighting," my professor urged.

Growing up on 96th Street, there was no question I had a plethora of material to reflect upon. Why didn't my Canadian friends feel the same? Canadian festivals and government grants promoted homegrown stories, not work like mine. *The Boy Test* was rejected from the Vancouver International Film Festival because it had no Canadian content. However, it screened in New York at Anthology Film Archives and at the Festival Internacional Latinoamericano, in Havana, Cuba, more culturally connected to me than British Columbia.

Simon Fraser University held racism workshops, which my White friends admirably attended. "Why don't you come along, too, Jen?" asked Natalie, a tall blonde poet with earnest eyes and wavy hair down to her belly button. I declined.

My whole life was a racism workshop, I thought, heightening my awareness I didn't quite belong.

Jacob and I filled #12N with things from my mother's place, like an old black sleeper sofa from my former bedroom turned guest room, which Gil, a friendly security guard I'd known for years, hauled from RNA's 150 side to our new apartment location on the 160 side. We took an extra rug rolled up under the piano, my 1960s Herman Miller steel-case dresser, and my father's tools, which we used to build shelves to store my books, *tchotchkes*, clothes, and photo albums.

Because Jacob was a student and I worked sporadically in the film industry, we managed to live part-time both in New York and Vancouver. In March 2001, Jacob and I were married in Vancouver by a marriage commissioner at a friend's loft with a stunning mountain view. In May, my mother held a party for us at the World Trade Center, destroyed four months later on September 11th. Around this time, my mother's partner, Reuben, had a stroke, losing complete function of his left arm, his left leg limping. He moved in with her so she could care for him. At sixty-five, she became his full-time caregiver, her bed the epicenter of his convalescence, where she took his blood pressure and helped him dress. With Reuben living in #14E, we were doubly appreciative to have our own apartment.

Though I was content dividing time between Vancouver and New York, Jacob wasn't. Being from cosmopolitan, politically complex Montreal, he'd found Vancouver boring, not therapeutic, as I had. He wanted to escape Canada, see the world. He applied and was accepted to a PhD program in Political Geography at UCLA and received more funding from this program than any other. I already knew what life was like in the US and didn't want to return full-time, especially not to George Bush's America or to Los Angeles, where we'd have to raise a baby without friends or family.

We were in opposite places.

After much discussion, I begrudgingly gave in. I figured one of us had to have a stable job with health insurance, especially if we were going to have a baby, though if we'd stayed in Canada for Jacob's PhD, insurance would have been a nonissue. Everyone is insured in Canada. No one goes bankrupt if they become seriously ill.

We prepared for our departure.

On September 11th, 2001, moving day, we woke up early, bleary-eyed. Most of our belongings were in boxes, but odds and ends were scattered about, and we needed to clean the apartment. The phone rang, startling us. It was my friend Monica, a fellow New Yorker, doing her master's in film studies at University of British Columbia.

"Turn on your TV," she said.

"It's already packed." I couldn't understand why her voice was strained.

"Unpack it."

I pulled the TV out of the box and turned it on. That's when I learned about the first and second planes crashing into the towers.

"Oh my god!"

"No one knows what's going on," she said.

"Have you talked to anyone in the city?"

"I can't get through. The lines are busy."

"I'm gonna try."

After we promised to be in touch, I hung up and called my mother, but couldn't reach her. I tried my sister, who lived downtown in an artist's loft in SoHo, formerly and coincidentally the site of our Grandfather Isidore's belt-making business, blocks from the towers. Her line was busy, too. On TV, we learned the border had been closed between the US and Canada and that we couldn't move that day. Maybe not for a few days or weeks or months. Nobody knew. I became immobilized, glued to the screen, dialing over and over again until I reached my family and discovered they were fine, though the air downtown was toxic, thick with debris and dust from the burning towers. "We're going to stay at 96th Street for a while," Elizabeth said.

Once again, as it had been for me, RNA house was a refuge for them. They'd gone there before when their Canal Street loft burned down in a suspected arson.

Jacob and I ended up visiting friends for a week on Gabriola, one of the Gulf Islands off British Columbia on the Georgia Strait. It was beautiful, tranquil, and as remote as possible from the New York attacks. We kayaked, trying to chill out, paddling rhythmically, in unison, taking deep breaths, the distant snow-capped mountain ranges still, solid, in contrast to us.

We sailed past a couple in a kayak and asked if they'd heard.

"Oh yeah," the man said. "There was somethin' on the radio about it, but I didn't pay much attention."

Months later, when I finally saw my mother, she said, "I believed in our architecture." It gave her strength, sustenance. It was her god. She came from bricks, mortar, cement, and pillars of steel. Her deity was toppled that day. I. M. Pei, the architect who designed Kips Bay Towers, the blueprint for RNA House, reflected those same values when he wrote: "Life is architecture and architecture is the mirror of life."[1]

Certainly New York City streetscapes acted as mirror and muse in my films. For the shiva scene after Jackie's father dies in *The Boy Test*, we positioned the camera by my #14E living room window, mounted a thick glass cup over the camera lens, and took a panning shot of the Upper West Side skyline looking south. The distorted, undulating buildings reflected Jackie's agitated state of mind. After Jackie learns about the Seaver trade, there's an extended take of her staring out the 7 train subway window en route to Shea Stadium. The Manhattan skyline fades into the background, as the exquisite graffitied 5Pointz Long Island City artist studio warehouse comes into view. In 2013, these murals were whitewashed in the middle of the night. High-rise luxury towers were built in the warehouse's place, yet another sign of the city's gentrification and loss of character[2]—architecture reflecting life.

How would I respond artistically to the LA streetscape? I didn't know, though I anticipated my life there with great trepidation.

Once the border reopened, Jacob and I moved into UCLA married student housing, a brand-new gated community with identical, nondescript, three-story buildings and manicured grass lawns flanking both sides of the 405 freeway. From the freeway overpass, I was floored by the twelve lanes of never-ending traffic, epitomizing, for me, everything that was wrong with the postwar development of cities. Repeatedly, I thought about planting a camera on the overpass to shoot the phenomenon, but never did. The view deadened me, stopped me in my tracks, both spiritually and creatively. I couldn't comprehend Los Angeles; it made no sense to me. The city's inhabitants were glued to their cars, invisible. Going anywhere required driving long distances on frightening highways to get to a pocket of interest. I missed New York City's spontaneity, walking down the street, reading the situation, knowing enough about the history and culture to explore a theme. I craved filmmaking's collective process. Maybe over time, I'd meet other filmmakers with whom I could bounce off ideas or collaborate, and I'd feel capable of commenting.

In the complex was a large Chinese population of young couples with babies and their nanny parents. Also living there was a sizeable South American community, some Koreans, Japanese, South Asians, and a handful of Europeans, Israelis, and Canadians. Most of the Americans were Mormons with lots of babies. In one way, the place reminded me of Mitchell-Lama housing. Families got apartments according to how many kids they had, and rents were subsidized. A newly built market-rate complex across the street featuring similar amenities went for twice the price. For the most part, class differences were masked, which I liked. Because we all lived under the same housing conditions, people were not judged by how much money they had. As Lynsey Hanley wrote in *Estates*, "Le Corbusier envisaged that, in the blankness of the collective machine-home, people would turn away from thoughts of individual improvement and instead concentrate on mutual improvement . . . that bourgeois society would wither and collapse if that seat of bourgeois life, the family home, were subverted or replaced by identical communal dwellings."[3] In fact, at UCLA married student housing, the opposite was true. Hardworking undergraduate and graduate students were pursuing professional careers, striving for or sealing their places within the bourgeoisie.

It took me a while to realize that many international students were the wealthy elites of their countries. I clued in when an Argentinian woman said: "I'm so proud of myself for taking care of the children on my own. But I can't wait to get back home and have help."

"What kind of help?"

"We have a live-in cook, nanny, and maid."

"Ah," I said, nodding.

Cars were an indicator of student wealth. New to Los Angeles, I didn't appreciate the importance of cars as a status symbol. We'd driven down from Vancouver in a beat-up Mazda, and most of our Canadian friends had battered old cars. At UCLA student housing, oversized BMWs, Mercedes, and Volkswagen SUVs monopolized the parking lot. If I'd been more cognizant, I would've picked up instantly on wealth disparities, but I wasn't. I liked believing we were all equal financially, even if we weren't.

The place was a baby factory. Everyone who moved in there got pregnant, as did I. I became friends with a Black stay-at-home actor/dad from Brooklyn and his South Asian wife from New Jersey studying law. I also spent time with a French-Canadian nurse and a German doctor. Skilled, they both managed to work part-time while pregnant and after they gave birth, an ideal situation, unlike mine. With morning sickness, I didn't feel up to working as a production assistant, as I'd done in Vancouver, on my feet all day stopping traffic. Demoralized and with zero connections, I sold flowers over the phone for Teleflora, an unskilled minimum wage job, with no maternity leave or part-time option.

Jacob and I decided to spend the first summer after 9/11 in our one-bedroom at 96th Street. I needed to observe, firsthand, that the city was functioning, that people woke up every day, went to work, ate, drank, and slept despite fears of another terrorist attack. Pregnant and lonely in LA, I was relieved to be in New York near my mother, sister, and old friends still living in the building. My dear friend Nina was living on the Upper West Side, having moved back from suburban Connecticut straight out of college. She brought her kids to RNA to visit me and others she'd known growing up. It was like a homecoming—to a closely-knit, egalitarian village that played by a different set of rules than the rest of the overpriced and impersonal city. Many of the original gang I grew up with had been reunited, acquiring RNA apartments of their own. Their children played together in the backyard, and some of the older folk got to see their grandkids grow up.

The doorbell rang, and I got up to answer it. There stood my gorgeous childhood friend Gina—thick, straight dark hair, brown eyes, high cheekbones, olive skin—carrying a big jug of water. Our families had moved into RNA House at the same time, and we'd grown up together, going to P.S. 75

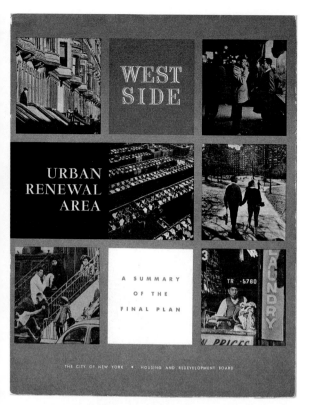

Left: West Side Urban Renewal Area: A Summary of the Final Plan, pamphlet cover.

Below: West Side Urban Renewal Area aerial view of targeted twenty-block Manhattan area to be renewed.

Thomas Airviews

The Target: 20 Blocks on Manhattan's West Side

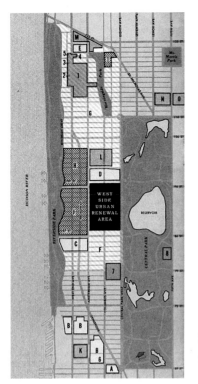

Left: West Side Urban Renewal Area graphic map of twenty-block Manhattan area adjacent to Central Park.

Below: West Side Urban Renewal Area land use plan.

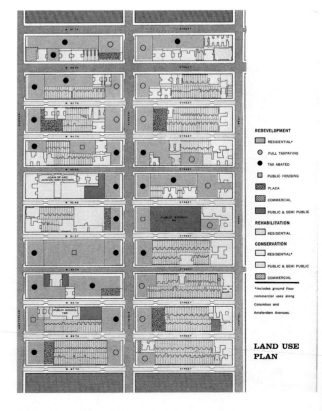

REDEVELOPMENT

▨ RESIDENTIAL*

○ FULL TAXPAYING

● TAX ABATED

▢ PUBLIC HOUSING

▨ PLAZA

▨ COMMERCIAL

▨ PUBLIC & SEMI PUBLIC

REHABILITATION

▢ RESIDENTIAL

CONSERVATION

▢ RESIDENTIAL*

▢ PUBLIC & SEMI PUBLIC

▨ COMMERCIAL

*Includes ground floor
commercial uses along
Columbus and
Amsterdam Avenues.

**LAND USE
PLAN**

RNA House
April 1st, 1965

RNA House
August 20, 1965

Left: Location for RNA House, 1965. Photograph by Carlos F. Meza.

Below: Leaflet announcing the groundbreaking ceremony for RNA House.

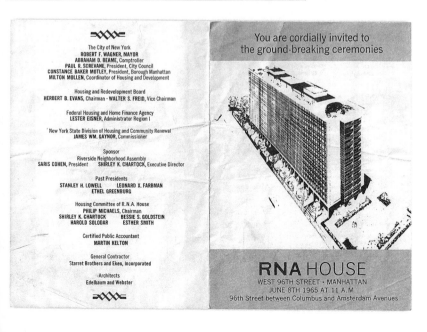

The City of New York
ROBERT F. WAGNER, MAYOR
ABRAHAM D. BEAME, Comptroller
PAUL R. SCREVANE, President, City Council
CONSTANCE BAKER MOTLEY, President, Borough Manhattan
MILTON MOLLEN, Coordinator of Housing and Development

Housing and Redevelopment Board
HERBERT B. EVANS, Chairman · WALTER S. FREID, Vice Chairman

Federal Housing and Home Finance Agency
LESTER EISNER, Administrator Region I

New York State Division of Housing and Community Renewal
JAMES WM. GAYNOR, Commissioner

Sponsor
Riverside Neighborhood Assembly
SARIS COHEN, President   SHIRLEY K. CHARTOCK, Executive Director

Past Presidents
STANLEY H. LOWELL   LEONARD X. FARBMAN
ETHEL GREENBURG

Housing Committee of R.N.A. House
PHILIP MICHAELS, Chairman
SHIRLEY K. CHARTOCK   BESSIE S. GOLDSTEIN
HAROLD SOLODAR   ESTHER SMITH

Certified Public Accountant
MARTIN KELTON

General Contractor
Starret Brothers and Eken, Incorporated

Architects
Edelbaum and Webster

You are cordially invited to
the ground-breaking ceremonies

RNA HOUSE
WEST 96TH STREET · MANHATTAN
JUNE 8TH 1965 AT 11 A.M.
96th Street between Columbus and Amsterdam Avenues

Left: RNA House under construction, 1966. Photograph by Erminio Gubert.

Below: RNA House, 1967. Photograph by Erminio Gubert.

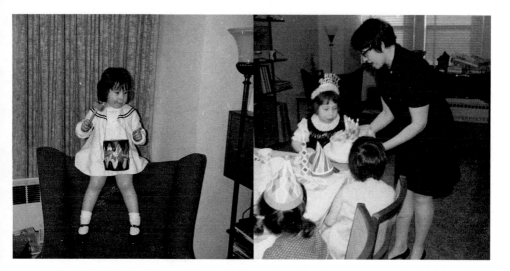

Jennifer Baum, four and five years old, with mother Judith Baum and cousins, in RNA House apartment. Photographs by Charles Baum.

Living Room in RNA House apartment. Photograph by Richard Bloomenstein.

Left: Childhood letters between Jennifer Baum and mother, Judith Baum, and childhood photos of Jennifer Baum. Photograph by Jennifer Baum.

Below: Jennifer Baum at RNA House apartment and on terrace. Photographs by Charles Baum.

Jennifer Baum with RNA House kids in backyard. Photograph by Erminio Gubert.

Kids with their mother in RNA House backyard playground. Photograph by Erminio Gubert.

Left: Charles Baum in RNA House backyard. Photograph by Judith Baum. Right: Judith Baum in RNA House apartment kitchen. Photograph by Jennifer Baum.

Teachers' Strike, Judith Baum, lower right corner. Vecchione Family Archives.

Left: Current view of 700 Columbus Avenue. Photograph by Jennifer Baum.

Middle: 700 Columbus Avenue kids selling lemonade. Bobby Broom Archives.

Bottom: 700 Columbus Avenue kids playing in backyard. Robert Cohen Family Archives.

Left: 711 Amsterdam Avenue backyard. Photograph by David Stokes.

Middle: Neighborhood kids, 90th Street and Columbus Avenue. David Owens Archive.

Below: Neighborhood kids across the street from RNA House. Photograph by David Baumbach.

Above: Emily R. K. Chester walking on roof of RNA House. Photograph by Ferdinando Holthaus.

Left: View from Tower West, RNA House on left. Photograph by Shelton Walden.

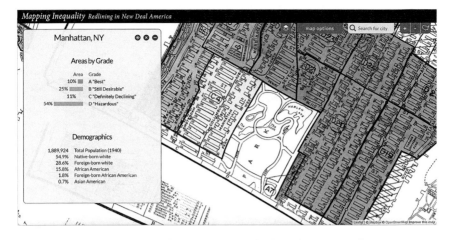

Mapping Inequality, Redlining in New Deal America, Manhattan's Upper West Side and Harlem. Richmond Edu Creative Commons.

East Harlem New York City Housing Authority tower-in-the-park buildings. Photograph by Jennifer Baum.

Commuter train northeast of 96th Street and Park Avenue with New York City Housing Authority buildings in background. Photograph by Jennifer Baum.

East Harlem New York City Housing Authority George Washington Houses. Photograph by Jennifer Baum.

Esplanade Gardens, Harlem Mitchell-Lama Housing. Photograph by Mondello Browner.

First Houses courtyard, New York City Housing Authority. Photograph by Jennifer Baum.

Above: WPA Dolphin Sculpture, First Houses courtyard, New York City Housing Authority. Photograph by Jennifer Baum.

Right: Hudson Yards and Penn South. Photograph by Jennifer Baum.

Above: Brutalist sculpture air vent, West Side Urban Renewal Area Mitchell-Lama. Photograph by Jennifer Baum.

Left: Puerto Rican flag, Columbus Avenue West Side Urban Renewal Area. Photograph by Jennifer Baum.

Former West Side Urban Renewal Area Mitchell-Lama tower converted to market-rate housing with Trader Joe's, 93rd Street and Columbus Avenue. Photograph by Jennifer Baum.

Left: Former West Side Urban Renewal Area Mitchell-Lama tower next to RNA House converted to market-rate housing. Photograph by Jennifer Baum.

Right: Former West Side Urban Renewal Area Mitchell-Lama tower converted to market-rate housing, 95th Street and Columbus Avenue. Photograph by Jennifer Baum.

Above: RNA House. Photograph by Jennifer Baum.

Left: Shopping cart in empty RNA House apartment, moving day 2014. Photograph by Jennifer Baum.

and CGPS, playing in the backyard and at each other's apartments. When we were kids, her swinging film editor dad read *Playboy Magazine*, hiding issues under the mattress. We dug them out and had a blast making fun of the ludicrous naked bunnies. Gina lived down the hall from us, still in the three-bedroom apartment with a terrace she'd taken over from her parents when they moved to Florida. Hers was identical to #14E's floor plan though reversed, facing west. Gina's brother, Peter, had moved out long ago, becoming a trapeze artist with the Vargas Family Flyers, performing at Ringling Brothers and Barnum and Bailey Circus. Now Gina had a baby and a husband and was excited about my pregnancy. I was happy and grateful she was so nearby.

"I brought this for you." Gina plunked the jug down on the kitchen floor.

"Why?"

"In case they poison the water," she answered. "I have a constant supply. So we're prepared."

"Seriously?"

"You guys should start saving. Everyone I know is doing it."

"Maybe we should." I looked at Jacob.

"We can talk about it later," he said, rolling his eyes.

So much for things being back to normal in NYC, I thought.

The year 2002 was the beginning of Bloomberg's first term as mayor, and nothing seemed normal. Bloomberg would ultimately serve three terms, the New York City council voting to extend the two-term limit for elected officials so he could run a third time, a move opposed by the majority of New Yorkers. Under his control, change would occur at a rapid pace. PEA dissolved because it could no longer raise money. The progressive head of the organization, Jeanne Frankl, my mother's boss, was forced to resign. PEA merged with the Center for Educational Innovation, which had its start at the right-wing, free-market Manhattan Institute think tank, the same place where, in 1995, a senior fellow predicted that all of Manhattan would be gentrified.[4] My mother quit and got a grant to archive PEA documents at Columbia University's Teachers College. She then started working at Advocates for Children, eventually writing an advice column about public schools for New York City parents called *Ask Judy*.

In my neighborhood, chain drug stores Rite Aid, Walgreens, and CVS appeared along Columbus and Amsterdam Avenue, but my exhausted caregiver mother remained loyal to Black-owned-and-operated Ivan Pharmacy, even though Ivan moved his business a few blocks farther south from RNA House. Whole Foods opened on Columbus Avenue between 97th and 98th Street, along a strip that had previously housed Woolworths and Mikell's, a jazz club frequented by James Baldwin, Toni Morrison, and Maya Angelou. Because Whole Foods was expensive, my mother hated shopping there and continued to go to the reasonably priced, less chic Food City, located in a one-story building on the grounds of a Mitchell-Lama plaza. Food City, however, was unable to negotiate a long-term lease and closed in 2013, the West Side Urban Renewal Area losing another affordable union-run business.

In a shocking development, soon after Whole Foods launched, a luxury tower with apartments smaller than those at RNA House, charging market rates, squeezed into the site of the former tennis courts at Park West Village. Whereas in the 1980s, two upscale buildings had been constructed on either side of 96th and Columbus, never before had a luxury infill project been crammed into recreational space. The Central Park playground at 97th Street was now populated by well-clad Parisian women in heels, chattering on benches as their children played, their French wafting throughout the grounds, eclipsing the Spanish I heard growing up. Bloomberg's agenda was clearly underway.

Still, it was great to be home. Though the neighborhood was becoming unrecognizable, the RNA House cooperators were the same, and it was comforting to be there. In the lobby, I bumped into Scott, one of the men with a schnauzer we'd met when first moving into the building. He'd split with James, his long-term boyfriend, but kept the apartment on the fifteenth floor above my mother's.

"I hear you're pregnant," he said.

I nodded, smiling.

"Is there a man involved?" he joked, and we laughed.

"I remember all those years you were trying *not* to get pregnant." He hugged me, and we laughed some more.

Outside the UCLA student housing laundry room, I sat on a bench, rocking infant Gideon in my arms, wishing I were back in New York with my mother. Shortly after I gave birth, she and Reuben had visited for two weeks. Without her company and support, I felt clueless raising a baby. I looked up and saw a middle-aged Korean man, father of a graduate student, gawking at me, mouth agape.

"How old are you?" he asked.

I'd turned forty the day before. I was the oldest mother in the complex.

"Is this baby yours?"

I nodded.

"How is this possible?"

He stared at me the way Westerners who go to faraway places scrutinize the natives. In his eyes, I was a freak, the exoticized other.

I frowned at him, both insulted and depressed, then went inside to check the laundry.

Later that day, I carried Gideon to one of the playgrounds scattered around the complex, bustling with babies and their mothers. It was early evening, a popular time to congregate outside. After being alone all day with my infant, I enjoyed this twilight ritual, in lovely weather, watching the golden LA sun disappear below the buildings before everyone went home to eat dinner. The collective experience reminded me of RNA House, though, in student housing the playground was padded; at 96th Street there were no soft landings. Another difference was the conversation. None of the student housing mothers talked politics, or anything else, for that matter, other than their kids, which left me feeling hungry for intellectual stimulation. I tried to change the conversation, chatting with a young, pretty second-generation Japanese American mother.

"You're from Houston, right? What do you think of Bush?"

It was April 2003. We'd just invaded Iraq. At the time, I was relieved I'd given birth in February before the war broke out. Otherwise, I feared my elevated stress level would affect Gideon's health.

"I like him," she said.

"Why?"

"He's a good guy. He owned the Rangers for a while. It was fun."

"What about the war?"

"We had to invade, because of 9/11. Hussein was responsible. He had weapons of mass destruction."

"That's not true."

She shrugged.

"What about abortion? He wants to make it illegal."

"Abortion will never be overturned." She paced around, looking for an exit strategy, clearly agitated by my questioning.

"What about the air quality? Isn't Houston one of the most polluted cities in the country? Bush wants to roll back environmental regulations."

"You know what? I hope your side wins because you seem to care so much about the issues."

With that, she scooped up her toddler playing on the grass, and left. I stood there, hands on my hips, in disbelief. How could this be? How could she be so disengaged, not care, like politics was nothing but a game with winners and losers, not understanding her life was at stake? I longed to raise Gideon at RNA, where being an older, politicized mother was the norm, not the exception.

When we lived in Los Angeles, downtown was in the throes of gentrification. The city was making a concerted effort to transform the area into an upscale residential, entertainment, and retail hub, the opening in 1999 of the Staples Center where the LA Lakers played marking the beginning of the transformation. As per usual, low-income people of color were being displaced. I mustered the motivation to start shooting a video about LA's makeover, braving the I-10 to drive downtown and conduct interviews with evicted residents. Obstacles abounded. I couldn't afford a babysitter. I didn't have the budget to rent equipment, or pay a crew, even a small one. Feeling powerless and trapped, I abandoned the project.

In LA, the friendly cooperative Vancouver and New York film communities where people volunteered on each other's projects didn't exist, or at least I couldn't find them. Perhaps if I'd gone to film school or worked in the industry, the story would've been different. Those I did meet didn't have the time or resources; everyone was scrambling to make a living, to pay the rent, to break into Hollywood. So I gave up filmmaking and became a writer. It was free. I wasn't dependent on anyone. I could do it anywhere. I could retreat into my own imagination. No budgets, actors, caterers, or locations required.

Still, it was a difficult transition. As a feminist, I was demoralized. I'd worked hard to become a filmmaker. It had given me great pleasure and purpose and was a huge part of my identity. Now, I was giving it all up for my husband's career. How could I have allowed myself to let this happen? Because I loved Jacob. I was thirty-five when we met. I wanted to have a baby. He was nine years younger than me and would've preferred waiting. If I agreed to move to LA for his PhD, he'd agree to start a family.

After spring semester ended, we returned to the city. The conditions in our apartment were not ideal. Six-month-old Gideon was on the verge of crawling, and I worried he'd nibble on the chipped linoleum breaking off the floors, so I put down blankets and fabric over all exposed areas. It didn't seem wise to renovate the apartment. How much would we actually use it? I yearned to live there full-time, but this would've meant splitting up the family. At least for this summer, I pretended we were permanent New York City residents. Downstairs, neighbors *kvelled* over baby Gideon. In good weather, older cooperators congregated in the backyard. When the building originally opened in 1967, the backyard was a wide expanse of concrete with a space-age steel and cement playground, cement benches, and a basketball hoop. But as time went on, wooden benches, flowerpots, and cushioned metal chairs and tables were added, making the space more appealing.

On a wooden bench, bundled in a heavy beige knit sweater despite the warm weather, sat 100-year-old Bea, who'd watched me grow up. "Jenny, *Mazel Tov*. Bring over the baby. Lemme get a good look."

I sat down on the bench next to her.

"Bring him closer. I can't see very well."

I placed Gideon in her arms, and she held him for a while.

"Precious," she said.

Eventually, my mother came downstairs, and the two of us strolled to Central Park, just a block and a half away, my mother pushing Gideon's stroller as we walked around the reservoir.

I relished being near my mother, visiting her frequently. She babysat Gideon, the two of them establishing a deep bond. When my mother raised Elizabeth and me, both her mother and mother-in-law lived in the city. Her sister was just across the Hudson River in New Jersey bringing up her kids. Childhood and college friends with babies were nearby, Kaila, the closest, living in RNA. Plus, she had support from the entire RNA House community. *This is how it should be. This is what I wanted.*

We tried to spend as much time as possible at RNA during the summer and breaks from UCLA. But in June 2005, when Gideon was two, we packed up to move to Paris for Jacob's PhD research. Having grown up in Montreal, Jacob was bilingual and thus comfortable reading and writing French. RNA House made an exception and granted us permission to sublet our one-bedroom to my Vancouver art designer friend, Dan, who was thrilled to live in the city and pay cheap rent. He stuffed our belongings into the front closet, and with the aid of thrift stores, magically transformed the apartment into a mid-Century modern oasis.

Going to Paris seemed like a great idea, much better than living in student housing. I loved France, having visited the city twice before. However, I wasn't a Francophile. I wasn't yearning to learn the language or absorb the culture. In fact, I'd been studying Spanish on and off, a language I'd heard my neighbors speaking in the backyard, at school, in the park, and from music blasting out of open car windows and in mom and pop stores.

What were my expectations of life in Paris? Mostly that I wouldn't be stuck in a homogeneous suburban gated community. Instead of driving, I could wander the city with no set agenda, and have spontaneous interactions, exploring bookstores, cafés, and *boulangeries*, my favorite way to meditate. That's what I'd done all my life in New York and what I sorely missed in LA, where you needed a destination, or you'd end up nowhere. I imagined meeting politicized, cultured women, willing to discuss critical issues of the day, that they'd introduce me to art and books and music, and that I could be myself again.

At the intersection of the 17th and 18th *arrondissements* (districts), we found an inexpensive apartment on Rue La Condamine in Batignolles, a quaint *quartier* (neighborhood) with narrow, winding streets and a square with a church and park, on the cusp of gentrification. The *agence immobilière* (realtor) wouldn't allow us to rent the place unless we had a *garant* (guarantor) who could sign the lease as well. Luckily, Jacob's friend and colleague Renaud Le Goix, professor of urban and economic geography at Paris Cité University, offered, and we got the small one-bedroom, with a tiny alcove we curtained off for Gideon. By French standards, we lived on the second floor, though Americans would call it the third. It had some accoutrements of a typical Parisian apartment, such as shutters, but no parquet floors. Instead, there was a stained carpet we tried but failed to scrub clean.

Jacob's and my bedroom overlooked a grassy courtyard, surrounded on all sides by apartment buildings. That winter, during a very gentle storm, Gideon encountered snow for the first time in the courtyard, forming the tiny amount into a few balls, then tossing them down on the ground.

Except for that one snowstorm, the neighbors didn't tolerate his playing on the grass, riding his tricycle, or kicking a ball. Maybe if other kids had lived in the building, we could've rebelled, but Gideon was the only one.

A mix of young people and older folk, all of whom were White, resided in the small five-story building, a former nunnery, with two apartments per floor and a narrow hardwood spiral staircase running through the center. They weren't unkind but didn't exude warmth either. Living there was in stark contrast to RNA House.

A stiff woman in her late sixties inhabited a ground floor apartment with a little garden next to the courtyard. Once she gave Gideon some apricots brought back from the country. But she also chastised him for playing on the grass. *"Il y a un parc juste à côté"* (There's a park just next door), she said. True, but it was *interdit* (prohibited) to play on the grass there as well. In the park was a designated playground, with a *manège* (carousel), swings, and go-carts where the gang of neighborhood kids congregated.

With *l'aide de l'état* (help from the state), France was in the midst of a baby boom. Because families were supported, there was no crisis of under-population as in Italy or Japan. Maternity leave was generous, nurses made house calls before and after the birth, health benefits included an exercise regime for women to restore their bodies, a monthly child allowance was granted for every kid in the family, and there was a free, government-run *crèche* (day care), though wait-lists were long.

Gideon would've been eligible to enroll in a crèche because Jacob was on a student visa, and thus entitled to such benefits for Gideon, as well as health insurance for the two of them. Ultimately, we couldn't get a spot, so we registered Gideon in a bilingual English/French *jardin d'enfant* (nursery school) called *Les Petits Dragons*. Married to a student, I wasn't eligible for anything and ended up *sans papier* (without papers). Soon after we arrived, I saw a nine-month, Teaching English as a Foreign Language certificate program advertised in an ex-pat magazine and quickly applied to begin that fall. *Sans papier*, I knew I could make money teaching private English lessons, a lucrative endeavor if you had access to a rich clientele.

Living on Jacob's meager fellowship, our budget was tight, and so I was grateful for the business, though the work gave me no chance to practice French. What I sorely needed was access to French people, to a commu-nity where I could interact meaningfully—i.e., a group of French mothers, a job, or volunteer work. Little did I know at the time how hard this would be or how important it would be to gain French literacy, to understand French culture, and to participate in French society.

My access to French people increased somewhat the following year when we enrolled Gideon in *L'École élémentaire Truffaut*, a public elementary school. In France, public education begins at age three as long as the child is *propre* (clean), meaning diaper-trained, a word whose connotations I found offensive. Most French parents were similar to New Yorkers—*très pressé* (in a hurry) and too busy for newcomers, especially ones who spoke little French.

"*Ça va?*" I'd call out to a mother rushing through the school hallway, after she'd dropped off her three-year-old in the classroom.

Turning her head, she'd shout, "*Oui, oui. Et vous?*" before disappearing down the stairs.

Eventually, I did make friends and learned to speak French, though not beautifully. *C'était une question de fierté.* (It was a matter of pride). I didn't want to return to the US unable to converse at all, like the American woman back in student housing who'd told me of her year in Brussels speaking only English. In Paris, there was no shortage of people who talked politics. Even the postman, once he learned I was American, would stop in the lobby to speak to me and voice his concerns. I listened attentively, absorbing as much as I could.

I became close to Marie-France, an artist with four kids and a Mexican husband. They lived in a small ground-floor one-bedroom at the foot of a courtyard; the apartment flooded when it rained. Apartment poor, they were social-benefits rich thanks to *l'aide de l'état*. Married to a marginalized Mexican who knew no French upon arrival, she was especially sympathetic to my plight. During the winter, when the sun barely rose above the five-story buildings, we walked to a neighborhood café and stood at the bar, sipping espressos, talking to the other parents, regular customers, or the bartender about *les émeutes* (the riots) in *les banlieues* (suburbs) that had racked France in 2005, President Sarkozy's corruption, and the disastrous Iraq war. If she or someone else spoke to me one-on-one, I could follow, but during a group conversation sprinkled with *argot* (slang), I was lost.

With Gideon in school and Jacob ensconced in his Geography Lab, I was left to my own devices. I'd teach a private English lesson, then explore the city alone. My favorite destination was the Centre Pompidou, designed by architects Renzo Piano and Richard Rogers, a modernist monstrosity in some people's eyes; for me, a fantastic futuristic utopian structure reminiscent of New York. On the façade were cylindrical glass-enclosed escalators snaking to the top floor, exposed brightly painted functional pipes, and scaffolding, like a work in progress, like never-ending New York City construction, a reprieve from Paris's historicity. In the late '70s, shortly after it'd opened, my mother, sister, and I visited. Going there always reminded me of them, of where I came from, where I belonged.

From the Pompidou's top floor, the golden pink late afternoon light illuminated the skyline, the black rooftops of the older buildings seeming close enough to touch. From there I'd wander to the Jardins des Tuileries, admiring the soft shafts of light trickling through the plane and chestnut trees losing their last leaves, a melancholy overwhelming me.

Again and again, my mother said, "It's romantic to be poor and lonely in Paris."

Though content in France, Gideon missed my mother. Often, he packed his bag and pretended we were flying to New York to visit her. I wished we were back in our RNA House apartment, too, near my mother, sister, and brother-in-law and their son, Malcolm, and old childhood friends raising babies. Holidays were particularly lonely. Many families we'd met at Gideon's school ran off *à la campagne* (to the countryside) to be with grandparents, underscoring how *déraciné* (rootless) we were.

Over the three years we lived in France, we managed to come home three times, staying at #14E with my mother because we'd sublet our apartment. We crowded into my sister's former bedroom, Jacob and I sleeping on a foldout couch and Gideon on a single floor futon squeezed between the couch and closet. During each visit, I brought Gideon downstairs to play in the backyard with Gina's two little girls and all the other new generation of RNA House kids frolicking about. I sat and chatted with old friends while Gideon and his cohort played handball with a beat-up pink Spalding ball found in my childhood closet. An Upper West Side public school had just opened a bilingual French/English program to serve the Haitian community, and I fantasized we could move back to 96th Street and Gideon could attend.

I knew we were fortunate to live in Paris, a walkable city where people congregated on the sidewalk, relied on public transportation, had access to great art, architecture, film, opera, music, dance, and theater, bought food at local markets, pushed their groceries home in *caddies* (carts), and sat at outdoor cafés sipping wine while observing the world passing by. Paris was more like New York than either Los Angeles or Vancouver. So, in a sense, I adapted very quickly, and I enjoyed my time there. But I couldn't shake my outsider status. If not for the language barrier and inability to work legally, I would've been right at home. Or mostly at home . . .

I adored Paris. But Paris wasn't *mine*. *My* city was New York, a realization growing stronger by the day. I longed for New York to be Gideon's city, too. I recognized he was turning into a French boy, while I still felt locked out of French society. It wasn't just a question of language. I wanted Gideon to grow up with the same beliefs, values, and experiences that had shaped me, so we'd have shared references. Thus, despite all the pleasures of living in Paris, in 2008, after Jacob had completed his dissertation and it was time to depart, *j'était soulagée* (I was relieved). Coincidentally, at this time the Parisian apartment owners refused to renew our lease. They claimed a family member wanted to move in, the only way they could legally evict us. In reality, no family member needed the flat. Instead, now that the neighborhood was in the throes of gentrification, they wanted to upgrade the place and hike the rent.

Packing up, I wondered if we could've afforded to rent a Parisian apartment in the same neighborhood in 2008, the year we departed, rather than in 2005, the year we arrived. Probably not. According to our guarantor friend and professor of urban and economic geography Renaud Le Goix, and his colleague Loïc Bonneval, *"Le sens général de l'évolution ressort sans équivoque: l'abordabilité, entendue comme le rapport entre les prix et les revenus, a diminué partout."* (The general direction of change is clear: affordability, understood as the relationship between prices and incomes, has declined everywhere.)[5] Just like in New York, market forces were pricing middle-income people out of Paris, affecting social cohesion.

"Ring the bell next door." My mother, in slacks and a T-shirt, her purse slung around her shoulder, her arms resting on her shopping cart, was ready to go out, but Reuben had fallen, a common occurrence, and neither me nor my mother could lift him. Reuben's health had been deteriorating, and he tumbled often. Back stateside from Paris before returning to California so Jacob could adjunct at UCLA while looking for a full-time job, this was my first time witnessing the event. Dan was still subletting our one-bedroom, so we were staying at #14E.

Sometimes my mother called 911, but if the next door neighbors were home, she asked them to help. In 2001, after the original #14F tenants passed away, a friendly Black family moved in. Selena, from Brooklyn, her husband Reginald, from Georgia, and their three boys—Jamal, Tariq, and Darius—lived in the three-bedroom opposite ours.

Selena answered the door in a bright red T-shirt and khakis, her long sandy brown hair tied in a ponytail. "Hey, Jenny. Good to see you."

"Reuben fell. Could one of the boys help?"

"Jamal," Selena called.

Tall and slender, Jamal came, towering over his mother. A trendy dresser, he wore black jeans, a Ralph Lauren polo shirt, Timberland boots, his hair a short fade. "What's up?"

"My mother's boyfriend fell. Could you please pick him up?"

"No problem." As Jamal left his apartment to enter ours, Rusty, their medium-sized gray dog, escaped and ran up and down the hallway. Five-year-old Gideon chased him, laughing.

Jamal navigated past the shopping cart into the narrow kitchen. "You all right?" he asked. He hoisted Reuben and installed him in the sturdy dining room chair, bought just for him.

"Thank you so much." My mother opened the door for Jamal. "Tell your mother I say hi."

With Reuben safely seated, we kissed him goodbye and joined Gideon in the hallway to wait for the elevator downstairs. My mother wiped her brow, sweaty from the humid New York summer and from the stress of Reuben's illness. "So glad they're next door. I don't know what I'd do without them."

"You could hire someone."

"Naah. We want our privacy. I can handle it."

But she couldn't. No one realized the toll caring for Reuben took on my mother. All attention was paid to him, the sick one, the one who'd become disabled after suffering a stroke.

In the lobby, Gil, the security guard, called out to Gideon: "Yo, buddy. Howya doing?" Gideon ran up to him, the top of his head as tall as the security desk, and pointed at the TV security screens. "What are these for?"

"They show all the public spaces in the building. Making sure there's no trouble," Gil explained.

"There's the laundry room. Grandma and I go there." That summer, one of Gideon's favorite activities was doing the laundry with my mother—sorting the clothes, counting out the exact change needed for each machine, sticking the coins in the slot, and watching the machines whirl.

Outside, on the sidewalk, we headed east toward Columbus Avenue. A tough-looking dark-skinned skateboarder dude decked out in a glossy satin jacket, big gold chains around his neck, sunglasses, sweatpants and Air Jordans whizzed toward us, weaving in and out of pedestrians. Gideon stepped right in front of him and stuck his hand out, obstructing his path. Much to my surprise, the dude stopped.

"Can I try?" Gideon asked.

The skateboarder helped Gideon on and patiently taught him how to ride.

At that moment, I was proud of Gideon's audacity. He behaved like he owned the streets as much as anyone else, just as I had growing up. He could easily become a New York City kid. If only we could stay. But we couldn't. It was 2008, the start of the Great Recession. Jacob had tried and failed to find work in the New York metropolitan region. A job, albeit a temporary one, was waiting for him at UCLA, and we needed the income. He'd invested too much time and energy in his academic career to give it up now. My earning potential was diminished. Aside from teaching private ESL lessons in Paris, I'd been out of the workforce for a while.

At the end of the summer, my friend Dan and I disassembled our one-bedroom. RNA House no longer let us sublet. The apartment was afford-able housing for people who needed it. Either we lived in the city full-time or sold the flat. We could've lied, as did others in the building who stayed away for long periods. But we were too ethical.

"I can't keep perpetuating the myth you're moving back for real," my mother said.

I was heartbroken. If we'd installed ourselves at RNA, we'd have been financially secure. Our maintenance would've been low, and, as stated by Mitchell-Lama policy, which grants apartments according to family size, we could've eventually upgraded to a two-bedroom. Further, my mother would have been nearby to help raise Gideon. He would've grown up a New York City kid, schooled in uniquely Upper West Side secular Jewish values. What could've been better? I longed for what my mother had—to be grounded, with roots, a history in a cosmopolitan walking city steeped in progressivism, to understand the nuances of everyday life, the politics, gestures, jargon, traditions. To be home.

The day before we flew to Los Angeles, Gideon and I made a pilgrimage with my mother to Coney Island. We stepped off the D train into the Stillwell Avenue terminal station and marveled at its beauty. When I was a kid, the station had fallen into disrepair, like many of the New York's subway stations. Now the new high-ceilinged metal arches reminded me of Paris's Gare de Lyon. "This is breathtaking." My mother pointed up. "Notice the solar panels on the very top."

We walked across the street to the amusement park, which was still derelict and funky, like when I was a kid, but now eerily empty on the cusp of change. Many lots had been abandoned, soon to be developed into shiny new rides. In September, outer space–themed Astroland would close, though the famous rickety wooden Cyclone roller coaster and the Wonder Wheel, designated landmarks, would remain. A few kiddie rides were open, which Gideon enjoyed. Thankfully, Nathan's was still there, so we bought a heap of oversized crinkled French fries made from freshly peeled potatoes and shared them.

Afterward, we strolled along the boardwalk toward the West End, where NYCHA developments were clustered. Postwar, the area went into decline with the advent of car ownership, suburban development, and the highways Robert Moses built to Long Island suburbs and beaches, considered more desirable for those with the means to leave the city. Pristine Long Island beaches became the rave. Jones Beach, one of Moses's major accomplishments, was difficult to reach by public transportation. When I was a little kid and my father was still alive, he liked to drive us there. As a teenager in the '70s, my friend and I ditched class and took the subway to the Long Island Railroad, and finally a bus to reach Jones Beach—a fun, though extremely inconvenient, all day adventure.

Meanwhile, Moses used eminent domain to bulldoze entire working-class Coney Island neighborhoods and construct high-density public housing towers. By the 1970s, the area had become neglected and dangerous. It wasn't that modernist high-rise public housing towers were inherently flawed. Rather, the problem was the isolation, the loss of retail, the segregation of the poor, the lack of sufficient funding, and the creation of federal housing and highway policy that aided Whites and discriminated against Blacks and people of color. The fact that the city built public housing in great quantities was inspirational. The way such housing was vilified, its tenants blamed for urban woes, was reprehensible.

My friends and I also skipped school to spend a day on subway-accessible Coney Island. While sunbathing alone, some girls asked me to watch their radio while they swam. I did my best until a man snatched it.

"Hey," I said.

He pulled out a knife and aimed it at me. "Say something, you'll get cut."

Perhaps if public housing in Coney Island had been well maintained and the neighborhood thriving, instead of swiping the radio, the knife-brandishing guy would've been sunbathing next to us.

As my mother, Gideon, and I continued walking on the Coney Island boardwalk, my mother explained that when she was young, she used to crawl under and dig for change. She pointed to the cracks between the boards. "People dropped coins that fell through to the sand."

"I wanna try," Gideon said.

We found a beat-up section of the boardwalk with space between the planks and room enough below to scavenge. Gideon crawled under but didn't last long. "It stinks of pee and poop," he said, scurrying out, nose pinched.

I squatted and saw a sleeping Black woman, her arm clutching a large stuffed garbage bag.

"It's very sad there are so many people who don't have homes," my mother told Gideon. To me, she added, "It's just getting worse under Bloomberg."

We turned back and started walking along the sand to a cleaner area of the beach and lay down towels I'd been carrying in my backpack. It was a humid, overcast weekday; there weren't many people around except for us and three homeless women.

"It's just like what happened in the Rockaways," my mother said. "In the 1940s, when I was a kid, we used to summer there. Even Grandma Helen went to the Rockaways growing up. It was a working and middle-class get away, lined with small beach bungalows where we slept. After the war, Moses razed the bungalows, decimating the neighborhood, and constructed NYCHA projects there. He turned the remaining bungalows into public housing, a terrible idea because they were unheated. No place to spend winters. Rockaway transformed from a vibrant beach resort rivaling Coney Island in its heyday to a run down, dangerous, isolated public housing enclave in the 1970s."

I couldn't imagine Coney Island or the Rockaways as vibrant vacation spots for the masses. Soon both areas would be in the turmoil of gentrification. When it was time to go, my mother and Gideon gathered some Coney Island sand into a baggie they'd brought from home.

"Close it tightly," my mother said.

Gideon meticulously ran his fingers several times along the seal. After he finished, he gave her the bag. "Hold it, Grandma."

My mother guarded the sand until later that evening when Gideon packed it in his suitcase to bring to California.

Chapter 11

No Next Time

IN 2012, WHEN we went to New York soon after Hurricane Sandy had destroyed large chunks of the city, I was relieved to find RNA House unscathed. By this time, we'd left Los Angeles and moved to Phoenix, where Jacob had been hired by Arizona State University. Thanks to Jacob's job, I began a tuition-free master's degree in Teaching English as a Second Language. I was glad to be back in school. But I still longed for New York.

In the RNA lobby, I noticed the security guard desk now said *concierge*, and the elevators had been refurbished. As we ascended, Gideon jumped to reach the newly illuminated fourteenth floor button and continued jumping, excited to see my mother.

"I'm going to leave my bag here," he said. "Okay?"

Jacob and I smiled and nodded. Once out of the elevator, Gideon tore down the hallway to #14E, rang the bell, and jumped some more, until my mother answered the door. They embraced and went inside. We were an afterthought. Fine by me. I cherished the closeness my mother and Gideon shared.

Once in the apartment, I asked my mother: "What's with the elevators? They're shiny and fast."

"They were in terrible condition. It's about time they were renovated, don't you think?"

Now smaller and silver-haired, she cleared a pile of the *Times* off the table and stacked them on a stool.

"Why does it say *concierge* at the security desk? Is the building privatizing?"

"RNA House? No, never!" She slapped the air. "It's not for the common good."

My gut ached. "What about the good of your daughters?"

She hugged me. "My daughters are doing fine."

"But we're going to lose this place one day!"

"Don't dwell on that, darling." She sorted papers into a recycling stack. "The next vote to privatize is in a few years when the mortgage is up for renewal. There's a secret group of tenants plotting, but I don't think they'll get enough votes. I'll never go along with it."

As the Upper West Side gentrified, the temptation to privatize increased as tenants realized they could buy their apartments at an insider's price, then flip them for a hefty sum. By 2012, of the over 260 Mitchell-Lama developments constructed as part of the Limited-Profit Housing Companies Act of 1955, only 98 were left.[1] The rest had privatized. However, the transfer process was costly. If RNA were to go private, it would have to hire expensive attorneys to seek government approval and would no longer be eligible for tax abatements and subsidized loans to finance its mortgage. Maintenance fees would rise. Tenants on fixed incomes would likely not be able to afford their apartments.

I had mixed feelings. I knew that if the building stayed public, when my mother died, I'd lose the apartment. Morally, philosophically, intellectually, I understood the building should stay public; privately, though, I was already mourning the loss of my childhood home.

"In the original 1955 Mitchell-Lama legislation, there was no buyout provision," my mother said. "It only happened in '59 when Rockefeller became governor and introduced the opt out/privatize option."

"Wow. I didn't know that."

Gideon grabbed a rubber band wrapped around the kitchen faucet and shot it into the garbage can.

"The housing crisis is reaching Depression levels. We need more Mitchell-Lama housing, not less. Around eighty thousand public school kids are homeless!" my mother said. "All Bloomberg's doing is building upscale towers. I can't wait to get rid of him."

Bloomberg's approach to the affordable housing crisis was to provide tax incentives and abatements to private developers to set aside a small portion of otherwise luxury apartments for middle- and low-income people. Those lucky enough to obtain affordable housing did so by competing in a lottery, an absurdity in itself.

In the *New York Review of Books*, Michael Greenberg explained that the tax break given to developers, 421-a, a relic from the 1970s when New York City was nearing bankruptcy and Whites were fleeing to the suburbs, was devised to keep bankrupt landlords from forsaking their properties. By the Bloomberg era, the city's financial condition was a hundred percent better than in the '70s, yet in order to urge development, builders were still exempt from paying property taxes if they were willing to designate 20–30 percent of their units as below market rate. The tax exemption period lasted for thirty-five years, at which point apartment rent would no longer be controlled.[2] In other words, the majority of housing was built for the rich. Everyone else rolled the dice to win what was left over, which they'd only be able to afford for a limited time, and the city lost tax revenue in the process.

Gideon and I followed my mother to her bedroom, plopped onto her bed next to a snoring Reuben, and watched as she got to work at her upright teak desk writing her Insideschools.org *Ask Judy* column.

"Play with me, Grandma. Gideon bounced up and down on the springy old mattress.

"In a sec."

I looked over her shoulder and read:

> The trouble is that the way schools measure progress is through standardized testing, which then leads to test prep, often at the expense of offering a broad curriculum. Just looking at the test results—or the letter grade on the school's Progress Report—will not reveal everything you want to know about the school. There are other components of the letter grade: the school's Quality Review and its Learning Environment Survey.

"I'll finish later," she said, standing up. Gideon sprang into her arms.

I leapt up to brace my mother before she fell backward. "Careful, Gideon!"

Back in Phoenix, I started to write about RNA House. It was my way of holding onto the building, belonging from a distance, immersing myself in a world that seemed to be slipping away, vanishing, both personally and globally. Little did I know I'd lose my mother and this universe much sooner than I could've imagined. I called my mother and asked her about RNA's early years, but she was reluctant to talk. Caring for Reuben was wearing her out, though she didn't want to stop. Every day she helped him shower, dress, do his physical therapy exercises, lifting his legs up and down and bending his knees to his chest, and took his blood pressure. She had high blood pressure, too, but she never bothered to monitor her own.

"I'm tired. I slept badly. All night Reuben needed help going to the bathroom. Then all day, I schlepped him to different doctors. Why can't you do the research? Why are you making me do all the work?"

"It's your memories, your stories that matter, Mama. Stories are what move people. Not just the facts. I can find the facts."

"Okay," she said, sighing into the phone. "I'll tell you what I remember." It was then she supplied me with anecdotes about the food and babysitting co-ops, Halloween and holiday parties, the fund for the workers at Christmas, the 1968 Teachers' strike, the early group purchases of appliances, the robberies, and the utopian Upper West Side Urban Renewal vision of housing for all. "It's hard to convey how different the ethos was then compared to now."

In the background, I heard chopping sounds.

"I'm making dinner," she said.

I used to believe that the success of the Mitchell-Lama Housing Program on the Upper West Side led to the area's inevitable gentrification. But as I researched the history of housing policy in New York, I realized my narrative was incorrect. Gentrification was not inevitable. It didn't have to play out this way. Just because an area became palatable for affluent White populations, it didn't mean that the working and middle classes had to be priced out. The government could have constructed more affordable housing on a large-scale basis as they did postwar. But they chose not to, especially under Bloomberg.

What the mayor did was rezone huge swaths of industrial land for luxury development with a miniscule proportion designated for affordable housing. *Vanishing New York* author Jeremiah Moss compared Bloomberg's megaprojects with those of Robert Moses. Like Moses, Bloomberg employed eminent domain to seize properties. While in power from 2002 to 2012, he bulldozed approximately 25,000 buildings, "almost triple the number demolished in all the years from 1990 to 1999 combined."[3] In 2009, Mario Mazzoni, head organizer at the Metropolitan Council on Housing, a tenants' rights organization, said, "If you are talking about building affordable housing, the way [Bloomberg's administration] conceives of it is as a massive subsidy to developers,"[4] a vision most evident at the waterfront.

Oddly, since water views are usually considered desirable, New York City historically housed poor populations in NYCHA projects along neglected, derelict sections of the coasts in East Harlem, the Lower East Side, the Rockaways, and Coney Island, an inverse of city planning since the 2000s where the coastline has been commandeered by luxury buildings. My travels between New York and Vancouver made me more acutely aware of this peculiarity and New York's subsequent transformation. Vancouver had its funky elements, but it was primarily a clean, new, orderly city, where the rich lived in glass towers and beautiful homes along gorgeous shores with breathtaking views.

New York City was becoming like Vancouver. At first, the change seemed positive, like a novelty, especially at the waterfront. Parks were safe and shiny. People kayaked, played volleyball and soccer and sunbathed, and children climbed state-of-the-art jungle gyms. But then the squeaky-clean promenades and new upscale towers kept encroaching on industry and old piers where barges docked and gay men cruised, pushing out working-class manufacturing jobs and the remaining traces of a counterculture. Anthropology and geography professor Neil Smith said, "It's no longer just about housing. It's really a systematic class-remaking of city neighborhoods. It's driven by many of the same forces, especially the profitable use of land. But it's about creating entire environments: employment, recreation, environmental conditions."[5]

This change was epitomized to me in 2014, when I went to the Williamsburg waterfront to see Kara Walker's site-specific installation of a monumental Aunt Jemima sphinx at the former Domino Sugar refinery, which closed in 2004. The refinery—the largest in the country—was a massive, rusted nineteenth-century steel warehouse dripping with molasses. Most of the refinery would be razed to build luxury residential towers with an 80/20 mix of upscale and moderate-income apartments, respectively. Remaining industrial bits would dot the playground and waterfront park. About the Domino Sugar Refinery, the *New Yorker*'s Hilton Als noted, "As recently as 2000, it was the site of a long labor strike, in which two hundred and fifty workers protested wages and labor conditions for twenty months. Now, the factory is about to be torn down and its site developed, and its history will be eradicated by apartments and bodies that do not know the labor and history and death that came before its moneyed hope."[6]

Just like Jenny Holzer's Times Square marquee project, this rezoned site was turned into art before being destroyed for corporations.

Meanwhile, under Bloomberg, income inequality widened, rents escalated, and homelessness increased, reaching Depression levels. During the first few years of his administration, he denied federal housing vouchers to the homeless, accusing families living in shelters of gaming the system.[7] In addition, his administration bought five hundred homeless families one-way tickets on trains, buses, and planes out of the city, because it was cheaper than sheltering them in the city.[8] His administration introduced the "Poor–Door" policy, whereby developers were able to receive tax abatements to build luxury towers, with amenities like gyms, water views, and doormen as long as they designated a token number of affordable apartments for tenants with no access to high-end comforts. The different classes would be housed in the same building, but segregated by entranceways, one luxurious, the other, small and functional. "It reminds you of who you are," said Daisy Fermin, thirty-four, in the *New York Times* about her living in the affordable section of her Williamsburg Tower, The Edge.[9]

Scant city resources were directed toward repairs for NYCHA developments, already underfunded at the federal and state level, or to check for lead paint poisoning.[10] During Hurricane Sandy, many waterfront public housing projects were damaged severely because their boilers and electricity were in the basement. Greg Floyd, President of Teamsters Local 237, which represents eight thousand NYCHA employees, said: "Sandy's effect on NYCHA put the icing on the cake. NYCHA was in decay already . . . Sandy came in and really finished the job—in the Rockaways, in Coney Island, in the Lower East Side."[11] It would take several years for federal aid to kick in to restore the projects, some of which were still not repaired as of 2019.[12]

In NYCHA housing, crime was rampant. Bloomberg's solution was to fingerprint residents, turning them all into criminals.[13] The Broken Windows policy initiated under Giuliani morphed into Stop-and-Frisk under Bloomberg, an aggressive controversial strategy which targeted people of color. "Students heavily exposed to stop-and-frisk were more likely to struggle in school . . . young men were more likely to experience symptoms of anxiety and depression . . . this exposure fostered cynicism in policing and government writ large and made residents more likely to retreat from civic life."[14] A public housing lawsuit claimed that the New York Police Department, which replaced the Housing Authority police, was stopping and arresting NYCHA residents without due cause. In 2013, Bloomberg's last year in office, in order to raise money, he proposed infill projects to construct upscale towers on NYCHA development land, which spurred on outraged protests from NYCHA residents.

"Jud*eee* . . . Jud*eee* . . . ," I heard Reuben yelling in the background.

"Gotta go, darling. Reuben's calling. Love ya. Bye."

The last time I saw my mother in June 2013, the year de Blasio was elected mayor, we took the subway at 96th and Broadway up to 125th Street and traversed Harlem's main thoroughfare toward the Metro North train station, en route to visit my mother's friend who lived in White Plains, a suburb of New York City. We stopped in a few stores along 125th Street, far enough east to be untouched by gentrification, my mother and I chatting with the storekeepers. Back in the '60s and'70s, my mother's sister, along with other relatives and many of her friends, moved to the suburbs; during New York City jaunts, they never took the subway. My mother, however, remained a true New Yorker, traveling by train through fiscal times both good and dangerous. On the way to White Plains, I noticed she was winded climbing the Metro North stairs, but she was 77, so I thought this was normal, and she seemed fine the rest of the day.

When it was time to leave New York City for Arizona, my mother escorted Gideon, my husband, and me downstairs, as usual, to say goodbye and take one last picture in front of RNA House, a tradition at the end of our visits. This time she forgot her camera.

"Should I go back up?" she asked.

"Nah," I said. "We'll get a shot next time."

There was no next time.

I couldn't wait to see my mother over winter break. I was busy that fall semester teaching composition to international students at ASU. Without much time to phone, I kept thinking I'd see her soon and we'd catch up. When we did talk, after perfunctory chit chat about our lives, she spoke about what really concerned her—the upcoming mayoral election. "I'm endorsing de Blasio. He's gaining in the polls. I have high hopes for him. We all do."

De Blasio campaigned on a "tale of two cities," promising to take New York back from corporate interests and return it to the people—as if! My mother lived long enough to see him win by a landslide but died in December before he took office. Upon de Blasio's victory, John H. Mollenkopf, director of the Center for Urban Research at the City University of New York said, "Liberalism is not dead in New York City."[15]

As it turned out, liberalism wasn't dead, but sputtering.

Instead of calling her, I stared repeatedly at a photo I'd placed on my desk taken the previous year of Gideon and my mother outside RNA House just before we departed. It'd been a mild February day, Gideon dressed in a light green jacket, my mother in a gray fleece. They stood cheek to cheek, haloed in sunlight, smiling blissfully, a cozy closeness between them. In the background, Jacob and a leafless tree were reflected in the glass lobby door, behind them a car and RNA's globed modernist streetlamps. At the very back, sun splashed onto the refurbished tenements across the street. Some kind of power radiated from this crisp, sharp, three-dimensional image, as if my mother's soul was yearning to connect, waiting for us to arrive. Maybe it was just me projecting anticipation. Either way I gazed at the photograph all the time, counting the days until we visited, knowing how happy we'd be to reunite.

The Friday my mother died, I took Gideon for an IQ test to see if he qualified for the Gifted and Talented program at the local public middle school. We missed the district deadline, so had to hire a private psychologist. As I waited for him, I thought about our upcoming winter holiday trip the next day to New York and Montreal, a voyage we'd made seemingly endless times. Visiting my mother wasn't easy. On the fourteenth floor, the city's cacophony crashed in from the main 96th Street thoroughfare. Televisions in different rooms simultaneously blared the PBS NewsHour, football, or *Mad Men,* to accommodate hard-of-hearing Reuben. When we went to Jacob's parents in Montreal, we entered a combination Victorian and Edwardian Village. My in-laws' 1914 semi-attached brown brick townhouse was like an upscale bed and breakfast. Jacob's Jewish Moroccan mother set the dining room table the night before, covering the dishes with napkins to keep out bugs and dust, and draped dish towels over bowls of fruit.

My mother had no time for such niceties, nor would she have felt compelled to behave this way if she did have a moment to relax. She was constantly stressed, pushed to the edge. Once, we'd forgotten a box of Jacob's mother's homemade chocolate truffles at #14E and we'd asked my mother to mail it to us. "Between work and taking Reuben to the doctor, I have exactly a window of one hour to bring it to UPS," she said, almost panting.

I felt terrible for making the request.

A sinking feeling overcame me. In the windowless waiting room, I started to pace. How long could my mother possibly go on this way? When would it end?

Then, suddenly, it did.

In retrospect, I wonder if this was the moment my mother died.

Gideon did very well on the test. He was, in fact, gifted. I had mixed feelings about this designation, as did my mother, who, as an education advocate, had created the first comprehensive list of gifted programs in New York City. I also knew that being in Arizona, where the state is 48th out of 50th in public education, it was important to do everything I could to provide Gideon with a good education. If he had to be segregated into a Gifted and Talented program, so be it.

I looked forward to telling my mother the news but never got the chance. It was on the drive home that my sister called. I was anxious to get back and finish packing for our trip. Rush hour now, the traffic was heavy on the freeway, and the carpool lane was congested, so I had to take it slowly, even if I wished otherwise. I hated driving, hated what it did to my physical body—the lower back aches and shoulder pain—and I hated what it did to Gideon's mind. He was growing up car-dependent, rarely walking and believing that driving was the norm, not the exception, making driving's environmental damage easily ignorable.

We exited the freeway and headed to our sleepy suburban neighborhood. In my mind I was already in New York, planning what museums my mother and I would visit, which friends I would meet.

"I can't wait to see Grandma," Gideon said.

"Me, neither."

But then the phone rang. "Mama's in the emergency room at Lenox Hill Hospital. She collapsed on the street. I got a call from a cop. He found my name in her address book. That's all I know."

I swerved the car, momentarily losing control, but it didn't matter. No one was around but Gideon and me.

"Malcolm and I are stuck on the subway in Brooklyn, but we're heading there now. The F train just went above ground. I'll lose you as soon as we go underground again."

"What?" I felt undone, disassociated, unmoored, trying to connect with my sister's disembodied, hard-to-hear voice over the screeching subway cars.

"You're flying home tomorrow, right?"

"Yes."

"Good. I'll call when I know more."

"No, wait," I cried, though it didn't matter what I said. She was slipping underground. When I got home, I phoned the Lenox Hill Hospital emergency room and tried to locate my mother but couldn't get through to anybody. It was busy, busy, busy. I dialed over and over again but finally gave up. No surprise. I didn't expect anyone to answer. It was New York City. The hospitals were overcrowded and underfunded. My sister would arrive there, but not me. I was across the country, removed, surrounded by ranch houses, strip malls, cacti, and dust instead of those, save my immediate family, who mattered.

Then, my sister called. "Mama died," choked my sister, incredulous. "She died."

It didn't register. Not at first. How could it? Moments ago, Gideon and I were happy, eager, content. We sat speechless on the futon couch, heads pressed together. Yanked into a nightmare, we began to absorb the devastating news. Finally, I picked up the phone. Nina, my oldest RNA House friend, was the first person I called.

Later, we learned my mother suffered a heart attack on an Upper East Side street after attending a colleague's funeral. Earlier that day, she'd written her last *Ask Judy* post for Inside Schools on fun things to do over the holidays:

> Holidays are upon us! If you are one of the lucky ones to have vacation days along with your kids—or if you are a high school student used to travelling around the city on their own, here are some ways to enjoy your time: At El Museo del Barrio, kids can ring in the holiday

season by making a crown for Three Kings Day, listening to stories, and taking in a concert by El Sistema. The main branch of the New York Public Library displays an exhibit of books from its collection celebrating the rich history of children's literature called, "The ABC of It: Why Children's Books Matter." New York Transit Museum's Holiday Train Show in Grand Central Station includes a 34-foot-long display, festooned with miniature versions of city landmarks such as the Brooklyn Bridge and the Empire State Building. The Department of Youth and Community Development lists community centers and other local groups that offer activities for kids during school vacations. And my favorite: check out the fanciful decorations in department store windows, and on shops and buildings up and down the main street in your borough. We'll be back in the office and online on Jan. 2, 2014! Happy holidays to all.

Judy

The following night we arrived at 96th Street in shock. The RNA house lobby was empty, except for Gil, the longtime friendly security guard who'd befriended Gideon, listening to jazz. "I'm so sorry, you guys." He said, hugging us and buzzing us in.

Usually when someone died in our building, the co-op board posted an official typed announcement on the lobby doors. But in the elevator riding to the fourteenth floor, I saw a handwritten notice in cursive green and blue magic marker. *Sad News. Beloved cooperator Judy Baum passed away.* I never learned who'd written it.

This time in the elevator, Gideon didn't jump. Once the door opened, I walked ahead down the hallway, unlocked the door, and embraced my sister.

Immediately upon my mother's death, Reuben's daughter, Rebecca, hired a full-time caregiver for Reuben, who was essentially helpless on his own. All the beds were taken so George from Georgia (the former Soviet state) slept that first week on the floor of my onetime-bedroom-turned-Reuben's-study/junk room in the stained 1960s sleeping bag my mother had kept all these years. No provisions had been made for Reuben's care, the expectation being my mother would outlive him. Now she was gone—the essential component, the stabilizer, the ingredient that bound us all together, and our lives were turned upside down.

Rain poured on the day of my mother's funeral, but that didn't stop an overflowing, standing-room-only crowd of family, friends, colleagues, people from the building, and others we didn't know, from packing the Plaza Jewish Community Chapel on 91st and Amsterdam. Many were parents of New York City public school children; a large wheelchair-bound Black woman said, "I came because your mother helped my kids."

My sister and I sat together, shell-shocked, and watched as people took the podium—a surreal, heightened, performative moment. All these educated, composed, self-assured women, and only women—my Aunt Susan (my mother's sister), friend after friend, colleague after colleague—an impressive array, celebrated my mother's life from childhood to the present. It felt both personal, like they were addressing my sister and me, and public as they wanted the world to know what an extraordinary person she'd been. She was in good company, they were in good company, I was so lucky to have her . . . how could this be happening, this replay how many years later, of my father's death? It made no sense. Would I die this way, too?

My first cousin Ellen Rosenbloom, her sister Laura by her side, recited her poem:

What a shocking exit—
but the party wasn't
over—over and over
you think about her
shopping, talking
working, laughing
all the regular things
day to day, then she
collapses in the street—
they told you it was
a heart attack
but she was healthy
always wide open—
to chat, have a meal,

laugh or just be—
daughter, sister,
wife, mother,
grandmother
partner, aunt
my dear
sweet aunt.

I was touched by Ellen's minimalistic poem. She'd captured the elemental, raw, unimaginable moment so precisely.

Once family and friends finished eulogizing my mother, her colleagues spoke. Jeanne Frankl, Executive Director of the Public Education Association (PEA), recounted how during the decentralization of the city schools, recurring elections required nominees and their representatives to know the arcane and annually revised New York election law. To support them, PEA issued a fifty-page manual that my mother prepared, updated, and had translated into Spanish. Jeanne said: "Judy was really brilliant, a great writer, someone who researched everything no matter how unfamiliar. I am particularly glad to speak about Judy, because I was concerned that family and close friends might not be fully aware of the depth and significance of Judy's professional life."

This was true, at least for me. I was blown away to learn about my mother's advocacy on behalf of public school kids. I'd been aware of her work but hadn't realized the extent of its reach.

Jeanne continued, "When PEA was closing, Judy was hired by Teachers College through a grant to collect and archive PEA's hundred-year-old collection of documents, the most complete collection in existence of documents about the New York City school system."

I knew Jeanne was speaking to the entire room, but it felt like she was gazing only at my sister and me.

Next up was Clara Hemphill, who recollected how she'd worked with my mother at PEA, Advocates for Children, and most recently at the Center for New York City Affairs at the New School. Clara said that for decades, my mother was the single best-informed person in the city about public education, a walking encyclopedia about schools and their history. She started this work during the fiscal crisis of the 1970s, when the city was threatened with bankruptcy, the public schools were in free fall, there were thousands of teacher layoffs, and the middle class was leaving for the suburbs.

Clara said, "Judy was interested in good schools for her own children and grandchildren, but it went beyond that. She wanted good schools for everyone's children. She was an advocate for poor children and new immigrants, and a willing listener for any parent caught up in the opaque bureaucracy of the Department of Education. She answered phone calls from anxious parents, from the most broken down and vulnerable parents to the most obnoxious and entitled parents. She would be calm, patient, reassuring. The schools are in much better shape now than when Judy started her work. Judy deserves credit for that."

I turned and saw the wheelchair-bound woman nodding and clapping.

Clara said: "Even in the city's darkest days in the 1970s, Judy held firm to the belief that good public schools were possible and essential to a functioning democracy. The problem now is not flight of middle class to suburbs and half-empty schools but overcrowding and gentrification that's pricing the middle class out of the city. Judy helped thousands of parents get a good education for their children and she passed her wisdom on to us. We plan to carry on her work for the next generation. So, Judy, past, present, and future generations of public school parents salute you."

Why wasn't my mother alive to hear these tributes? It was absurd, I lamented to myself.

After the service ended, I stood outside in the heavy rain with Daphne and another old CGPS friend, Gabe, who held an umbrella over my head, the rain gushing as if the world was weeping for my mother, her family, friends, colleagues, and all of New York City's Public school children. Dazed, I kept stepping away, sometimes moving underneath the edge of the funeral home awning where larger drips fell on me, and Gabe kept moving the umbrella to protect my head.

"That was the *real* Upper West Side shit, man," Gabe said.

"Why *did* you go to private school?" Daphne asked me.

"It was my father who wanted us to go," I said.

When my sister, her husband, Tim, Malcolm, Jacob, Gideon, and I gathered in the hearse to take us to the cemetery, I almost said, "Everyone's here except Mama. We need to wait for Mama."

At the New Jersey cemetery, I saw my mother buried next to my father, and even though I didn't believe in an afterlife, the symbolism comforted me; after all these years apart, my mother was back by my father's side where she belonged. Fiercely secular, I wondered what my mother would've thought about my sentiment. She'd always said funerals were an important ritual to process death and grieve, but she never said anything about cemeteries. We rarely visited my father's grave. It was almost as if it didn't exist. My mother preferred to remember him alive, not in the ground.

After the burial, we returned to the apartment to sit shiva, beginning the ritual of nonstop socializing for seven days to ensure that we were never alone in our grief. We remembered, cried, and laughed, and at the end we reemerged into our everyday lives, though nothing felt regular about them. On the third evening, a tiny elderly Black woman entered the apartment, a White man by her side. "My name is Evelyn Rich," she said to me. "I was a colleague of your mother's. This is my husband, Marvin."

I took their coats, tossed them on top of the mound of jackets and scarves on my mother's bed, and led them into the crowded living room. It was Christmas Eve. Evelyn looked like she'd just come from church in her red-feathered pillbox hat, navy woolen buttoned-down blazer, and long purple skirt, festive compared to our mourner's black.

"Please gather around." She gestured to the crowd. "Nobody here knows me, but I came tonight because I wanted Judy's daughters to understand what a great person their mother was."

My sister and I looked curiously at each other. People got up from their seats and came closer. Marvin stood humbly by her side, his hands clasped.

"I first met Judy Baum when I worked for the Educational Priorities Panel, and she worked for Advocates for Children. The Panel was created in 1976, the year of the New York City fiscal crisis, to ensure that sufficient educational funds actually went to children in classrooms rather than being siphoned off for 'other' administrative purposes at the (then) New York City Board of Education."

The chatter in the room died down completely.

"Judy represented Advocates for Children on the panel whose members formed a coalition of nonprofit, civic organizations. Advocates grew out of the two 1968 strikes which the United Federation of Teachers led in opposition to increasing demands for community control of schools by minority groups and others convinced that New York City's school children were being shortchanged on any number of fronts resulting in failing schools and poor educational outcomes."

Evelyn fixed her gaze on my sister and me, then scanned the room drawing everyone in. Though petite, her voice resounded, and she held us captive, breathless.

"Judy became a fountain of information about schools during her tenure at Advocates. I would call Judy regularly as parents and others sought me out for advice about schools, programs, principals, superintendents, city policies, and practices. Advocates defended all kids—especially minority, poor, disabled, gay, lesbian, bisexual, and transgender kids. Judy was an effective spokesperson and an ardent supporter of them."

I wanted to shout *Amen.*

"When I became principal of Andrew Jackson High, a failing school in Queens, and when I had a problem with a child who didn't fit in, I contacted Judy, and together we figured out the best place for the child in a different school. At Andrew Jackson, I often had to suspend students. The students went to Advocates for help and Advocates came with the students and parents to the suspension conference, requesting reinstatement. So frequently Judy and I were on different sides of the aisle, but I always knew we were allies."

She raised her fist.

"Many of us know the *famous* educators—if not personally, at least by name. I was lucky to know one of the *truly* famous educators, unknown to many in the halls of power, but known and widely respected by those of us who work in the trenches, as well as many of the actual students and parents she helped. Her name was Judy Baum, and I am proud she was my friend."

Everyone clapped.

"I've said my fill. Let's go, Marvin."

They gathered their coats and left.

My aunt said Evelyn was like a fairy godmother, waving her magic wand, bringing my mother back to life for a few minutes, blessing herself and us, and having done her work, disappearing. To me, her homage was like the finale of a three-act play. Act I was my mother's sudden death a day before my arrival, Act II the funeral, where family, friends, and co-workers eulogized my mother's life and profound impact on New York City public education. Act III was the shiva, where everyone sat, ate, mourned, and reminisced about my mother. Then, the finale—Evelyn, small in stature but powerful in praise, going out of her way to proclaim that everything my mother did mattered.

Chapter 12

***

Relinquishing the Apartment

ONE WEEK AFTER the shiva, Elizabeth and I had to face the reality of relinquishing our beloved childhood apartment. Because we grew up in subsidized middle-income housing, we had no inheritance rights, and had to empty the apartment in a hurry for the next family on the wait-list. We couldn't stop to contemplate the tragedy of our mother's sudden death, couldn't linger or ruminate over forty-seven years of ephemera symbolizing the early years when our father was still alive, or mourn the loss of our cooperative apartment, the wellspring of our values of social and economic justice.

Reuben's daughter, Rebecca, moved Reuben back to his New Jersey condo, where most of his belongings were, and where my mother and he went on weekend jaunts. At first, he was resistant, thinking he could stay on at RNA. He couldn't. Even though he'd been living in #14E since 2001, he had no legal claims to the apartment because of Mitchell-Lama rules and regulations. He wasn't a New York City resident, nor had he been declaring his income to the New York City Department of Housing Preservation and Development, necessary stipulations to retain the place. Though my sister and I were on the original lease, we had no legal claims, either. In two weeks, I was due back in Phoenix to teach composition to international students, and we didn't know the deadline to vacate the apartment. So, we began the harrowing, heartbreaking task of extracting our mother's spirit, smells, life, our lives, our father's life from the apartment, unimaginable while mourning, but required by law.

Raw and sick with grief, we set aside a few prized 1960s Marimekko dresses and dashikis to divvy up later. Then, like street sweepers, we vacuumed out the rest of her clothes closet, her body odor, perfume, and talcum powder permeating the air we barely had time to breathe. Through nasty, icy winter weather, we lugged her jam-packed shopping cart down the hill to Broadway and 96th Street to donate her suits, blouses, and slacks to Housing Works, a thrift store that helped people with HIV/AIDS. Next, we gave away years' worth of coats, hats, gloves, and scarves, feeling emptied, like flat tires forced to continue down the road.

On our mother's bed, we displayed Danish modern furniture catalogs, a letter from Hubert Humphrey thanking our parents for their campaign contribution, a menu from Eastern Gardens Chinese restaurant on Broadway and 100th Street advertising Mo Go Gai Pan for $3.50, typed carbon-copied notes from PTA meetings at P.S. 75 when Luis Mercado was the first Puerto Rican principal, an RNA newsletter congratulating my sister and another girl for their graduations from Hebrew school, flower power stickers, Impeach Nixon buttons, and our father's agenda where he noted that fateful Father's Visiting Day and his impending, never-kept doctor's appointment. The rest of the agenda remained blank, unused, my mother keeping it as proof. Shaken, we put these remembrances in a "to save" box to divide up later and tackled more expendable objects like warped Tupperware spilling out of kitchen cabinets.

After I returned to Arizona, Elizabeth and I learned that we'd normally have only three months to move. But because we were the original tenants at RNA House, the co-op board made an exception and extended the deadline to the end of June. They understood what a dedicated, beloved cooperator my mother was, and how, over the years, my parents fostered RNA's collectivist values and resisted the tide of privatization.

In Arizona, I was more bereft than I could've possibly imagined because no traces of my mother existed in this politically reactionary state. In New York, I'd felt her presence in the apartment, building, subway, streets, air, sounds, music, history, people, especially people—those who loved, understood, and admired her and those thousands of kids and families affected by her work. In Phoenix, virtually no one knew her except ten-year-old Gideon, my husband, and me. I longed to be back in New York City more than ever.

In my absence, my sister took on the herculean task of sorting through more things alone, determining what was important, what was junk, what to give away, what to divvy up, making as much progress as possible without me. Occasionally, the dust in the apartment was so thick from forty-seven years of accumulated soot, she wheezed, needing a dust mask to excavate paper mountains from deep inside closets.

At the beginning of May, I came home to help my sister finish dismantling the apartment. I felt like I lived in New York City again, as if at #14E I was finally home, though I knew it was temporary, that I was packing up, letting go. Elizabeth and I wanted to save everything that wasn't junk, what we admired of our parents' taste, savvy, intelligence, and progressiveness. We longed to hold on to what they valued, to keep what was ripped away from us, first with our father's untimely death, then our mother's unfathomable repeat ending. Tense and distraught, we rolled dice to decide who went first, dividing up the Danish modern furniture, precious paintings by Harlem Renaissance artists Jacob Lawrence and Charles Alston, soapstone carvings, memorabilia, *tchotchkes*, and a library's worth of books—MIT Press's black-with-white lettering *Bauhaus* tome, an artwork in and of itself, Howard Fast's *The Passion of Sacco and Vanzetti*, Rachel Carson's *Silent Spring*, Lewis Mumford's *The Culture of Cities*, Eleanor Roosevelt's 1937 autobiography *This Is My Life*, inscribed, *To my daughter-in-law, Judith. Love, Gertie. December 1958*, the year my parents were married.

I tackled my former bedroom. Initially, it'd been my father's office, where he stored his tools, telescopes, cameras, and liquor. My sister and I'd shared a room, but once I turned six and my sister eight, my parents separated us. As the small room was already crowded with his things, my father built another closet for me with sliding shoji screen doors. My bed, bookcase, dresser, and desk squeezed into the 13′ by 15′ space, my electric train set nailed to a board leaned up on the wall behind the door, my gymnastics mat squished under my bed. After my father died when I was ten, my mother left his belongings intact because they reminded her of him. Some objects were useful—the liquor, hammers and nails, and my father's large turquoise homemade telescope, the one he used to show the neighborhood kids the stars. Others became obsolete, like his slide projector and 8mm film camera. Still others, like his micrometer caliper or his tungsten carbide rod saw, we hadn't a clue how to use.

Once I moved out, my room had become the guest room. My mother removed my desk and replaced my bed with a fold-out sleeper couch for visitors. Because I was transient, living in tiny spaces in Manhattan, Brooklyn, Vancouver, Los Angeles, and Paris, many of my possessions remained, among them coin and button collections, books, photo albums, journals, and the letters my parents, sister, friends, and I exchanged over the years. My mother also began adding her own books, clothes, and papers in the room as well.

After Reuben was installed in the apartment, my former bedroom turned guest room became his study. A long plywood Ikea desk spanned much of the wall where my desk and dresser had once stood. The office was now stuffed with his mail and clothes squeezed into the already full shoji screen closet my dad had built long ago. By the end, terminating in my mother's sudden death, my former bedroom had become more like a dumping ground, a place my mother stored things she had no energy to dispose of. She'd always been on top of decluttering, until she wasn't, until the stuff controlled her. She was so spent, so wasted, so exhausted taking care of Reuben, shopping, cooking, maintaining two homes, plus working as an education advocate that she had little time to care for the apartment or herself. The beautiful closet my dad built for me bulged, the doors no longer staying on their track, the shoji screen panels torn.

Dust mask on, I gingerly opened the shoji screen, trying not to make the damage worse, even though I knew the closet wouldn't be preserved. I sorted through old clothes I meant to give away, my white feathered sequined tutu with no sequins remaining, crumpled wrapping paper, old toys, childhood paintings, report cards from elementary school, thirty-year-old stained sleeping bags, my *War is Not Healthy for Children and Other Living Things* and Picasso's *Peace Dove* posters, and mounds and mounds of sooty documents to be shredded. I found numerous toiletry kits, soap containers, travel-sized shampoos and mouthwashes for my mother's trips to visit me; she was too busy or tired to dig them out, so she kept buying new ones instead. I also discovered heaps of bags—plastic bags, reusable canvas bags, shopping bags from department stores like Macy's, B. Altman's, Lord and Taylor, Saks, and Bloomingdale's. It was as if she were leaving them there on purpose, or perhaps subconsciously, for us to use to clean out the apartment once she was gone.

Though under intense time pressure to dismantle the room, I paused to read childhood letters. Grabbing a pile from a cabinet, I sat down in the lotus position on the bare linoleum, my purple shag rug long gone, and searched for envelopes with my mother's handwriting.

July 31, 1973—Dear Jenny, It's early morning now—Daddy just left for work . . . I'm going to put away a lot of junk so the painters can get to the walls. The living room is already bare of tchotchkas . . . The flower box on the terrace is still sad looking but the fern and the new Florida plants are fine . . . Today I get a bonus—Watergate begins at 9:30 instead of 10!

Aug 3, 1973—We are nearing the countdown stage in the great apartment painting caper. Boxes are everywhere—also junk, dust (sneeze, sneeze) and dirty walls. Daddy is busy every night dismantling shelves which are attached to the wall . . . Can I throw away the Lucy Tea Party set? What about Operation? You sure can use the space in the closet . . . Fishy is now living in the kitchen—We had to move him for the painters, and I think he likes the company.

Aug 17, 1973—Progress is being made putting books back in place. But I'm not going to restore everything exactly in your room until you come home because you might find a way to get rid of some things (even though you did a good job of it before you went to camp). Maybe you should un-clutter the room somewhat. I'm working on keeping the wood and Daddy's charts out. Also—no more unicycling in the apartment!! The walls are spot free—they should stay that way!!! This is serious!! Work on it in the out-side hallway. When you learn to do it without holding on, you'll be allowed to ride in the house again. I'm going to be neurotic about the walls for a while. Heh! Heh!

The following summer, four months after my father died:

July 25, 1974—Your letters are fabulous. They are well written, inter-esting and sometimes funny too. I enjoy reading them until I get to the crying parts. You seemed to have gotten over that and then I came to visit and spoiled it all!

On the way back, I paid, get this, 69 cents for gas! But I really had to get some for the trip home. Enclosed are some Mets clippings to cheer you up. They won!

I have been watching the debate about impeachment—This is by the Judiciary Committee of the House of Representatives. If they vote for im-peachment, then the entire House of Representatives will vote for it. Then the Senate holds a trial. The debate is televised and at times boring—but you know me!

The Mets lost again, and I won't even discuss it.

Loads of people have been asking for you, including Murray the Butcher.

June 29, 1975—I started packing up your room for the painters and have done all the little things on your shelves—but the damn books will take many boxes. Only 1 ½ shelves done and two boxes already filled!! I'd better do a few shelves every night I'm home or it will take forever!!!

Your shag rug needs a cleaning. I will NOT buy you another rug. Your antic of spilling orange juice only made your room smell.

The sad news is that the Mets lost two.

August 8, 1977—Dearest Jennifer, I am sitting in a corner of the dining room. To my right all of the contents of your room, mine and the hallway and bathrooms are piled—sprawled —lumped all over the living room. My body aches from having gotten them there and it aches even more at the thought of putting them back. Elizabeth has been a super terrific help and I hope you'll be also when you get home. Arturo is here but wasn't when we needed him—I hope he will show up next week—especially to undo the hi-fi. He was all tied up with his music this week and caused everyone great concern by not being reachable—so the phone calls flew back and forth. Peter, Nicky, Hayward, his mother, his father.

I could've stayed on the floor forever, immersed in my mother's voice, enraptured by her wit, warmth, and optimism, avoiding the task at hand—decluttering, cleaning, throwing things out, mimicking my mother's actions, but this time with finality.

I forced myself to get up and go back to work.

On the way to buy moving supplies, in the RNA lobby I saw Scott, the man with a schnauzer who lived above us on the fifteenth floor. As a young child, Scott had calmed me down when I got stuck in the elevator, and as I grew up, joked with me about boyfriends. Now, in his eighties, he still looked fit, muscly, and handsome.

"I'm so sorry, Jenny," he said, and kissed me on the forehead. "Your mother was a great woman."

Even then, though grieving, I wanted to keep writing about the building, the experience of coming of age there. It was a distraction, as well as a necessity. I needed to create, comment, critique, in order to cope at this moment and in life, so I asked: "If you have time, could I interview you for a book I'm writing about RNA? In the early years, what it was like to be openly gay in the building and in the city?"

In the '60s, throughout the country, sodomy was illegal. In New York City, the gay community was systematically harassed by the New York Police Department, culminating in the 1969 Stonewall riots.

Scott paused, studied my face. "Sorry, Jenny. I don't want to be a poster boy for the Gay Rights Movement." He kissed me again.

I understand, I thought, although feeling hurt. Growing up I knew him not as *gay Scott*, but as another caring cooperator. *I guess he wants to be remembered that way. Still, it would've been great to hear his perspective.*

Similarly, I tried to interview the numerous mixed-race families I'd grown up with about their experiences in the late '60s when RNA first opened. By then, the Northern States had overturned anti-miscegenation laws, but interracial coupling was rare and frowned upon. They too declined, although I'm not sure why. Maybe they didn't want to be poster children either. Or maybe they'd felt defined by their race too often in the past and didn't want it to happen again.

I pushed my mother's shopping cart down Broadway to Staples on 81st, along the route noting numerous Starbucks, banks, luxury high-rises, an AMC movie theater, and a Banana Republic. Fortunately, a few old-time stores remained like Zabar's, Murray's Sturgeon shop, and the Cuban-Chinese Restaurant *La Caridad*, but they were few and far between. In the middle of the day, Staples was virtually empty, an eerie suburban vacuousness permeating its two floors. When I was little, of course, big box stores like Staples didn't exist. Now, I would've preferred to shop elsewhere, but the only option was a more expensive UPS, hardly an improvement. *At least I wasn't ordering from Amazon*, I thought, as I stocked up on boxes, tape, and environmentally unfriendly Styrofoam peanuts.

I preferred to walk home on less gentrified, grittier Amsterdam Avenue with a mix of NYCHA and Mitchell-Lama housing, tenement buildings, and graffiti scrawl like *Kill Your Masters* sprayed onto a dark green traffic counter box on a streetlight pole. On 93rd, across from a stand-alone NYCHA building, a newish addition to the neighborhood was kosher *Sunflower Café*, with sidewalk seating, reflecting the neighborhood's changing demographics. While historically, there has been a significant Jewish population on the Upper West Side, it was comprised largely of secular, politically progressive Jews. Since the '90s, though, the area has seen an influx of Orthodox Jewish families, who lean Republican, have a lot of children, are anti-abortion, and against same sex marriage, a trend I didn't understand. I wondered if this move toward conservatism could ever threaten the neighborhood's tolerance and people like Scott. *No way*, I thought. *Not on the Upper West Side*.

I didn't sleep over often at 96th Street. It was too upsetting. After spending hours sorting, shredding, packing, donating carts filled with unwanted stuff to Housing Works, and schlepping yet more moving supplies from

Staples, sometimes with Elizabeth, sometimes solo, I needed space from the apartment and social contact, so I stayed with friends and family as much as I could. Other times, I slept at #14E, inviting Vancouver folk to visit the city and keep me company. Once, I ran out of options and spent a night in the apartment alone, curling up in my mother's bed, hoping for a good night's sleep.

I dreamt there was a summer thunderstorm, the best kind. The weather had been so hot, the air heavy, damp, humid. I had to wash my face every hour to get the soot out of my pores. Finally, the rain came and brought relief to the city. I was lucky the apartment had a terrace, so I could go outside to watch the storm. I sat on the heavy iron chair, not bothering to clean it off, not caring that the layers of soot would soil my clothes. The rain came down hard and everybody ran for cover, no one left on the streets except one lone passerby. I leaned over the edge of the railing, my head getting soaked, but I didn't mind. I saw the rain hitting the cement, bouncing off and forming huge puddles. I lifted the binoculars from the glass table and spotted a smokestack in the distance spewing out thick black smoke. I tried to focus. The smoke kept on changing form, billowing out, diffusing, then the smokestack would spit out more. *It's rare to see this now. The landlord was supposed to clean it up. He's violating the law*, my father said. *I don't care*, I shrugged. His big warm cheeks sank in disappointment. *If you continue with that attitude, I'm not going to show you anything.* I stood on my tiptoes, grabbed his arms, and looked up at him. *I'm sorry, Daddy. Show me.* He shook his head. *Too late.*

I didn't know where to focus, so I searched for a new object, but the rain came down so fiercely, I could see the drops through the lens. I kept on trying to get past the rain, to focus on the building facing mine, but the huge streaks of water streaming down from the sky, crashing onto the sidewalk, distracted me. In the background, black smoke disappeared into the atmosphere. I saw ten-year-old Christina, wearing her Catholic schoolgirl white blouse and plaid skirt uniform, jumping at a window in her apartment in the building facing ours, her blonde pigtails bouncing up and down. *It's something she likes to do the way you like to do gymnastics*, my mother said. I went back inside the apartment and placed the drenched binoculars on the dark brown dining room table, puddles forming on the Formica surface, dripping onto the cherrywood floor my parents had laid down.

I woke up, had a shower, got dressed, and made coffee. A moving company representative was scheduled to come over with an estimate for shipping costs to Phoenix, and I needed to prepare. I set my computer on the dining room table and turned it on, feeling composed, like I could handle things, could cope. I'd had a restless sleep, but it wasn't as bad as I'd imagined. I turned on the faucet, filled a large glass of water almost to the brim—I drank water constantly then, thirsty from all the labor, brought the glass to the table, tripped on the table leg, and spilled the water all over my laptop. Immediately, my composure disappeared, and I was frantic. My entire information age life had been on my computer—photos of my mother, Gideon, Jacob, and me from Paris, LA, New York, writings about RNA House, my teaching second language composition research, and emails from everyone.

At that moment, the buzzer rang. It was the moving guy. I screamed into the intercom: "Don't come up. I can't deal with this now. I need to reschedule. Sorry."

I ran back to the table and mopped up the drenched computer with paper towel, then went onto the terrace, turned the laptop upside down, and shook it furiously. It was a brilliant sunny day, the air clean from the heavy rains the night before.

In the *New Yorker* essay, "The Mind-Expanding Ideas of Andy Clark," Larissa MacFarquhar wrote, "Some musicologists say that playing an instrument involves incorporating an object into thought and emotion. . . . If a person's thought was intimately linked to her surroundings, then destroying a person's surroundings could be as damaging and reprehensible as a bodily attack."[1] My thoughts, identity, and sense of place in the world were intimately linked to 150 West 96th Street, #14E. Dismantling the apartment felt like a bodily attack. Now I was twice besieged, losing my RNA and computer lives simultaneously.

I tore out of the apartment and brought the computer to the closest Apple Store. A crazed week passed before I found out most of my data could be salvaged. Once I knew, I regained a semblance of normalcy, if one could call this period of time normal. I took a deep breath and continued packing.

While emptying out my mother's desk, I discovered E. B. White's *Here Is New York*, written in 1949, the same year the Truman administration's seminal Housing Act passed. On the inside cover, my father inscribed to my mother: *For Judy, With Love, Charles.* I climbed onto my mother's bed and flipped through the book. Reading *Here Is New York* consoled me, made me understand even more my parents' commitment to the city as a work in progress for the benefit of all its citizens, not just themselves. Or at least that's how New York used to be when they came of age.

E. B. White marveled at New Yorkers' ability to intermingle. He pointed to the New York Housing Act integration provision, absent in the rest of the country, to demonstrate progressive legislation bringing more tolerance, not less. He delighted in New York neighborhoods soon to be destroyed by Slum Clearance: "Each area is a city within a city within a city. Thus, no matter where you live in New York, you will find within a block or two a grocery store, a barbershop, a newsstand, and shoeshine shack . . . a dry cleaner, a laundry, a delicatessen . . ."[2]

White recognized the value of the old as well, ending his book by paying tribute to a tree: ". . . there is an old willow tree . . . long suffering and much climbed, held together by strands of wire but beloved of those who know it. . . . If it were to go, all would go—this city, this mischievous and marvelous monument which not to look upon would be like death."[3]

Though White acknowledged forward-thinking aspects of the Housing Act, the Act's Title I slum clearance provision did exactly what he predicted and dreaded—brought death to sections of the "mischievous and marvelous" city. It's true. Neighborhoods were ruthlessly destroyed, people were displaced, as well as ghettoized. But at least the government funded public housing on a grand scale. *If only we could return today to the ethos of a decent home for all,* I thought.

I closed *Here Is New York*, put it in the "to keep" pile, and looked south out the window at all the grayish-white brutalist cement Mitchell-Lamas, bland brick NYCHA projects, brownstones, and luxury towers that defined the current Upper West Side skyline, wishing the government would build subsidized housing en masse again so I could afford to move back. I tried to be philosophical about not having a place in the city anymore. As my mother said after Hurricane Sandy, "My daughters are doing fine." She was right. I was doing fine.

The doorbell rang. It was my mother's friend Betty Gubert, an original RNA House tenant, here to make a condolence call. Betty was parent to childhood playmates Emily and George for whom she bought McDonald's Hanukah gift certificates when the fast food restaurant first opened, and one of my favorite RNA House moms growing up. Emily's best friend,

Julie, lived just above Emily on the fourth floor. They spent so much time together as kids that they imagined breaking the ceiling between apartments and building a staircase to connect them.

Betty was a few years older than my mother, but she looked younger. Though her tightly curled black hair was now gray, her olive skin was still wrinkle-free, unlike my mother's weathered face. They were both gatherers and organizers of research, my mother at PEA, Advocates for Children, and the Center for NYC Affairs, and Betty as librarian at the Schomburg Center for Research in Black Culture. Betty was also the author of *Invisible Wings: An Annotated Bibliography on Blacks in Aviation, 1916–1993*, and co-author of *Distinguished African Americans in Aviation and Space Science*.

I led Betty to a cobalt blue Formica end table by the living room's south facing windows where a cluster of potted house plants remained. We'd been watering them religiously, hoping to find them good homes. My sister had taken a few, but I, of course, couldn't ship them to Arizona. Betty selected a bloomscape, clutching it to her chest. "This will be a great way to remember your mother. I can say, *Oh, look how well Judy's plant is doing*, and think nice things about her."

I smiled.

"Something else of yours is also at 96th Street, not *living* but certainly appreciated. When you moved out of your one-bedroom, at your moving sale I bought your aubergine-shaped salad bowl and huge aubergine platter. During RNA holiday parties, I've used the bowl for Italian cole slaw," Betty said. As she left, she added: "Your mother must've loved your remembrance of growing up on 96th Street. Be glad you wrote it and that she read it."

Betty was referring to the first essay I wrote about the building, which I never could've completed without my mother's help. My mother read the piece but died before it was published. Later that day, when my sister was over, Selena, who lived in #14F, directly opposite our apartment, paid her respects. The conversation turned to my mother's Brooklyn upbringing.

"That's why she was so cool," Selena said.

We made coffee and sat around the dining room table.

"When Judy asked if one of the boys or my husband was home to pick up Reuben after he fell, every time they'd help Judy without hesitation."

"It's great you were available," Elizabeth said.

Selena sipped her coffee. "It was a Friday afternoon when Jamal came to me and said, *Ma did you know Ms. Judy passed?* It completely shocked me. I'd just seen and talked to her that morning. When I opened my door to go out on a walk with Rusty, Judy was picking up her newspaper. 'Time for Rusty's constitutional?' She grinned. I replied, Time for a spin. Judy said, 'Rusty has such a majestic stride. Enjoy your walk.' Jamal doesn't take to all, but he liked Judy. As he said to me years ago, 'Ma, Ms. Judy is a really nice lady.' Judy took time to talk with Jamal, especially about education. Jamal knew Judy had a kind spirit."

Selena chose a fern. "I'll take good care of this," she promised as she left.

It was comforting that my mother's plants lived on in the building, Selena even naming her plant Judy in homage. Both women subsequently sent photos of the plants to show how they were flourishing.

I did the laundry in the RNA basement for the very last time. The dreary room was still the same except for the upgraded laundry machines. Now they were larger, more energy efficient, and took cards rather than coins. Not a good way to learn basic math, I thought, remembering Gideon's pleasure counting laundry quarters with my mother. One positive change, however, was the adjoining bathroom, now clean and furnished with toilet paper. Danny, the friendly maintenance man who'd been working at RNA House for decades, was repairing a machine. Over the years, whenever I ran into him in the lobby, he'd open doors for me and say, "Alright. Howya doing? Give me that gorgeous smile of yours."

Now he said: "I'm real sorry to hear about your mom's passing."

I thanked him and told him she had worn herself down.

He came closer. "One time, when I was working in the backyard, I saw your mother's boyfriend fall off his chair and he asked me to pick him up."

I used to wonder if my mother would turn into one of the old folks. gossiping on cushioned chairs out back, though I couldn't picture it as she was always so active.

The building had become an unofficial NORC—a Naturally Occurring Retirement Community. Many original tenants aged there, instead of moving into assisted living or leaving the city for warmer climates. Beginning in 2020, with City Council Member Helen Rosenthal's support, RNA acquired NORC funding for one year, which supported ten hours per week of an onsite Social Worker. If RNA were to privatize, the NORC could continue, but it wasn't clear whether the City Council would provide funding to a private co-op.

Danny continued, "So I lifted him up. He was a big man."

I nodded, "It took a lot out of my mother to care for him."

"Ya know, the building was on the verge of telling him he no longer had permission to drive."

"Really?"

In 2001, after Reuben's stroke, his left arm wasn't functional, so he got a knob installed on the steering wheel of the car he shared with my mother to drive one handed. Over time, as his health deteriorated, his driving became more erratic, and he occasionally got into minor accidents in the garage such as denting RNA neighbors' cars. My sister and I constantly feared he'd get into a terrible accident one day, that this would be the tragic end to what seemed an unsustainable living arrangement. Instead, our mother collapsed on the street.

Danny hugged me.

"Alright, give me a smile now. It'll be alright."

On June 30, 2014, my sister and I sat on the floor of our childhood home, fiddling with the familiar keys, waiting to hand them over to the RNA House board, emotionally and physically spent. The day before, two sets of movers cleared out the boxes and furniture, half going to Elizabeth's downtown loft, the other to Arizona. We'd tried, to no avail, to sell or donate the piano, but it was too old, out of tune, and expensive to move, free or otherwise. Instead, we watched with dismay as the movers destroyed it, turning it into scrap wood to be sold or dumped.

The last item to go was our mother's bed. I shipped her Danish modern headboard back to Phoenix. No one wanted her lumpy old mattress, but we gave the box spring, still in decent shape, to Housing Works thrift store, where we'd donated all her unwanted possessions. Once her bed was removed, it truly meant we could no longer sleep there, whether we wanted to or not. We no longer had a choice. The apartment and our mother were gone.

Al Kurchin, the round-faced co-op treasurer, arrived and remarked he'd known my mother from the beginning. He went room to room inspecting, taking notes on a clipboard, as if the apartment was just another co-op in the building, which, of course, to him it was.

"We'll have to dismantle the cabinet," he said, pointing to the broken but once beautiful shoji screen closet. "You'll get most of the equity accrued, minus the repairs."

In 1967, my parents had bought the apartment for $3,800. In 2014, we got $34,000 back. After fifty years, the typical private postwar three-bedroom in the area sold for a $1.5 million.

We spoke about the upcoming privatization vote, something on the minds of all the tenants. Al recapped my sentiments—how the Mitchell-Lama program was one of the most successful urban planning projects in Manhattan's history, and how it changed the neighborhood into a thriving, diverse community, affordable to low- and middle-income people. "Now people want to walk out with a profit on no investment by privatizing, ending the affordable housing they enjoyed for years. It's a disregard for the people waiting fifteen years on a list, which becomes obsolete," he said.

I nodded, swallowing my mixed emotions. As my mother aged, the reality that we'd lose the apartment became more pronounced, and I'd found myself partially holding out hope for privatization, not due to the attraction of a real estate sale windfall, but to keep the apartment in the family. My personal attachment to the apartment contradicted the faith my mother had taught me in the common good.

"It is my hope they vote 'no' in the next election and realize the folly of their dreams of profits," he said. "Your mother was against privatization. She had a *gute neshuma*."

"What's that?"

"A good soul. Look it up in the Yiddish dictionary."

We gave him the keys and he departed, allowing us a moment alone to linger. The building that seemed so fair, that shaped our values about inclusion and social and economic justice, which we grew to love, didn't in the end feel just at all. We thought of the apartment as ours, though in the back of our minds, we had always known it wasn't. Its sudden, unceremonious loss echoed how our mother abruptly disappeared from our lives, in the same way our father did when we were kids, taken by massive cardiac arrest.

There was nothing more for us to do. We left, leaving the door unlocked behind us.

Later, we learned from a friend in the building how appreciative the next family in line was to get such a great apartment high up, with southern exposure and a view of the skyline, opposite noisy 96th Street. In my mind, I wished them well, though I knew I could never visit to see how they transformed apartment #14E to make it their own.

■■■

In Phoenix, I recreated #14E as much as possible, arranging furniture and hanging artwork mirroring my parents' design. Perhaps my desire to hold on to #14E was extreme, but I was traumatized. It wasn't as though Jacob and I had set up a beautiful home with exquisite belongings that I undid. Up until this point, we'd been transitory, constructing plywood lives only to dismantle them. Recreating 96th Street pleased, consoled, and stabilized me. Fortunately, in Phoenix, we could afford a house large enough to accommodate #14E belongings, something I appreciated about living here. Such wouldn't be the case if we moved back to the Upper West Side.

In the living room, my parent's auburn, white, and, blue geometric rug with decorative flourishes covered the tile floor, the elegant Hans Wegner couch lined the wall, a small brown Navajo rug bought by Grandma Gertie and Grandpa Isidore ages ago thrown on top, the teak floor lamp with tripod legs and steel-blue funnel-shaped shade next to the couch, my sister's black-and-white textured photo of tulips scrawled on a chalkboard and a colorful abstract painting from Jamaica hanging above, the Charles Alston watercolor of a woman's face on the opposite wall. Resting on an older, more formal end table with a marble top, also from Gertie and Isidore, stood a pitcher filled with dried roses, just as my mother had placed, above Elizabeth's abstract painting in varied green-blue hues.

The teak headboard from my mother's bed fell apart, so I hired a neighbor who transformed it into two end tables and one lower coffee table with hairpin legs, where I displayed the sacred Bauhaus tome. Near the entrance, the cool cherrywood rectangular glove box with curved ends hooked to the wall, the black-and-white swinging op-art piece overhead, in the corner, the turquoise telescope accenting the colors in Elizabeth's painting. In the vintage steel-frame Herman Miller dresser, from long ago in my RNA House bedroom, I stored the heaps of childhood letters my mother had saved. Whenever I missed my mother, I opened the drawer and read a letter, her voice, love, concern, intelligence, and sharp wit momentarily coming alive:

Aug 1, 1977—On the way back from a weekend in the Berkshires, we went to Alice's Restaurant. The original one (about which the song was written) burned down and the new one is just a few feet up the road from Tanglewood. Apparently, Arlo Guthrie was convicted for littering and so the army refused to draft him. He wrote a song about the irony of being thought too immoral for littering to kill the innocent in Vietnam . . .

I went to Saks with Aunt Susan for their sales, and you would be proud of me: I bought a strappy, blousy, batiky (brown, black, gold) mid-calf-length BRALESS DRESS! My letters are so hasty and messy, they will never do for my published edition!

All you need is love love love love love love.

Je t'aime beacoup. Ta mère

September 1981 (After I'd arrived at Oberlin College, near Cleveland)— I guess it's hard to move away (even if it's temporary) from the bosom of your family . . . As you know, I never did it myself. My first independence was when I lived at home with Aunt Susan and my parents went away!

Since Grandma and I got to Cleveland, we've had nothing but sweetness and light. It's the biddy capital of the world. You must come to this house. It's a gem! As kitschy as its possible to be—you'll flip over it. And Aunt Mabel Rose would be delighted to have you stay over if you need a change of scene. Downtown Cleveland is quite a city, but everyone is so fearful of crime! Apparently, there is great hostility between the races. So be cautious when you travel in.

⟍ Did you get your absentee ballot? You know the NYC primary was post-poned because of legal challenges to the redistricting plan, so there's going to be a city wide primary on Sept 2 and then another for city council at a later time. What anguish! What gnashing of teeth! I don't know if my absentee ballot counts or not.

October 1981—Reuben and I went to see Cloud 9, an off-Broadway play—a farcical commentary on gender confusion and feminism. It was terrific.

Last week was my high school reunion. The major change in everyone was that instead of being nasty, sarcastic, jealous and competitive, everyone was nice to everyone else. We all seemed to have become mature women at ease with ourselves at last. Life may very well begin at 45.

I exchanged my Ikea desk for my mother's upright one, reserving a shelf for photos shot on film. Prominently displayed was a photo Gideon took of my mother and me—a close-up, our faces filling the frame, the edges of our foreheads, eyebrows and cheeks touching as we smile down at him looking up at us behind the camera lens. There's depth and texture to the image. He captures our wrinkles, shiny skin, wavy hair, the flare of our noses, our delighted smiles, and engaged eyes. Tangible expressive body parts. Alive, not buried, not starved, not gassed. Alive.

Others included the one of Gideon and my mother cheek to cheek in front of RNA House, of them admiring a cup they filled with snow from the #14E terrace, of my newly married parents, of my sister and mother cleaning their glasses in the kitchen, and of Jacob, me, and baby Gideon. Center stage was a newly discovered black-and-white photo my father shot of four-year-old me in the RNA backyard, staring defiantly into the camera, wearing a striped A-line jumper, headband, white knee socks, Mary Jane shoes, the hoop of a Footsie around my leg, the cup attached to the hoop with a plastic cable in hand, ready to hop.

Chapter 13

The Crucial Necessity
of Affordable Housing

SINCE LOSING RNA HOUSE in 2014, I often stayed with my friend, Mark, who lived in Penn South, also called Mutual Redevelopment Houses. Located on 8th Avenue and 27th Street, his high-rise was part of a ten-building, 2,820 apartment, redbrick tower-in-the-park, limited equity cooperative built in 1962. It was sponsored by the International Ladies Garment Workers Union in collaboration with the United Housing Foundation (UHF), "a real estate investment trust founded in 1951 to oversee cooperative housing,"[1] and designed by Herman Jessor, the architect behind the massive Mitchell-Lama developments Co-op City in the Bronx and Rochdale Village in Queens. At the time, the president of the UHF was Abraham Kazan, whose involvement with cooperative housing dated back to 1927 when Amalgamated Houses was constructed, a result of the 1926 New York State Limited Dividend Housing Companies Act. Kazan declared, "I am a cooperator, interested only in building the cooperative commonwealth,"[2] highlighting the collectivist ethos of his day.

When Mark first moved in, I told my mother he'd gotten an apartment there after years on the wait-list.

"Good for him," my mother said.

Penn South hired roaming security guards for the ten-building complex. Visiting Mark after dark felt less secure than going home to RNA House, where a guard greeted me, preventing anyone from following me in or from lurking in the lobby. Still, at Penn South the lobby was well lit, the front door locked, and the intercom system worked. Riding up to his apartment, I felt an immediate solidarity with the folks in the elevator. They were New Yorkers from a different era, relics from the past. They weren't slick, manicured, or sporting designer clothes, but *haimish*, old school, rough around the edges, with thick New York accents. Maybe they were teachers, actors, or firefighters. One man carried an armful of *Forward* magazines, a Jewish leftist journal he was donating to the library in the laundry room. I wanted to tell them I grew up in a building like this one and that I'd recently lost my childhood home after my mother died, but the sentiment seemed too intimate to discuss with strangers on an elevator ride.

Unlike at RNA House, Penn South elevators hadn't been refurbished. *No danger of privatization here*, I thought. But then, the complex wasn't in an upscale neighborhood—yet. It spanned from West 23rd to 29th, between 8th and 9th Avenue, adjacent on one side to the Chelsea-Elliot NYCHA housing projects, on another, the brutalist Fashion Institute of Technology, and on the edge of bustling, raucous, truck-laden midtown. However, gentrification was creeping in, the flower district disappearing, making way for boutique hotels, upscale housing, and a major refurbishing of Penn Station and its environs. Maybe Penn South residents, sensing enormous financial gains, would one day vote for privatization, too.

After college, Mark lived in an East Village tenement. His apartment was dismal, the kind of place my paternal grandparents grew up in, with faulty heat and only two small windows on either end of a narrow railroad flat—one window facing the street and the other butting up against another tenement, with barely enough room for a pigeon to lodge on the windowsill.

At Penn South, Mark paid $500 maintenance for a spacious studio apartment on the nineteenth floor with a separate kitchen big enough for a table. Looking through his large northwest facing windows, I couldn't miss the colossal shimmering luxury skyscrapers under construction at Hudson Yards. Reaching twenty-one floors, Penn South buildings used to be considered tall for the neighborhood. Now they were dwarfed by the ninety-two-story Hudson Yards towers. One hundred seven units of the upscale apartments were set aside as rentals for moderate income people, part of the deal given to developers who received 421-a tax breaks. James Parrott, director of economic and fiscal policies at the Center for New York City Affairs at the New School (the last place my mother worked) said, "We are still giving tax breaks to a development that enriches billionaire developers and high-rise commercial and residential development that is not benefiting ordinary people in New York."[3]

Started under the Bloomberg administration, and with $6 billion in tax breaks, Hudson Yards transformed sixty blocks on Manhattan's far west side. Previously, the area was a wasteland dotted by a few warehouses, gas stations and taxi garages. The Long Island Railroad tracks were operational, but the highline tracks were abandoned. Office space for major corporations, a shopping mall, hotel, school, an arts center and apartments selling for $9.5 million plus were set to open soon. It's "the biggest private real-estate development in US history. The last development of this magnitude in New York was Rockefeller Center, completed 80 years ago."[4]

Who needs this kind of luxury mega development in an already congested city struggling to house its citizens? It's grotesque. As of 2019, more than 114,000 New York City public school students were homeless,[5] up from 80,000, the number my mother quoted in 2012. Hudson Yards could have been built as an affordable housing mecca, the largest development in the history of the US for middle- and low-income Americans. But this is no longer the mentality of New York City.

While at Mark's I did laundry, pushing my cart across the landscaped park where an integrated mix of kids climbed the playground's jungle gym, middle-agers walked dogs, and older folk schmoozed on benches. Unlike RNA, which didn't receive status until 2019, Penn South was the city's very first official NORC. Established in 1986 by the philanthropic United Jewish Appeal (UJA),[6] NORC services available at Penn South included a Blood Pressure Clinic and Parkinson's Support Group. Also on offer, to name a few, were community drawing and painting, meditation, yoga, and drama classes.

Looking for something to do, I skimmed the books in the laundry room library. Much to my delight, I found Oscar Hijuelos's 1990 Pulitzer Prize winning novel, *The Mambo Kings Sing Songs of Love*, about the lives of Cuban émigré musicians in postwar New York City. When it was first published, my mother held up a copy and said, "You should read this because it's based on musicians like Arturo's father, Chico."

At that moment, I felt like New York City cooperative housing was exactly where I belonged, and I didn't want to leave. I grabbed the copy from the bookshelf, parked myself on a laundry room bench, and began to read.

I got to see Arturo once more when his band, Arturo O'Farrill and the Afro Latin Jazz Octet, played at Tempe Center for the Arts in early January 2017, shortly after the calamitous presidential election. Conceived by local architecture firm Architekton, in collaboration with Los Angeles–based Barton Myers Associates, Tempe Center for the Arts was a stunning angular concrete, copper, and glass performance and gallery space, reflecting the regional design of the Anasazis' (an ancient civilization dating back to 1500 BC, who lived in cliff dwellings in the Southwest) Chaco Canyon Pueblo Bonita Great House plan.[7] Tempe, contiguous to Phoenix and home to Arizona State University, was where I actually lived, but no one outside Arizona recognized the city's name, nor could they pronounce it. They added an "H" at the end, so it sounded like Tempeh, the Asian soy product. It was easier to just say Phoenix.

I loved hearing Arturo play the piano again—the edginess, experimental deftness, his nimble fingers dancing up and down the keyboard, sometimes fast, sometimes slow, with bangs and starts, producing soothing quiet melodies and piercing dissonant sounds, transporting me back to when I was a stoned teenager lying on the living room rug doing homework while he practiced. He looked in character in his yellow-and-black African printed jacket and was funny, engaging and political on stage. "I was told not to talk about politics in Arizona. So, I won't tell you what side I'm on," he said, between pieces, the audience laughing. "I'm Mexican, born in Mexico City."

The audience clapped.

"We're playing songs filled with immigrant chords and refugee notes."

More clapping.

"For some what's happening now is the best thing ever, for others it's the coming apocalypse."

More laughter.

"This could last four more years, eight more years, or maybe six more weeks. I still haven't told you what side I'm on."

Laughter and applause.

After the performance ended, I waited eagerly for him to finish with his fans. The last time I'd seen him play was at Summerstage in Central Park in the '90s. He'd kissed me on the cheek, asked about my sister, and said: "Your mother saved my life," before moving on with crowds clamoring for his attention. This time, he hugged me repeatedly, and led me to a bench in the corner, where we sat close.

"So amazing to see you. It takes me right back," he said.

I immediately told him my mother had passed away.

"Your mother was a loving soul to take me in."

A woman my small size with long brown hair approached. "This is my *tia*, my mother's sister," he said.

She shook my hand. "Who are you? A former girlfriend?"

"No, the girlfriend's sister. Art lived with us during high school."

"You knew him during the wild years." She smiled and wandered off.

I told him Elizabeth was an internationally renowned photographer and that she'd shown at the Guggenheim, Met, Whitney, and Jewish museums. "Doesn't surprise me at all. All you Baums were so brilliant."

"You too, with the piano," I said.

"It's easy to impress with the piano. I was so crazy back then. We were all crazy. You Baums really shaped me more than anyone else, I think. Your mom especially. She was so industrious."

Growing up, I hadn't considered whether Arturo was grateful to come home to us. I'd only contemplated my loneliness when he was with Elizabeth behind closed doors and my mother was off with Reuben. I was so vulnerable and insecure back then. I left the concert hall and walked to my bicycle parked around the corner. I'd changed a lot. I was more confident now than I'd ever been, having directed films, gotten married, had a baby, and written published essays. However, my politics hadn't transformed. I still held on to my utopianism, though without rose-colored glasses. I knew the political reality. RNA cooperators pushing to privatize epitomized it. Now, even some NYCHA projects, desperate for funding, were in the throes of privatization.

In 2014, when de Blasio became mayor, "he inherited a public housing emergency."[8] NYCHA had "an annual operating deficit of $77 million and a roughly $17 billion capital need for infrastructure repairs"[9] due to years of neglect under the Bloomberg and Giuliani administrations and the state and the federal government. NYCHA officials failed to inspect for lead paint poisoning, residents suffered from asthma due to leaky apartment mold, buildings were rat-infested, boilers were broken, security doors in lobbies didn't function, and crime was rampant. In response, de Blasio installed security cameras in lobbies, "relieved the authority of its annual policing fees"[10] and "allocated $101 million towards reducing crime in public housing developments."[11] He used federal Hurricane Sandy relief funds to repair NYCHA housing, fixing over one thousand apartments, raising heating systems to rooftops, and constructing floodwalls at the Ocean Bay development in Far Rockaway.[12]

The mayor received praise for his endeavors from NYCHA scholar Nicholas Bloom: "He has made it a point to visit public housing. . . . His office has been engaged."[13] However, Bloom was critical of de Blasio, too, suggesting that the city should invest even more funds into NYCHA housing. In order to do this, the state must relinquish control of NYCHA and make it a city agency "to incentivize the city to better allocate funds for the struggling housing authority."[14] Nonetheless, NYCHA remains under state control.

Problems in NYCHA housing remained so dire that, in 2018, the federal government began to monitor the authority. Bronx councilman Ritchie Torres, who grew up in public housing, noted the irony in this relationship. "Given the decades of federal disinvestment from NYCHA, the city should be suing the federal government rather than the other way around."[15] In 2019, the federal monitor approved a New York State plan to allocate $450 million to repair boilers and elevators in NYCHA housing, a major victory, but still insufficient to restore crumbling NYCHA buildings, facing a $32 billion shortfall.[16]

Desperately lacking funds, de Blasio followed through with Bloomberg's contentious infill projects on NYCHA tower-in-the-park properties. The plan was to build both market-rate high-rises and affordable housing on available land deemed expendable, such as parking spaces, playgrounds and landscaped green areas. In gentrified Chelsea, near the Highline (flanked by such gems as Zaha Hadid's futuristic residential building selling condos for $50 million), Google's office tower, art galleries, Penn South, and the Chelsea-Elliot NYCHA development, an infill project was underway at NYCHA's Robert Fulton Houses. Two 11-story NYCHA buildings were to be demolished, replaced by a tower, 70 percent dedicated for upscale apartments, 30 percent for public housing tenants.[17] The Rental Assistance Demonstration Program (RAD), created under the Obama administration, would fund the project, by "converting traditional public housing subsidies to Section 8 vouchers and turning over management of the sites to private operators,"[18] a slippery slide toward privatization. As Noam Chomsky tweeted: "That's the standard form of privatization. Defund, make sure it doesn't work, people get angry, you hand it over to private capital."[19] So, in other words, demonize public housing for its failures, rather than pointing the blame at governments that fail to provide adequate funding.

Many NYCHA residents were skeptical of the infill project, fearing they would be displaced, as had happened historically during slum clearance programs. Further, they were angered that new upscale towers would cram into open green spaces which enhanced livability. Housing scholar Bloom wrote, "Infilling NYCHA with new structures will not only take away some of the city's last open spaces, and tree canopy, but will further undermine the remaining quality of life for current NYCHA residents. Less air flow, fewer trees, and reduction in permeable surfaces seems like a bad idea for a warming city."[20] It's an affront to and assault on public housing residents.

After learning about these infill projects, I recalled walking with my father past East Harlem tower-in-the-park NYCHA developments, and I decided to visit the neighborhood again. En route to the East Side, I made a pilgrimage to the Central Park reservoir, starting at 96th Street. Circling the path, I paused to admire how the San Remo defined the Central Park West skyline. Over the years, I'd photographed it during the icy blue of winter and the warmer hues of summer, the towers sometimes shaded, sometimes bright, but always visible, their image reflecting in the water. This time, I simply marveled that I once had access to the building and wished I still had an excuse to enter.

In 2019, I stopped at my cousin's Upper East Side two-bedroom high-rise luxury rental on 95th Street between 2nd and 3rd Avenue, just south of the 96th Street redline. Looking out from the twenty-second-floor window facing north from her apartment, I saw miles of East Harlem projects, 164 acres, a total of twenty-four developments—the largest collection of public housing in the city.[21] Starting inland and adjoining the Harlem River Drive, the buildings were easily identifiable—monotonous, brownish-red cruciform-shaped brick towers with small windows and no terraces, most in a tower-in-the-park setting. It was remarkable how green the East Harlem terrain looked, oak, maple, and linden trees among the varieties dominating every available space, butting up against the bland towers, providing beauty and oxygen to an otherwise depressed area. *Better the trees monopolize the landscape than the developers*, I thought.

Gentrification had encroached above the East 96th street redline, as tenements were replaced, not by public housing, but by market-rate towers. Fortunately, these upscale high-rises could only invade so far because NYCHA projects, starting at 98th Street, were like fortresses, keeping the upscale buildings at bay. I strolled past a beautiful stone wall, up steps leading to green grass, a community garden, and a playground filled with kids and a *Pre-K for All* banner scribbled with graffiti, to Lexington Houses, a four building complex constructed in 1950, each tower fourteen stories high, housing 448 people. A wooden stand-alone sign, *Welcome to Lexington Houses*, with a pair of decorative calligraphic flourishes underneath, a Dodger Blue background, and white vinyl decals peeling and curling off, was partially obscured by overgrowth. Paint chipped off banisters leading to the entranceway, which had a broken stone awning and steel front door evoking a prison. An NYPD car parked in the resident parking lot. The building façade needed a cleaning.

Nearby, at equally shabby George Washington Houses (1957), a fourteen-building development housing 1,510 people, I spotted a wooden hand-painted sign in red letters: *Welcome 2 Mad Fun Farm!* with a green 2 through the middle, nailed to a chain-link fence. Peering through, I saw a large field with benches and garden boxes growing leafy vegetables. The grounds of these two projects were lovely, albeit not manicured. *If only they could be funded properly*, I thought. In retrospect, what was once considered disastrous public housing—placing low-income tenants into towers with abundant greenspace and no businesses, causing isolation, rootlessness, and segregation—today seemed miraculous and revolutionary. What an insult it would be to these NYCHA residents if luxury infill towers were constructed on their property.

I remembered recently privatized Stuyvesant Town, an early example in Manhattan of Le Corbusier's *Ville Radieuse*, financed by the Metropolitan Life Insurance Company and granted property tax breaks to keep rents low. I ventured downtown to check it out, walking past the magnificent modernist geometric Islamic Cultural Center of New York on Third Avenue between 96th and 97th Street, and hopped on the train at the newly opened 96th Street Second Avenue Subway station, a public works project that took too many years of planning and investment to complete.

Started during World War II, completed in 1949, Robert Moses bulldozed eighteen racially integrated slum blocks in the Gas House District, from 14th to 23rd Street between 1st Avenue and Avenue C on the Lower East Side to construct Stuyvesant Town, consisting of 110 standardized cruciform-shaped brick towers over eighty acres. The complex contained 11,250 whites-only low-income apartments, priority given to WWII veterans, and eventually integrated in the 1950s. I hadn't been to Stuyvesant Town since it privatized back in 2006, when, under Bloomberg's watch, the complex was sold off to speculators, who evicted tenants, refurbished apartments, and raised rents astronomically, causing a great public outcry.[22]

I was appalled when my mother told me the development was no longer subsidized. How could this plain functional bastion of affordability be turned into luxury housing?

The 2006 buyers went into debt and lost the property. Touting their deal to save affordable housing, de Blasio, Governor Cuomo, and Senator Schumer reached a new agreement for the sale of Stuyvesant Town with the Blackstone Group, a "Wall Street Investment firm and one of the country's largest landlords."[23] By dropping the $77 million in mortgage recording taxes and providing Blackstone with a $144 million low-interest loan, the deal preserved "nearly half the 11,232-unit complex for middle-class families, . . . ensuring that a block of 5,000 apartments would be affordable for the next 20 years for teachers, construction workers, firefighters and others who have traditionally made their homes at Stuyvesant Town,"[24] and with the promise that no new infill towers be built on green space. However, as part of the deal, tax breaks would only last until 2020, at which point more affordable units would be phased out and replaced by 1,200 market-rate apartments.[25] It was hard to see how this was a victory for affordability when the city lost revenue and only a small portion of low-rent units would remain, while the rest would become market-rate.

Was this really the best New York could do on behalf of its citizens?

Fortunately, in 2019, new rent regulation laws went into effect, making the deregulation of 5,000 units impossible.[26]

Growing up, I hated visiting my friends there. It felt bleak and isolated, park benches rotting, grass patchy and unkempt, pigeon poop splattered on entranceways. Looking at it on this visit, however, it was an oasis. Tall plane trees shaded the scrubbed brick buildings and the winding, landscaped pathways and restored benches. Adirondack chairs were positioned artfully on the well-maintained lawns, like an American version of a Parisian park, a lusher green due to subsequent climate-change induced rainfall. Hydrangeas, hostas, and caladiums beautified the property. The elegant circular fountain in its center, there from the beginning, rivaled Washington Square Park's. In the '70s, my friends and I splashed in the water. Today the fountain was off-limits. Five Stuy Café offered espressos and salmon over sautéed spinach. Sales agents advertised: *Downtown's answer to Central Park.*

The landscape was remarkably beautiful, but the buildings in this now upscale development were identical to the East Harlem tower-in-the-park NYCHA housing projects I'd just visited—cruciform-shaped brick high-rises, no terraces, and small windows and lobby doors. The difference, of course, were the accoutrements added to fancify the property. At

Stuyvesant Town, the window frames were painted an emerald green, in contrast with the dark drab brown at Lexington and Washington Houses. The black paint on the banisters leading to entrance ways wasn't chipping off. Emerald-green lobby doors had large windows and matching green awnings. A large slick glass entrance was designed for employees, *proudly serving* Stuyvesant Town. How great NYCHA projects would be if they were rehabilitated to look like the new Stuyvesant Town and provided decent services to residents yet remained public.

My last stop for the day was at First Houses (1935), NYCHA's original housing project. I remembered learning about it in high school but had never thought to go. Now, I was curious to see how it compared with tower-in-the-park housing. The initial idea for First Houses, designed by progressive architect Frederick Ackerman, contrasting Moses's bulldozer approach, was to rehabilitate existing tenements, but so much structural damage occurred when every third tenement was razed to provide light and air that most of the buildings had to be entirely restructured. The results were 122 three-room or four-room apartments in eight small, human-scale, identical redbrick buildings, four to five stories high, surrounding a courtyard, on two blocks of the city grid on the Lower East Side between East 2nd and 3rd Street and First Avenue and Avenue A.[27]

Unlike the tower-in-the-park model, First Houses blended into the partially rehabilitated and gentrified East Village/Lower East Side low-rise tenement landscape. Just like RNA House, the development now had gates to block off access to its courtyards to keep out the undesirables, the "unworthy poor." I wondered if they were installed in the early '70s around the same time RNA House constructed fences, when New York City was near bankruptcy and crime and heroin were rampant.

As I entered through the gate behind a trusting tenant, I was struck by how charming, hidden, and private First Houses was. The cobble and hexagonal stone courtyard was like a Parisian *impasse*, one side partitioned from 2nd Street by a wall with stone forms of animals in relief set into the brick. Sculptures by local Works Progress Administration artists—a delightful dolphin resembling an Inuit soapstone carving, two horses, and two bowing abstract figurines—were scattered around a children's empty wading pool. There were cast iron lamps lighting picturesque doorways with flat awnings and wooden pillars painted the same emerald green as Stuyvesant Town, matching the fire escapes. Wooden benches were scattered around the courtyard, and an upright piano abutted a wall that led to a trendy Avenue A restaurant. On a brick façade, an iron plaque marked First House's 1974 landmark designation:

THE NATION'S FIRST PUBLIC HOUSING PROJECT. ON NO-
VEMBER 21, 1934, THE CITY BEGAN ITS BATTLE AGAINST
THE SLUMS WHEN THE NEWLY FORMED NEW YORK CITY
HOUSING AUTHORITY OBTAINED THE RIGHT TO DE-
MOLISH AND REBUILD THE TENEMENTS ON THIS SITE.
THESE BUILDINGS, FIRST HOUSES, REMAIN A FITTING
MONUMENT TO THE BEGINNING OF THE PUBLIC HOUS-
ING PROGRAM IN THE UNITED STATES OF AMERICA.

In the courtyard, I met Nala, a friendly young Black woman with
braided hair, who'd recently moved into the complex and felt lucky to be
there. Previously she'd lived in another project where she was sexually
assaulted, plus she'd had medical problems, so she was given priority at
First Houses, considered one of the safest, best functioning NYCHA developments in the city.

"I used to live in a project like over there," she said, pointing to a high-
rise brick and concrete tower looming in the background. "People did
drugs in the hallways. This place is too small for that. Once I walk into the
courtyard, I feel protected. People who live here have jobs. Know what I
mean?"

I nodded. I, after all, grew up in a tower, too, and would've preferred
to live in a more intimate environment. The problem, though, wasn't the
size of the project she'd lived in, but its lack of financial support and the
demoralization of its tenants subjected to systematic racism.

Nala said there were a variety of people in the building—Blacks,
Whites, Asians, Spanish-speaking. "It's good to have a mix in the building,
but I don't feel comfortable in the neighborhood. There aren't many Black
people around. In my last building almost everyone was Black, and I grew
up in Bed-Stuy."

She was on the tenant committee and wanted to get NYCHA to fix the
kids' wading pool, but she was a newcomer and couldn't be too pushy.

"Do you mind if I ask how much your rent is?"

"It's all right. I have a one-bedroom and I pay 30 percent of my income,
so it's $800 dollars a month. That doesn't include utilities. All added up
with food, it's $1400 a month. I work two jobs, at Macy's and around the
corner at a grocery store, and I barely get by."

"At least you know you won't be evicted if you can't pay the rent."

"That's right."

She invited me upstairs to her apartment. We walked through an emerald-green door with a white outline of a mezuzah on the doorframe. I pointed it out. "I bet a Jewish person lived here before."

"Yeah, maybe," she said.

Nala showed me the original oak hardwood floors, an archway in the hallway, sash windows, real wood closet doors, vintage furniture, and the antique sewing machine her great aunt gave her. It felt like a quaint country cottage. Despite what looked like utopia, she said there were lots of problems NYCHA didn't fix. "It's a good situation, but there's a ceiling leak damaging the floor and the heat doesn't always work."

Nala talked about mismanagement and apathy at NYCHA. She started paying rent in her new apartment, but NYCHA kept on insisting she still lived in the old project and claimed she was defaulting on rent. "NYCHA employees don't care," Nala said. "They know they're getting their next paycheck, so they don't do anything."

What a shame that due to governmental abandonment, NYCHA's work culture had been poisoned, although not entirely. Even with major problems, NYCHA was still considered the best public housing authority in the country, providing apartments to over 400,000 New Yorkers, with long wait-lists to live there. My nephew, who worked on housing issues for Manhattan Borough President Gale Brewer, told me there's an annual NYCHA Family Day attended by local politicians, and described the president of the NYCHA tenant association as amiable, diligent, and well-respected. Despite its bad press and subpar conditions, for many public housing residents there is a growing appreciation for project living as a salve against soaring rents and the ultra-rich takeover of the city.

I recalled a writing class I'd taken in Phoenix, where I developed ideas for this memoir. After I read a segment about the necessity of government financed affordable housing, a former army nurse, also in the class, said, "Thank you for showing me that government can do good."

I looked at her with confusion and disbelief, then remembered I was in Arizona, she was in her 80s, from Kansas, living in a society propagating the notion that government was bad, we need less of it, not more, public housing equaled "the projects," blamed for all center city woes. She'd adhered to this belief despite having enjoyed the fruits of her government job. I, of course, was shaped in an entirely different milieu, trusting that government existed for our benefit, not to harm us, my Mitchell-Lama housing experience proof. *I changed her mind*, I thought, *I accomplished something*.

Jonathan Finkelman, an Upper West Side friend who hung around 96th

Street and gave me guitar lessons, recalled how public housing granted his parents housing security and dignity:

> My parents had both grown up in poverty in the Williamsburg section of Brooklyn. My father was forever scarred by the sight of neighborhood families' entire belongings, furniture and all, being dumped out on the street because they couldn't pay the rent. At ninety-five years old, he just recently recalled to me once more the trauma of those memories, as if it'd happened yesterday. His father had lost his job in the Depression and never really recovered from that loss, a shadow of his former self to the end. My mother was born just weeks before the crash of 1929. She'd been raised, along with four older siblings, by her single mom, whose husband had died while she was pregnant with my mother. My grandmother struggled to keep the wolf from the door, working as a secretary and stenographer. After my parents were married, they moved into Kingsborough Houses, a NYCHA complex of 16 six-story buildings built in 1941 in Crown Heights, Brooklyn, where my older brother, David, was born in 1951.

"That's such an evocative, poignant story, Jon."

"It clearly haunted him throughout his life. Long after he'd become reasonably well-off, thanks to the G.I. Bill, he would still frequently make remarks along the lines of *If only I had more money*. Not at all in a greedy way, but as though he felt that having more money would assuage his anxiety."

"Your dad's story reminds me of my friend's affluent Holocaust survivor father who would circle and circle Manhattan blocks searching for a free parking spot to save money. No matter what level of financial security he obtained, he never felt confident it would last."

Jon's brother, David, added: "My parents saw Kingsborough Houses as a step up from the tenements where they'd grown up. My sense is that public housing didn't have the stigma it does today."

"That's right," I said.

In 1941, at Kingsborough Houses' opening ceremony, progressive Mayor Fiorello La Guardia stood before hundreds of future tenants, suggesting they "put a little ribbon on the curtains and a little flower on the dresser"[28] in their new apartments. He said: "It is always a thrill and a source of great satisfaction to me to see . . . a plan come to fruition . . . and where housing is concerned, to see a dream come true."[29] He thanked the federal government for funding: "It is true that we have spent $140,000,000 on public housing, but it is also true that we have $140,000,000 worth of value for it. There was no political real estate speculation in these projects. There were no favored contractors. We would not stand for it."[30] How decent, honorable, revolutionary!

Eighty years later, Kingsborough suffers from the same problems as other NYCHA projects, lacking sufficient resources to fix faulty heaters, mold from "water intrusion, chipping and peeling paint, insect infestations, and inoperable appliances and facilities."[31] These failures are inexcusable. Public housing used to equal an "investment in better citizenship," and a "suitable living environment for every American family." Society must again return to these common good beliefs and construct and maintain affordable housing, so people can live with dignity. The pandemic, which has devastated jobs and incomes and the ability of millions to pay their rent, only makes the need for affordable housing more obvious.

What better time than the present to dream up another such revolution—one that takes lessons from the belief in public responsibility, investment in citizenship, and dignity in housing. Clearly, we're in need of massive intervention from the federal government on the scale of the 1949 Housing Act. New York can seize this moment to return to its progressive roots when it was a work in progress for the benefits of all its citizens and built more affordable housing than any city in the US. We need visionary politicians, and the political will to construct public and subsidized housing on a grand scale. For the survival of New York and American society, people once again must find dignity in housing, to feel they have a stake in the collective, to be civically engaged, and to have agency to determine together the well-being of all.

Chapter 14

Battle over Privatization

WHEN I VISITED New York City, entering RNA House or simply passing by was too painful, so I skirted 96th Street between Amsterdam and Columbus. From afar, I allowed myself glimpses of the medium-scale beehive building, spotted from various perspectives, such as on the side street at 95th, where a triangular slice appeared between structures. Sightings weren't obvious; I had to dig. As I wandered, however, evidence of Mitchell-Lama privatization was apparent.

In the neighborhood, one of the first buildings to leave the Mitchell-Lama program was one of the first to be built: Columbus Park Towers, a massive twenty-six-floor tan brick co-op high-rise with white concrete terraces on West 94th Street, next door to my grandma's building. In 1984, the high-rise formed a board committee to explore privatization.[1] The city tried to prevent the tower from converting, arguing that because "of its location on an urban renewal tract, any so-called privatization of the project would be counter to the city's original urban renewal goals."[2] But in 1991, a state appeals court overruled the city,[3] setting the process in motion. However, because of infighting among cooperators about the ethics of privatization, it took years for the conversion to be completed in 2009.

I got in touch with childhood friend and photographer David Baumbach, raised in Columbus Park, to gauge his perspective about privatization:

I go to the neighborhood all the time. My mother still lives in the building. There's been a lot of renovation, and the lobby and outdoor area is fancy-looking. On the second floor is a gym. In the old days everything was utilitarian. The new folk are all people who can afford a million dollars plus for an apartment, but there are still some of the old guard who've been there for fifty years. From a political standpoint, the paucity of affordable housing on the Upper West Side is appalling. From a personal standpoint, the family obviously benefits financially from the buy-in.

One difficulty with Mitchell-Lama apartments was a prohibition against a child or significant other taking over the apartment if the titleholder were to pass away, unless they had proof that they'd lived in the apartment for a minimum of two years. This was problematic for many who'd been in the apartments for most of their lives, as it felt like their family homes were being taken away. I also think if apartments had been made available to family members, then a buyout may have been much less likely.

"I agree. It was really hard for my sister and me to give up our apartment. I'd contemplated living with my mother full-time, but her boyfriend was there, the place was overrun with stuff, and I would've had to leave my husband and son. It wasn't realistic."

"I know my mother, despite being a liberal and respecting the repercussions of privatization, wanted to keep the apartment and felt a sense of ownership and entitlement after having lived there for fifty years."

"It's complicated. When we were growing up, it wasn't hard to get a Mitchell-Lama apartment, so there was no need to cling to one. Now, I know people who have done all kinds of unethical things to hold onto subsidized apartments that should've gone to the next person on the list. In fact, after our mother died, a neighbor on the fourteenth floor suggested we bribe management to keep the place, which of course we didn't do, and which wouldn't have worked anyway."

"I don't recognize the Upper West Side as the funky, eclectic place it once was," David said. "It now seems indistinguishable from the East Side, which we always looked down upon with a kind of reverse snobbery, and I honestly don't care much about it as it is now."

"I don't like it much either, but I feel attached, nonetheless. Going there reminds me of my parents, my childhood, my history. Just sighting my building, even from a distance, comforts me. It's like sacred territory. I would hate for it to privatize. Then, my past would really be erased."

Antar Jones, also raised in Columbus Park, is an estates and trusts attorney who sits on the New York State Bar Association Committee on Diversity, Equity, and Inclusion and lives and works in Brooklyn:

> My mother was against privatization because the building helped a lot of people like my family who could never afford to live in a really nice building without the subsidy Mitchell-Lama buildings naturally provided. If it was privatized, that wouldn't happen anymore. My parents bought their apartment for a song. I agree with my mother. Privatization has changed the building in the exact same way New York has changed—it's really hostile to folks who don't have money, or worse yet, generational money.

Another Mitchell-Lama to opt out early on was Columbus House on 95th Street and Columbus, a thirty-four-floor concrete rental tower, where The Cellar jazz club used to be. On Columbus House's façade, a purple banner with white letters now boasted: NO FEE LUXURY RENTALS. In 2006, when the Witkoff Group bought the building for $68 million, they sued the city to raise rents. In 2009, however, the New York State Supreme Court argued in favor of current tenants, protecting their rights to pay affordable rents. Only those obtaining apartments after the conversion were subject to market rental rates, setting a precedent for other tenants in former Mitchell-Lama rental buildings turned private.[4]

I asked Kwame Kitson, who grew up in Columbus House and still lives on the Upper West Side but in a market-rate apartment and who became a family doctor, his thoughts about privatization:

> With privatization came division. My mother remained living in the building under subsidized conditions, but when she died her apartment became market-rate. Over the years when I visited her, the newbies were cold and distant. They hardly talked to each other. There used to be almost the feel of a small village in that building, great small talk in the elevators. I knew and spoke to everyone on all thirty-four floors. Today the feel is entirely different.

This is what would happen to RNA, too, if it were to privatize, I thought.

Two blocks south at 100 West 93rd Street and Columbus, an even larger white banner with green trim now advertised: BRAND NEW LUXURY CONDOS FOR SALE. According to *West Side Rag*, in 2018, after Trader Joe's launched in the building's ground floor commercial space, real estate prices in the tower "jumped more than $300 per square foot, a one-bedroom listing for $1.241 million."[5] All three brutalist slabs had been constructed as part of the West Side Urban Renewal Area plan. Today they were upscale high-rises. The population along Columbus was still heterogeneous, evidenced at 93rd Street by a Puerto Rican flag waving in the breeze, suspended on a cord above and across the avenue, from one lamp post to the other, and by Blacks, Whites, Latinos, and Jews walking the streets. How long would the diversity last?

Farther south on Columbus Avenue and 90th was St. Martin's Tower, a twenty-seven-floor concrete co-op. In front of the building stood a one-story high brutalist sculptural air vent with a broad base, tapered on top, and blocks that jutted out like appendages, matching the building's concrete terraces, reminiscent of an upright battleship and Darth Vader. David Owens, Director of Operations at New York Grays Baseball Club and Sales Agent at Halstead Real Estate Company, grew up and still lives in the tower: "Today the Upper West Side remains diverse, but we are losing a great deal of the area's original feel due to a lack of affordable housing. It is important to have a balance between progress and history. I welcome new people and businesses to the area, as long as we protect and fight to preserve the past."

"So does this mean you want St. Martin's to remain public?"

"Our building is conducting a feasibility study to assess the issue, and I haven't yet made my final decision. I don't believe that whether our singular building privatizes or stays in the Mitchell-Lama program would have an impact on affordable housing. We turn over four to six apartments a year. It doesn't put a dent into the need."

"That adds up, though."

"If our building were to go private, it would stay affordable for the 178 families presently here. I believe the city and state need to be building more affordable housing units. They need to incentivize developers using tax abatements. If not, you'll only have low-income NYCHA tenants and very high-income families living in the neighborhood."

"This is reason enough for your building to stay public then, right?"

"Well, there are benefits of privatization: autonomy from government agencies, total control of our apartments in terms of succession rights, gaining equity on an asset that many have been paying into for fifty years, ability to have limited subletting, and raising excess money when a newly privatized apartment is sold from flip taxes—money returned to the co-op for building improvements."

"Sounds like you're leaning toward privatization."

"I'm not sure."

"At RNA, the battle over privatization is tearing the cooperators apart. Is this happening at St. Martin's?"

"There is a small residual effect of the feasibility study relative to tension/hostility at St. Martin's. For the most part, we have a decent amount of harmony in our building."

Since speaking with David, I learned that the vote to privatize at St. Martin's failed.

I checked in with professor, writer, disc jockey Jonathan Goldman, another St. Martin's cooperator who also grew up and remains in the tower. He was more definitive:

I believe we should remain in the Mitchell-Lama program. The question is: what kind of New York do I want to live in? And I know the answer is one where my neighbors are Mitchell-Lama people: culturally and economically diverse. There's a continuity in the Mitchell-Lamas, and public housing in general, that is important for New York City neighborhoods. My family and families like it are devoted to the life and community of the building and surrounding neighborhood. As an example of supporting local businesses, we shop at Mani Market instead of Trader Joe's.

"My mother did the same. She remained loyal to the African American owned business Ivan's Pharmacy, even though at least three chain drugstores were closer to RNA House."

"My life, my partner's life, are both absolutely enabled by our residence. We are middle-class people: a social worker and a professor/musician, not the kinds who draw big salaries. There is no way we would be living in the neighborhood if not for subsidized housing."

I wondered what was doing at my grandmother's building, so I messaged Bobby Broom. It turned out he knew my old building friend Gina, because he had played with Gina's boyfriend, Jon Herington, in the band Steely Dan. He also knew Arturo, my sister's former boyfriend, from Music and Art High School. Bobby said:

I think residents are pushing for privatization at 700, too. I think that it should remain Mitchell-Lama. That sentiment is held over from my childhood. I know what the building meant for all of us growing up and that wouldn't have been possible if not for its affordability. The opportunities that were provided for working families to raise their kids in a healthy, diverse, and safe environment were invaluable. I feel so fortunate to have grown up there and would consider raising a family in a similar situation.

Yvette Marsh, who grew up next door to me in 733 Amsterdam Avenue, said her mother was still living in her childhood building:

Now it's private and most of our friends have moved on. They privatized in the '90s, moving the entrance and changing the address to 175 Amsterdam Avenue. Management wanted my mother out and offered her money. But she didn't want to leave, so she went to court and won the right to stay on condition the owners wouldn't upgrade her apartment. Since it privatized, the community feeling disappeared. The old timers knew each other. We went to each other's apartments to play or have dinner. It's no longer like that, sorry to say. I believe the building should've stayed Mitchell-Lama for affordable housing people like me who worked all their lives and should be able to live, not fancy, but comfortably.

I checked in with Elissa Vecchione Scott, who grew up at 711 Amsterdam Avenue, went to P.S. 75, and knew kids from RNA House. As an adult, she moved to Oregon and became a writer:

My parents, still living there, are against privatization, and said there was some talk about it a while ago, but not in recent years. People really believe it should remain affordable. Don't forget, we have long lists of applicants waiting for affordable housing here. Many Mitchell-Lama lists have been closed, because of their length. The city seems to have become WAY too divided between the rich and poor, whereas I feel growing up there was a range of middle class from low to high. While I would love to inherit a 4-bedroom, 2-bath apartment on the twenty-fifth floor overlooking all of Manhattan with spectacular western views of the Hudson River and New Jersey, along with a doorman-guarded building and private garage, it wouldn't be fair. It should stay Mitchell-Lama and go to those who live, work, and raise families in Manhattan who need affordable living! The city is becoming too exclusive, and forgetting we were once the entry city for inclusivity to our nation!

"Very well put," I said.

In June 2019 while visiting New York, I attended a 100th birthday commemoration for St. Gregory's Church priest Father Henry J. Browne (1919–1980), who led the crusade for affordable housing on the Upper West Side in the '50s and '60s. The event was held on West 90th Street in the West Side Community Garden, one of the last remaining community gardens in the neighborhood, as well as in the plaza of the Wise Towers NYCHA project, and at St. Gregory's Church. The church was housed in a 1912 four-story brick building intended only as a temporary location for the congregation, but a proper chapel was never constructed, so the church remained on the first floor, with a creaky staircase that led to a Catholic school and rectory on the top floors.

I loved mingling with housing advocates, old-time lefty politicians like Councilwoman Ruth Messinger, whose son was in my class at the New School, newer leftwing politicians like Manhattan Borough President Gale Brewer, and RNA House neighbors. I was home where I belonged, with people who agreed on the previous housing policy and understood the desperate need for affordable housing moving forward. As *New Yorker* writer Masha Gessen wrote: "A common sense of past and future, a broad agreement on organizational principles, trust that your neighbors near and distant share a general understanding of reality and current events—all of these are necessary for any kind of politics to function."[6] Gessen was referring to the dire political lies that incited the January 6, 2021, insurrection at the US Capital, but her analysis also applies to housing policy principles and perceptions. There must be a consensus, by the public and politicians, that housing is a human right, that earlier legislation funding affordable housing was beneficial to the common good, and that we need similar legislation today.

At the commemoration, I met Beth Rosenblum from Strycker's Bay Apartments at 66 West 94th Street. Her mother, Doris Rosenblum, had been president of Strycker's Bay Neighborhood Council, the organization Father Browne founded to advocate for affordable housing, civil rights, tenants' rights, and peace. Beth was short, had cropped brown hair, and was welcoming. I felt like I already knew her, as I did with the heterogeneous Upper West Side crowd of Blacks, Puerto Ricans, Dominicans, and Whites of various European descent.

As one of the event organizers, Beth was distracted, so later I emailed her more questions. She said:

I moved back in with my father this past summer to help with his care. He is ninety-two years old and recently lost his eyesight. I am now once again a part of the Strycker's Bay community. Everything has been updated. The A/C was added to the laundry room, the hallways and lobby and community room were remodeled, and the building looks more attractive. The neighborhood is cleaner, safer, less gritty, and unaffordable. I miss hearing children playing outside; I miss the local neighborhood stores; I miss the spirit. As this is a cooperative, there are board meetings that are relatively well-attended, although I've noticed most who show up are older residents; the younger ones aren't represented. My building remains committed to staying in the Mitchell-Lama program. I understand that while I was living away, this discussion topic came up, but was quickly dismissed. I see no reason to privatize as we are benefitting from living in a great neighborhood in affordable housing in the midst of market-rate unaffordable housing. I worry that as the original tenants and old timers pass on, the newcomers will raise this topic again and force the privatization movement on us.

Like most of those I interviewed, I felt deeply invested in preserving West Side Urban Renewal Area Mitchell-Lama towers. I wanted the neighborhood I cherished to retain its diversity, inclusivity, and social justice mission.

I wondered how much Harlem had changed. I knew it was gentrifying, that churches, ballrooms, and local businesses were demolished, African Americans were being displaced by affluent White people who were moving into upscale towers, and a Starbucks and a Whole Foods had opened up on 125th. I was curious if Esplanade Gardens, the Mitchell-Lama where Mondello grew up, had resisted the tide of privatization, so I asked him.

"Where do you live now? Are you still in Harlem?"

"My family and I live in West Harlem, about a twenty-five minute walk away from Mom at Esplanade Gardens. I live on the fourth floor of only seven floors; three apartments per floor in a co-op made up of two buildings that wrap around a street-avenue corner. I've been here for over twenty years."

"Is Esplanade Gardens still a Mitchell-Lama?"

"Yup. As far as I know, there are no significant stirrings to privatize. Around 2010, E.G. became a NORC—a Naturally Occurring Retirement Community, meaning the city provides social services to aging residents who remain living in their buildings. Most of the folks I know/knew moved there in 1967–1968 and are staying put."

"That's great. Why would anyone move out? Everyone should have the opportunity to age in a stable affordable community with neighbors they know, and services provided. What are your thoughts about privatization? I assume you're against it, but maybe not."

Mondello said:

I very much want Mitchell-Lamas to remain viable choices for middle-class residents. I do realize that many long-term residents would like to be rewarded for their patience and longevity with the ability to sell out, or I guess to get home equity loans, based upon market-rate values. But this ability is at the expense of the current crop of financially struggling, aspiring folks who have one less set of economic ladders to use. There are no plans on the horizon in New York to increase the supply of Mitchell-Lama housing.

A while back, I ran into a co-op owner who lived in my building about twenty-five years ago. She was a maître d' at a midtown restaurant, and a flipper of sorts. Somehow within three years of joining our co-op, she managed to move twice. She bought a unit, then I guess traded for another, and then sold that one and left. When I saw her, she asked me about the changes in the neighborhood. I told her I was concerned about long-time residents who had stuck out the bad times being economically driven out now that things were improving. With a sunny, fa-la-la disposition, she replied, *That's okay. They can just move to the South Bronx.* I was pissed.

I can't look at privatization without considering gentrification and equity. Change is inevitable. The unseen hand of capitalism is mighty strong. The flipper's attitude was only one example of callousness I've witnessed in my building. Maybe some of the cold-heartedness I've witnessed has been made inevitable by the plight of gentrifiers who were pushed out of their own neighborhoods. Given the differential between my predecessors and my own social and economic status, I might have been considered a gentrifier myself.

Since 1989, "nearly 20,000 of the city-supervised co-ops and rentals in Mitchell-Lama buildings have left the program."[7] De Blasio ran on a campaign to support affordable housing. Upon assuming office in 2014, he made saving Mitchell-Lama housing a top priority, allocating $250 million into a new initiative to protect the program. De Blasio said, "From Coney Island to the Upper West Side and for decades, hundreds of Mitchell-Lama buildings have offered stable, affordable homes for New York working families. We can't afford to lose one more of these homes. We're investing to protect them for the seniors and families who helped build our neighborhoods, and for generations to come."[8] His initiative "preserved, or extended the affordability, of 30 Mitchell-Lama developments with 11,000 residences. Of the approximately 100 remaining developments, with more than 45,000 homes, about two-thirds are affordable cooperatives, representing a significant source of affordable homeownership opportunity for New York City. The others are affordable rental apartments."[9]

Despite these encouraging efforts to preserve Mitchell-Lama housing, a faction of RNA House residents continued to push for privatization. A former co-op board member said, "In 2016, I sat on the board, and we voted 5 to 4 to accept a low-interest, city-sponsored loan. This would pay for 10 years of capital projects which we still need to this day. The deal included a lock in agreement to remain in Mitchell-Lama for twenty years. The board president reneged on the vote because he claimed, if we went ahead, it would alienate his pro-privatization friends. The board composition changed in 2017 and the pro-privatization folks voted to explore converting to a market-rate building."

The year 2017 was also RNA House's fifty-year anniversary. The co-op celebrated amid growing tensions over privatization. For the anniversary celebration booklet, one cooperator wrote:

We moved into RNA House in 1972, when I was 9 months pregnant with my first child. Many of those first shareholders were also young families with one or two children, living as we did on one low or modest salary. Usually, the mother stayed home raising the children while the father worked at entry level or civil service jobs, and/or pursued degrees in law, medicine, finance, etc. The mothers and children socialized in the backyard and park playgrounds, made good friends, shared babysitting, and had a strong support group.

In my forty-five years in RNA House, my maintenance has not even doubled while market-rate rents in the area have exploded. On the money I've saved living in a three-bedroom apartment in a nice, well-kept building, in a great area, on one civil service salary, I have been able to send both my kids to college and graduate school, made the down payment on my son's house, and done many other things that would have been impossible if not for Mitchell-Lama. Ironically, several of my neighbors who moved in at the same time and have benefited as I did in the Mitchell-Lama program, now wish to privatize.

By late 2017, the movement to privatize accelerated. My Stay-in-Mitchell-Lama friends and those leaning this way kept me abreast of the conflict, confiding their fervent feelings, and sending me flyers and emails about the evolving situation. I learned the family who moved into our apartment were in favor of converting, leaving me gasping, as though I'd lose #14E all over again. If RNA remained public, my mother's common good values and spirit would live on, and apartments would continue to go to families in need. If it were to privatize, all that my mother stood for would vanish.

A neighbor on the 150 side wrote:

> Hi Jenny,
> We are in a decision-making mode at RNA about the direction of our future. As I'm involved with the group known as "RNA Cooperators to Preserve Mitchell-Lama," I'm working toward that goal.
> Our group numbers about 50% of the building's apartments and the outspoken Privateer group about half that amount.
> So, at this time about 25% of the building is still "On the fence" so to speak. But we are two years away from a final decision since we signed an agreement with HPD to remain in Mitchell-Lama to December 2019.
> Financial greed has a way of rearing its head. Middle income people, who for 50 years built a diversified community, are now beginning to split into two camps. One can feel the tensions between the two sides where previously there was harmony and laughter at RNA.
> Fortunately, our saving grace is, to privatize, the house needs 2/3 of the apartments (about 139) to vote for privatization and maybe now they have about 50 apartments.
> It's difficult to convey to younger shareholders what we went through in building RNA into the shared equity cooperative based on the Rochdale Principles or understand what the Upper West Side looked and felt like in 1967.
> But we persevere.

A battle ensued over whether RNA should fund an expensive feasibility study to assess privatization viability. In January 2018, about 40–50 cooperators gathered in the RNA House community room to hear, "Thoughts about a Feasibility Study for RNA House," a presentation by Richard Heitler, an executive board member at Cooperators United for Mitchell-Lama, and board president of his Mitchell-Lama co-op, Village East Towers, in the East Village.

Heitler explained that costs would increase dramatically under privatization. For example, RNA House presently paid a subsidized tax of about $155,400/year to New York City. At market rate, that tax would be approximately $1,077,744. Further, since a private co-op cannot collect surcharges, the current surcharges that give RNA House about $200,000/year would be lost. All told, if the co-op went private, it would have a deficit of about $1.5 million. The pro-privatization camp believed they could fill this gap with flip taxes, when a newly privatized apartment was sold. If a private RNA House could sell six apartments every year with a 30 percent flip tax, it might be able to avoid raising carrying charges for a few years. However, in later years, when some apartments would be second sales (at say 3 percent flip tax) the flip tax income would be insufficient and carrying charges would have to increase.

"Who wants to sell their apartments in the next few years?" he asked.

No one raised a hand.

"If you plan on moving soon, privatization will help you leave with more money. But if you want to stay at RNA House, privatization will increase your current expenses."

Heitler quoted Abraham Kazan's vision: ". . . through cooperative efforts we can better the lot of our co-workers . . . where all personal gain and benefit is eliminated, greater good can be accomplished for the benefit of all."

He concluded: "That is the real Mitchell-Lama deal. Your economic benefit comes while you live here, not when you leave."

The pro-feasibility contingent advertised the study as simply a way to assess whether privatization would serve the interests of the whole community. It was not a vote in favor of privatization. They insisted that RNA was a cooperative, committed to taking care of one another. If the building were to privatize, they promised the cost of living would remain affordable to all cooperators, even those on fixed incomes or those opting not to buyout, who would then become renters.

The contingent distributed pro-feasibility leaflets and organized meetings, imploring cooperators to attend. One issue at stake was financing for an energy conversion project. The New York City Housing Development Corporation (HDC) offered RNA very low interest financing for the project but would require RNA to be locked-in to the Mitchell-Lama program for years. Those seeking the feasibility study found this problematic, though it's hard to understand why, unless their true motivation was privatization, in which case they should've owned up to it. What were they ashamed or afraid of?

A good friend of my mother's wrote:

> I am going to vote against the feasibility study. I want to continue the legacy of M-L, of providing affordable housing to people with limited resources. I am stunned by the hard-driving campaign of those who want the study. There are almost daily flyers, women canvassing, giving tutorials or seminars, even noting instances of corruption at some of the government agencies as evidence we don't want them telling us what to do.

In late January 2018, the pro-feasibility camp won, voting YES 81 and NO 73 to spend up to $65,000 for the initial phase of the study. Concurrently, the co-op held a Board of Directors election. For the first time ever, candidates ran on slates, a revolutionary change; five contenders supported privatization, and five wanted to remain in Mitchell-Lama. The pro-privatization bloc won. My mother's friend said: "The 5 who won are great on paper—young, old, White, Black, Latina, South Asian. The 5 who lost are mostly (4 out of 5) old and Jewish. Intellectually, I think I should be with the first group. Emotionally, I am with the second. It's a quandary. So now the building is divided, and the privatization bloc will continue their efforts."

Meanwhile, in the thick of the struggle, RNA tried to sustain a cooperative atmosphere, its Spring 2018 newsletter harkening back to the old days: "Many years ago, we had a "Help Your Neighbor" program, and we would like to bring it back. Helping your neighbor might include reading to someone with impaired vision, accompanying a person to the doctor, doing errands, helping with homework, babysitting, or pet sitting."

Another suggestion was to have a Backyard Movie Night: "An old classic movie perhaps, or maybe a family favorite. There will surely be something for everyone!"

News about the Garden Committee, Curbside Organics, and Bike Storage Room were also included.

I was glad the 150 side Bike Room was opening again. I remembered how excited I felt as a kid retrieving my bike from the jam-packed room off the lobby, riding sans helmet in the backyard or along the Central Park bicycle path to the East Side and the Harlem Meer, then back to 96th Street. Cars had unrestricted access to Central Park roads until 1966, when Mayor Lindsay closed the park to cars on Sundays. In 2018, the city banned all cars from the park.[10] Today, the city was too expensive, but it was also more livable for those who could afford it.

The feasibility study took months to complete. The co-op hired an attorney from Holland & Knight, a real estate firm specializing in co-op conversions. By fall, the study was concluded. The attorney in charge held a two-hour meeting in P.S. 163's auditorium on 97th Street, answering questions from cards submitted by cooperators. Under law, the RNA board was required to show the study to the Department of Housing Preservation and Development (HPD). HPD found it faulty and raised the issue with the building. The study inaccurately claimed that if RNA House stayed in the Mitchell-Lama program, monthly maintenance would increase to pay for structural improvements. In fact, the opposite was true.

The next stage in the process was to vote for the Red Herring, a common term for a draft offering plan for a stock about to go public. In the Mitchell-Lama co-op privatization process, voting YES to the Red Herring meant allocating $220,000 for the preparation of a draft offering to inform HPD that RNA planned to dissolve. HPD was upset with how the feasibility study diminished the value of the Mitchell-Lama program and asked that the study be corrected before it would allow a vote. In addition, HPD insisted that the announcement of the Red Herring be crystal clear—a YES vote meant the dissolution of RNA as a Mitchell-Lama co-op. NO meant that the building remained in the program.

A friend my age with mixed feelings reported: "The community is being torn apart over this. The privatizers want to beautify the lobby as an investment in the building. They see it as a retirement fund. Older people are afraid that costs will rise, everybody pulls to their own side." Another friend wrote, "I'm a socialist and I believe in social responsibility. At the same time, I'd like to leave my kids something."

While making corrections, the pro-privatization contingent continued to push to convert, now more openly. Using military rhetoric, they wrote, "We need to keep our power by *arming ourselves* with knowledge."[11] They cited the disrepair at the Bronx's Co-op City, the largest cooperative in New York, as evidence that public housing was neglected. This, of course, was a false argument, because Co-op City voted to stay in Mitchell-Lama Housing until 2052 and benefit from de Blasio's Mitchell-Lama funding legislation to fix structural repairs in its massive complex.[12]

The pro-privatization group circulated English/Spanish flyers in bold red, white, and blue letters with black background: "FAKE vs. REAL OWNERSHIP/ FALSO vs. REAL PROPIEDAD," highlighting the difference in value between a subsidized RNA House Mitchell-Lama apartment and equivalent RNA House market-rate apartments. The contrasts were stark. Under Mitchell-Lama, apartments ranged in price in 2019 from $25,000 to $35,000. At market rate, they could sell for between $700,000 and $1.5 million.

They couched the struggle in terms of the powerless versus the powerful, as if somehow the city, which had provided affordable housing, was the enemy: "OWNERSHIP IS POWER/LA PROPIEDAD ES PODER. Once women and minorities couldn't own land. The goal was to keep them from becoming independent and free. That has changed in the U.S. It's time that changed for us." This was a logical fallacy. While it was true that women and minorities were once denied ownership, their lack of rights didn't apply to this situation.

They twisted the argument to suggest that RNA House cooperators were somehow scapegoated by a city at fault, distributing to each apartment an enlarged copy of a dollar bill with *Million* stamped on it:

> Go ahead, shred it. Have you asked . . . Why is the city asking me to shred $700,000, $1 Million, $1.5 Million? The city has failed in its responsibility over the past few decades to adequately provide middle income housing to the residents of our city. In order to claim to have made good on campaign promises they have failed to deliver; the city is asking each of us to sacrifice REAL OWNERSHIP of our apartments. Do you want more information? If you do, vote "YES," when it's time to vote.

Again, they were blaming the city as an excuse to privatize.

Manhattan Borough President Gale Brewer spoke at a meeting in the RNA House community room attended by approximately 50–60 cooperators about the importance of preserving Mitchell-Lama Housing. As she knew some of the pro-privatization folks, she didn't make a strong case. Nonetheless, she hit a nerve. An African American pro-privatization cooperator, whose child I played with growing up, and whose wife cared for me in the backyard when I scraped my knee, stood up and said: "You want to prevent me, a Black man, from the chance to make a million?"

I sympathized with his position. Historically, there was systematic housing discrimination against African Americans whose neighborhoods were redlined and who were denied low-cost government mortgages, like what happened to Mondello's mother. Real estate agents would not sell homes to Blacks in White neighborhoods. Blacks were segregated and unable to accumulate wealth through homeownership. If they did manage to buy, their homes were worth much less than the equivalent properties in White neighborhoods. *The Color of Law* author Richard Rothstein explained:

> In many hundreds of instances nationwide, mob violence, frequently led or encouraged by police, drove Black families out of homes they had purchased or rented in previously all-white neighborhoods. Campaigns, even violent ones, to exclude African Americans from all but a few inner-city neighborhoods were often led by churches, universities and other nonprofit groups determined to maintain their neighborhoods' ethnic homogeneity.[13]

It wasn't until the 1968 Fair Housing Act that "racial discrimination in the sale and rental of housing [became] unlawful for private actors as well as government."[14] By then, however, segregation was entrenched. "Patterns were set and have been difficult to reverse. The enormous black-white wealth gap, for example, responsible for so much of today's racial inequality, is in large part a product of Black exclusion from homes whose appreciation generated substantial equity for White working-class families with FHA and VA mortgages that propelled them into the middle class."[15]

One way to ameliorate the situation and allow this African American cooperator a chance to accumulate wealth was for RNA to privatize. It was a question of personal benefit versus the common good. Of course, the African American position in the building was not uniform. A Black friend in her forties, raising kids on the 150 side, said: "I agree with your mom. RNA needs to stay under the Mitchell-Lama program. There are many elderly cooperators who have resided in RNA for years, living on fixed incomes. This is their home, and they should not be frightened and constantly badgered about privatization."

My mother's friend said: "I think the YES for privatization folks are getting more desperate. They used to send out well-written, beautiful flyers, i.e., "Cookies and Conversation." Now they are meant to alarm, or imply we are dumb for not getting a million when we can. They say we can become an SRO (a single-room occupancy, where residents share kitchens and bathrooms) or HPD can place the homeless in RNA apartments."

In an email to me, a pro-privatization acquaintance bolstered this fear: "HPD is threatening to install homeless people in the building. Furthermore, income limits to move in have been reduced, thus allowing "less desirables" to become neighbors. They're not the same kind of people we knew growing up."

Her accusations shocked me. I'd never heard or experienced any kind of antagonism or prejudice against anyone at 150–160 West 96th Street. *So much for my utopian perspective,* I thought. I asked an African American friend if she'd experienced racism in the building: "Once we relocated to RNA, the boys loved their new home. As far as RNA being a supportive community though, not so much. There was one upsetting incident where my boys were falsely accused of vandalizing RNA property. If my sons were performing these acts of crime, why didn't someone ring my bell to alert me? Instead, I received a letter from management."

The Stay-in-Mitchell-Lama group circulated a petition asking people to keep RNA House public, distributed leaflets to each apartment explaining how new members of the board were deceiving residents into supporting privatization and pushing hard for a "yes" vote, and, in stark terms, explained the advantages of the Mitchell-Lama program:

> Imagine staying in M-L for the next 30 years. Low interest loans, very little increase in maintenance, money to fix our garage, garage fees won't go up, decrease in electric bills via energy savings, pay very little taxes, all financial decisions overseen by HPD.
>
> Imagine living in privatization forever, not turning back. Dependent on bank loans, maybe even balloon mortgages, no voting rights if you don't go private but turn into a renter, a board of private individuals not overseen by anyone, a board that will control your hard earned money, you must pay more taxes, very little diversity.

A newer middle-aged cooperator emailed: "The city is desperate to support programs like Mitchell-Lama, which provide middle-income affordable housing in a gentrified city, to be inclusive of working people. This makes the opposition furious because they just want to cash in and leave New York City. In opposition."

In the RNA House Newsletter, an elderly Stay-in-Mitchell-Lama cooperator framed the battle in moral terms:

> We, in Mitchell-Lama, have been given an extraordinary gift of living in Manhattan at reasonable housing costs. Voting for privatization means there is one less working-class property available to other workers in the future. If we stay in Mitchell-Lama, we return the favor we've benefitted from and enjoyed for decades and cede it to other working-class folks and to the next generation. Otherwise, Manhattan becomes increasingly for the rich and that decreases our valuable diversity. By privatizing, we will be helping to further establish and maintain the de-facto segregation of Manhattan. Do we really want to do this? I don't want to be party to increasing the already

horrific levels of discrimination in this city. Choosing privatization is tantamount to choosing "self-imposed deportation" of working-class people from New York City for all generations to come. Do we want to contribute to the increasing gap between the "haves" and the "have nots" in our country? Do we want to support and grow working-class solidarity that is so necessary to win any improvements in health care, jobs, education, and housing?

Her powerful heartfelt argument was the most persuasive yet to remain in Mitchell-Lama.

As the Red Herring vote in January 2019 approached, my mother's friend reported hearing murmuring against privatization. "My reading may be off bigly, but I think the privatizers will lose. It will be a close vote, I'm sure."

I waited with bated breath to hear the results. Finally, she reported: "Good news. The resolution didn't pass! It needed 138 apartments to vote YES, and only got 108. The NO votes totaled 65. So, we are still in Mitchell-Lama. Until next time, whenever that is."

I felt much better and called my sister immediately to relay the news. "Whew," she said.

Another Stay-in-Mitchell-Lama cooperator mused that the '50s and '60s battle to keep this neighborhood affordable for lower-income people reminded him in some ways of today. Will those here now be able to stay in the future? Who will fight for that to happen the way Father Browne, the Strycker's Bay Neighborhood Council, Riverside Neighborhood Assembly, and other local democratic clubs did then, making the West Side Urban Renewal plan one of the most just in the city?

The struggle today *is* the same as during the postwar era. In 1952, the *New York Times* reported: "Unless something is done on a large scale to provide more apartments for middle-income families, most housing experts believe, New York will become an urban core inhabited by those wealthy enough to afford luxury apartments or poor enough to remain in slums or qualify for public housing."[16] This refrain from seventy years ago is now being heard once more throughout the city.

Two years after the Red Herring vote, in Spring 2021, the New York State Legislature passed the Mitchell-Lama reform bill making it harder for Mitchell-Lama co-ops to privatize. The legislation "raised the threshold needed to voluntarily dissolve [from 66.6 percent] to 80 percent of all dwelling units"[17] and prevented "back-to-back dissolution votes by imposing a five-year moratorium following a failed dissolution vote."[18] An alliance of three organizations—Mitchell-Lama Residents Coalition, Cooperators United for Mitchell-Lama, and the Brooklyn Mitchell-Lama Task Force led the fight with the help of Assemblymember Linda B. Rosenthal and State Senator Brian Kavanagh. An intensive lobbying campaign began to convince Governor Cuomo to sign the bill. Finally, in January 2022, Governor Hochul enacted the law. This was encouraging news. I knew, at least today, that this legislation made it more likely that Mitchell-Lama housing would remain public. Now, it was imperative for New York State to not only preserve Mitchell-Lama buildings but construct more of them.

On a recent New York City trip, I took the #1 train uptown to meet my friend who grew up in the El Dorado, the magnificent Emery Roth Art Deco building on Central Park West between 90th and 91st Street. The El Dorado was where *Marjorie Morningstar* took place, the 1955 novel about a young Jewish woman's quest for assimilation through economic success and shedding of old country ways. "By moving to the El Dorado her parents had done much, Marjorie believed, to make up for their immigrant origin"[19]—the opposite goals of my progressive parents, who strove for social justice, not social success.

Why was I still so attached to the city? I asked myself, as I walked toward the 23rd Street and 7th Avenue subway station past empty storefronts, boutique hotels, luxury towers, and homeless people. New York had abandoned the ethos of my youth, when fair play, collectivism, and the idea that housing was a human right guided politics, urban design, and planning. I jogged down the subway steps, swiped my Metrocard, and waited for the train. Many dear friends remained in the city, from childhood, high school, Oberlin, and, of course, RNA House. My friends at the Collective for Living Cinema and Film/Video Arts had all left the city. It's hard to imagine either place opening today. Would I yearn to live in New York if my roots weren't here? I'm not sure I'd want to be a newcomer forming relationships in an overpriced city where only rich people could live comfortably.

The scrubbed subway car transported just a few masked passengers, our heads bent, staring into cell phones. The current COVID crisis required transformative change that would put people over profits, I thought. But would the post-COVID recovery actually produce a more just city?

I got off the train at 96th Street and Broadway, my childhood stop. FOWAD, the discount clothing store where Nina and I took shelter from muggers in the '70s, and years later, I filmed a scene for *The Boy Test* and bought my wedding dress, was long gone, closed due to rising rents. On my *Growing Up on the Old Upper West Side* Facebook group, I discovered that FOWAD had been owned by an Egyptian man, whose first name was *Fouad*. In Arabic, the word *Fouad* meant *heart*. Spectrum, a chain of internet and mobile phone stores, now occupied the space.

Through the Spectrum window, I stared at the latest cell phone models. As of 2021, nearly two hundred storefronts sat vacant on the Upper West Side,[20] much of what was meaningful to me had vanished—the arthouse cinemas, independent bookstores, Chinese-Cuban restaurants, Murray the kosher butcher, Holocaust survivors kibitzing on the island in the middle of the boulevard, Grab Bag, the jammed-packed clothing store with a communal dressing room, H & H Bagels, West Side Camera. The Museum of Natural History remained, as did Symphony Space and the Thalia, though not in their original formations. Most of my friends, except those at RNA, had left the neighborhood, priced out like the mom-and-pop stores.

Activism and the progressive spirit were still alive on the Upper West Side to some degree, however, which consoled me. An RNA House friend mentioned a demonstration at a neighborhood building by Local 32BJ, a branch of the Service Employees International Union, for fair treatment and union coverage of building staff workers. For months after George Floyd was murdered, he added, a group of Upper West Siders gathered at 5 p.m. on Fridays at the 96th Street and Broadway subway entrance to hold a *Say Their Names* vigil. For a few weeks after the murder, some RNA cooperators stood outside the building every night at 7:00 p.m., holding *Black Lives Matter* signs. Likewise, in Upper West Side apartment and store windows, *Black Lives Matter* signs and rainbow flags could be spotted. Community social support groups held street fairs, attracted volunteers, and did neighborhood outreach. Activists welcomed homeless people to the Lucerne Hotel, opposing those who fought to have the homeless sent to other neighborhoods. Finally, he said, pro-Mitchell-Lama advocates living in West Side Urban Renewal Area co-ops, buoyed by the support of Manhattan Borough president Gale Brewer and other progressive state and city lawmakers, lobbied to protect Mitchell-Lama Housing.

En route to meet my friend, instead of avoiding RNA House, as I'd done until now, I found myself walking east on 96th Street up the hill toward my building. At Amsterdam Avenue I kept going, past a former subsidized low-rent super-slab, built as part of the same urban renewal movement as

RNA, where Rust Brown, the jazz club popular with Knicks stars like Walt Frazier, Willis Reed, and Earl "The Pearl" Monroe, used to be.

When I was growing up, the kids in this tower threw stones at us from their backyard, looming above the concrete wall separating our building from theirs. Terrified, we scattered, then regrouped, only for them to hurl rocks at us again. Even in utopia, classes were divided. Over two decades ago, the building had been converted into a luxury high-rise. Later, the sidewalk outside was narrowed, making way for storefronts in this now-pricey neighborhood, where developers were squeezing every inch of available land into profitable commercial property. The last time I saw my mother, in summer 2013, she and I navigated single file past the construction obstacles, debris, noise, and crowds. "Terrible, just terrible," my mother sighed.

I continued east up 96th Street toward Columbus Avenue and my building. As I approached, I saw the large glass RNA lobby windows stretching across the entrance. Gil, the amicable security guard who'd watched me grow up, was sitting at the front desk. I tried to make eye contact, but didn't try too hard, and went unnoticed. I watched him chatting to a neighbor as usual, like he was where he needed to be, like all my memory was in order, intact.

Just then, I had a vision of my mother. She was outside in front of the lobby, smiling and pushing her cart down the two front steps, on her way to buy groceries. She didn't look ahead, didn't see me, but she was there, in the heaven of her Just City.

The End

Acknowledgments

I CAME TO WRITE *Just City* because I was fascinated by RNA House's socialist system and how it shaped my family, neighbors, and friends. I don't hold a PhD in urban history, so in the course of researching this book, I educated myself about New York City's housing reform movement, affordable housing crisis, architecture, and planning. For historical accuracy, I relied on historian Peter Eisenstadt, author of *Rochdale Village: Robert Moses, 6,000 Families, and New York City's Great Experiment in Integrated Housing,* and Robert Snyder, Professor Emeritus of American Studies and Journalism at Rutgers University–Newark and Manhattan Borough Historian. I am extremely grateful to both of them for their encouragement and support. Thank you to Fredric Nachbaur and the entire editorial and production team at Fordham University Press for believing in this project. I want to thank all the Upper West Side Mitchell-Lama and NYCHA dwellers whom I interviewed, especially Mondello Browner, Bobby Broom, and Beth Rosenblum. Thank you to cooperators Betty Gubert and Jay Hauben for bestowing information about current events at RNA House as well as the history of Riverside Neighborhood Assembly, RNA House's sponsor. Thank you to David Ment at the New York City Municipal Archives, and the NYU Furman Center for Real Estate and Urban Policy for filling in the gaps.

I owe great thanks to several people who helped guide the personal side of this book. From the outset, my dear cousin Annie Steinhardt, a great writer and inspiration, taught me the nuts and bolts of creative writing.

From there, Meg Lemke, brilliant and caring Editor-in-Chief of *MUTHA* magazine, nurtured, edited, and published in *MUTHA* excerpts from *Just City*. Throughout this ten-year journey, Joe Miller was a dedicated, meticulous reader and a great friend. I'm not sure I could've written this book without him. I want to thank Amy Silverman and Deborah Sussman, leaders of the Mothers Who Write workshop in Phoenix, for their personal essay writing prompts, which propelled this manuscript forward, and to all the Mothers Who Write participants who gave me feedback. Thank you to Ariel Gore, founder and editor of *HipMama* magazine and teacher at School for Wayward Writers at the online Literary Kitchen, and the entire Literary Kitchen community. Many, many thanks to Lauren LeBlanc, my astute, conscientious, reassuring developmental editor, who helped me shape the final draft of this book.

Thank you to my dear childhood friend Phoebe Farber, who gave me valuable instant feedback at crucial moments. Thank you to Michael Frank, who believed in this project and helped me develop it, and to Penelope Green, who convinced me I should turn my essays into a book. Thank you to Jonathan Finkelman, who helped me through the home stretch with his compassion, patience, and expert editing skills. Thank you to Jenny Horn and John Steinheimer for photo editing, book cover collaboration, and emotional support. Thank you to my sister, who traveled this road with me. Thank you to my cousin, Ellen Rosenbloom, for encouraging my personal writing and for her poignant poem about my mother, included in *Just City*. Thank you to Catha Abrahams for her remembrances of the early years at RNA House and of my mother. Thank you to Jennifer Low for her constructive, shrewd feedback. Thank you to Henry Sivak for his French translations and critique. Thank you to my precious son for his love and enthusiasm. Finally, thank you to Jo Anne Schlesinger, Betsy Sokolow Sherman, Linda Pressman, Lisa Asche, Nancy Lauro, Nancy Abrahams Shefrin, Emily Gubert, Tom Reingold, Gina Gold, Craig Levine, Pam Dick, Adeena Karasick, Eve Schaenen, Ross Frommer, Jack Kaufman, Talia Antrobus, Elizabeth Greenstein, Dore Hainer, Juliet Douglas, Lois Stover, and Randi Hoffman for their friendship, support, and kindness.

NOTES

1. Moving into the Just City

1. Éva Forgács, "Between the Town and the Gown: On Hannes Meyer's Dismissal from the Bauhaus," *Journal of Design History* 23, no. 3 (2010): 265–274.

2. Annemarie Sammartino, "Mass Housing, Late Modernism, and the Forging of Community in New York City and East Berlin, 1965–1989," *The American Historical Review* 121, no. 2 (2016): 492–521.

3. This amount conformed to the terms of the Mitchell-Lama Housing Program. "Mid-Income Co-op Due on West Side: Plans Are Made for 14-Story Structure on 96th St.," *New York Times*, November 19, 1961.

4. W. H. Auden, New Year Letter, 1940.

5. Pamela Robertson Wojcik, *The Apartment Plot: Urban living in American film and Popular Culture, 1945 to 1975* (Durham, NC: Duke University Press, 2010), 213.

6. C. S. Lewis, *The Lion, the Witch, and the Wardrobe*, illus. Pauline Baynes (New York: Harper Trophy, 1994), 112.

7. Barbara Stewart, "Adventure Goes Out of Style; Deemed Unsafe, 60's Playgrounds Are Being Replaced," *New York Times*, May 20, 1999, https://www.nytimes.com/1999/05/20/nyregion/adventure-goes-out-of-style-deemed-unsafe-60-s-playgrounds-are-being-replaced.html.

8. Annemarie Sammartino, *Freedomland: Co-Op City and the Story of New York* (Ithaca, NY: Three Hills, 2022), 10.

9. Nicholas Dagen Bloom and Matthew Gordon Lasner, eds., *Affordable Housing in New York: The People, Places, and Policies That Transformed a City* (Princeton, NJ: Princeton University Press, 2016), 203–204.

10. Charles G. Bennett, "Mayor Cites Need for Pollution Aid," *New York Times*, August 5, 1967, https://www.nytimes.com/1967/08/05/archives/mayor-cites-need-for-pollution-aid.html.

11. Carl Glassman, "There's Still a lot of Dirt but Less Than Before," *New York Times*, July 18, 1976, https://www.nytimes.com/1976/07/18/archives/theres-still-a-lot-of-dirt-but-less-than-before-theres-still-a-lot.html.

12. Peter Kihss, "City Gains in Controlling Air Pollution," *New York Times*, March 8, 1970, https://www.nytimes.com/1970/03/08/archives/city-gains-in-controlling-air-pollution-city-reports-local-gains-in.html.

13. Glassman, "Still a lot of Dirt."

14. Sarah Crean, "The Bronx Is Breathing," *Transform, Don't Trash NYC*, February 20, 2015.

15. Adam Rome, "Give Earth a Chance: The Environmental Movement and the Sixties," *Journal of American History* 90, no. 2 (2003): 525–554.

16. Environmental Protection Agency, *The Guardian: Origins of the EPA*. 1992. EPA Historical Publication: 1. (Washington, DC) Spring 1992, https://www.epa.gov/archive/epa/aboutepa/guardian-origins-epa.html.

2. Community, Collectivism, and Tolerance

1. Dana Goldstein, "Remembering Ocean Hill-Brownsville," *Nation*, October 13, 2014, https://www.thenation.com/article/archive/tough-lessons-1968-teacher-strikes/.

2. Goldstein, "Remembering."

3. On the Street

1. Interview with Hilary Roberts, November 2017.

2. John Darnton, "96th and Broadway Typifies Essence of a Changing City," *New York Times*, May 29, 1972, https://www.nytimes.com/1972/05/29/archives/96th-and-broadway-typifies-essence-of-a-changing-city-96th-and.html.

3. Darnton, "96th and Broadway."

4. Darnton.

5. Darnton.

4. Breathing Life into the Sanitized Columbus Avenue Strip

1. Clara Hemphill, *A Brighter Choice: Building a Just School in an Unequal City* (New York: Teachers College Press, 2023), 29.

2. Laurie Johnston, "At Columbia Grammar, an Era Ends," *New York Times*, May 29, 1981, https://www.nytimes.com/1981/05/29/nyregion/at-columbia-grammar-an-era-ends.html.

3. Jennifer Hock, "Political Designs: Architecture and Urban Renewal in the Civil Rights Era, 1954–1973" (PhD diss., Harvard University, 2012), 145.

4. Jane Jacobs, *The Death and Life of Great American Cities* (New York: Vintage, 1961), 373.

5. Hilary Ballon and Kenneth T. Jackson, *Robert Moses and the Modern City: The Transformation of New York* (New York: W. W. Norton, 2007), 255.

6. Stephen Menendian, Samir Gambhir, and Arthur Gailes, "The Roots of Structural Racism Project," Othering and Belonging Institute, June 30, 2021, https://belonging.berkeley.edu/roots-structural-racism.

5. Class Consciousness

1. Eric P. Nash and Norman McGrath, *Manhattan Skyscrapers*, revised and expanded ed. (New York: Princeton Architectural Press, 2005), 67.

2. Gerald C. Fraser, "Neighborhoods: The Horne of Harlem's Affluent," *New York Times*, June 29, 1970, https://www.nytimes.com/1970/06/29/archives/neighborhoods-the-home -of-harlems-affluent-neighborhoods-the-home.html.

3. Mapping Inequality, Redlining in New Deal America, https://dsl.richmond.edu/panorama /redlining/#loc=15/40.794/-73.967&city=manhattan-ny.

4. Richard Rothstein, "A 'Forgotten History' of How the U.S. Government Segregated America," interview by Terry Gross, *NPR*, May 3, 2017, https://www.npr.org/2017/05/03 /526655831/a-forgotten-history-of-how-the-u-s-government-segregated-america.

5. Samuel Zipp, *Manhattan Projects: The Rise and Fall of Urban Renewal in Cold War New York* (New York: Oxford University Press, 2012), 260.

6. Zipp, *Manhattan Projects*, 255.

7. Le Corbusier, "A Noted Architect Dissects Our Cities," *New York Times*, January 3, 1932, https://www.nytimes.com/1932/01/03/archives/a-noted-architect-dissects-our-cities-le-corbusier -indicts-them-as.html.

8. Hilary Ballon and Kenneth T. Jackson, *Robert Moses and the Modern City: The Transformation of New York* (New York: W. W. Norton, 2007), 108.

9. Zipp, *Manhattan Projects*, 255.

10. Richard Plunz, *A History of Housing in New York City* (New York: Columbia University Press, 2016), 273.

11. Plunz, *A History of Housing*, 274.

12. Piri Thomas, *Down These Mean Streets* (New York: Alfred A. Knopf, 1967), 298.

13. Zipp, *Manhattan Projects*, 350.

14. Zipp, 339–344.

15. Plunz, *A History of Housing*, 295.

16. Fraser, "Neighborhoods."

17. Zipp, *Manhattan Projects*, 339.

18. Mike Mishkin, "These Upper West Side Buildings Stick Out Like Sore Thumbs," *6sqft*, March 27, 2019, https://www.6sqft.com/these-upper-west-side-buildings-stick-out-like-sore -thumbs/?utm_source=6sqft+Weekly+List&utm_campaign=8938a8ffoe-EMAIL_CAMPAIGN _2017_05_26_COPY_01&utm_medium=email&utm_term=0_24f851d35f-8938a8ffoe -262670026.

19. Richard Price, "The Rise and Fall of Public Housing in NYC," *Guernica*, October 1, 2014, https://www.guernicamag.com/the-rise-and-fall-of-public-housing-in-nyc/.

20. Plunz, *A History of Housing*, 313.

21. Glenn Thrush, "With Market Hot, Landlords Slam the Door on Section 8 Tenants," *New York Times*, October 12, 2018, https://www.nytimes.com/2018/10/12/us/politics/section -8-housing-vouchers-landlords.html.

22. J. S., "Why the Pruitt-Igoe Housing Project Failed," *The Economist*, October 15, 2011, https://www.economist.com/prospero/2011/10/15/why-the-pruitt-igoe-housing-project-failed.

23. Nicholas Dagen Bloom, "Maintaining NYCHA: Debunking the Myth of Unmanageable High-Rise Public Housing," *Urban Omnibus*, April 22, 2015, https://urbanomnibus.net/2015/04 /maintaining-nycha-debunking-the-myth-of-unmanageable-high-rise-public-housing/.

24. Luis Ferré-Sadurní, "The Rise and Fall of New York Public Housing: An Oral History," *New York Times*, July 9, 2018, https://www.nytimes.com/interactive/2018/06/25/nyregion/new-york-city-public-housing-history.htm.

6. Grappling with Death

1. Sam Roberts, "Infamous 'Drop Dead' Was Never Said by Ford," *New York Times*, December 28, 2006, https://www.nytimes.com/2006/12/28/nyregion/28veto.html.

2. Chris Brooks, "Labor and the Long Seventies," *Jacobin*, February 25, 2018, https://www.jacobinmag.com/2018/02/lane-windham-interview-knocking-on-labors-door-unions.

3. Ronald Reagan, "Inaugural Address," *Ronald Reagan Presidential Foundation and Institute*, January 20, 1981, https://www.reaganfoundation.org/ronald-reagan/reagan-quotes-speeches/inaugural-address-2/.

4. Christopher Gray, "Streetscapes/40th Street between Fifth Avenue and Avenue of the Americas; Across From Bryant Park, a Block with Personality," *New York Times*, August 4, 2002, https://www.nytimes.com/2002/08/04/realestate/streetscapes-40th-street-between-fifth-avenue-avenue-americas-across-bryant-park.html.

5. Camp Trywoodie Campers, "Letter to President L. B. Johnson," *Camp Trywoodie Yearbook*, Summer 1964, http://daithiobroin.ie/Trywoodie/wp-content/uploads/2012/10/1964.pdf.

7. Salvation in Socialism

1. Angela Davis, *Angela Davis—An Autobiography* (New York: Random House, 1974), 110–111.

2. Edward Bellamy, *Looking Backward, 2000–1887* (Cambridge, MA: The Belknap Press of Harvard University Press, 1888), 148.

3. Gerald W. Sazama, "Lessons from the History of Affordable Housing Cooperatives in the United States: A Case Study in Affordable Housing Policy," *American Journal of Economics and Sociology* 59, no. 4, (2000): 573–608.

4. Sazama, "Lessons," 573–608.

5. Joshua Benjamin Freeman, *Working-Class New York: Life and Labor Since World War II* (New York: New Press, 2000), 110.

6. Nadine Brozan, "Postings; A Historical Look Back at Working-Class Housing," *New York Times*, November 7, 2004, https://www.nytimes.com/2004/11/07/realestate/postings-a-historical-look-back-at-workingclass-housing.html.

7. Brozan, "Postings."

8. Brozan.

9. New York Legislature, *Report of the Tenement House Committee as Authorized by Chapter 479 of the Laws of 1894* (J.B. Lyon, state printer: 1895).

10. New York Legislature, *Report of the Tenement House Committee*.

11. New York Legislature, *Report of the Tenement House Committee*.

12. New York Legislature, *Report of the Tenement House Committee*.

13. New York Legislature, *Report of the Tenement House Committee*.

14. Richard Plunz, *A History of Housing in New York City* (New York: Columbia University Press, 2016), 47.

15. Plunz, *A History of Housing*, 208.

16. Landmarks Preservation Commission, November 12, 1974, Number 6 LP – 0876, http://s-media.nyc.gov/agencies/lpc/lp/0876.pdf.

17. Plunz, *A History of Housing*, 209.

18. Plunz, 209.

19. "'First Houses' Open, Roosevelt Hails New Slum Policy," *New York Times*, December 4, 1935, https://www.nytimes.com/1935/12/04/archives/first-houses-open-roosevelt-hails-new-slum-policy-east-side-block.html.

20. "'First Houses' Open."

21. Kevin Baker, "The Death of a Once Great City," *Harpers*, July, 2018, https://harpers.org/archive/2018/07/the-death-of-new-york-city-gentrification/.

22. Roland Wood, "Vast Housing Plan Envisaged for City," *New York Times*, December 8, 1935, https://www.nytimes.com/1935/12/08/archives/editorial-article-1-no-title-vast-housing-plan-envisaged-for-city.html.

23. Robert Caro, *The Power Broker: Robert Moses and the Fall of New York* (New York: Vintage Books, 1975), 613.

24. US Department of Housing and Urban Development, https://www.hud.gov/sites/documents/LEGS_CHRON_JUNE2014.PDF.

25. Samuel Zipp, *Manhattan Projects: The Rise and Fall of Urban Renewal in Cold War New York* (New York: Oxford University Press, 2012), 269.

26. Hilary Ballon and Kenneth T. Jackson, eds., *Robert Moses and the Modern City: The Transformation of New York* (New York: W. W. Norton, 2007) 106.

27. Ballon and Jackson, *Robert Moses and the Modern City*, 106.

28. Ballon and Jackson, 106.

29. Ballon and Jackson, 106–107.

30. Annemarie Sammartino, *Freedomland: Co-Op City and the Story of New York* (Ithaca, NY: Three Hills, 2022), 8.

31. Nelson Rockefeller quoted in Samuel Bleeker, *The Politics of Architecture: A Perspective on Nelson A. Rockefeller* (New York: Routledge, 1981), 113.

32. Ballon and Jackson, *Robert Moses and the Modern City*, 305.

33. Nate Schweber, "A Community Erased by Slum Clearance Is Reunited," *New York Times*, October 9, 2011, https://www.nytimes.com/2011/10/10/nyregion/reunion-for-a-vanished-neighborhood.html.

34. Schweber, "Community Erased."

35. Schweber.

36. Interview with historian Peter Eisenstadt, November 2022.

37. Interview with historian Peter Eisenstadt, November 2022. For a discussion on Jane Jacobs and gentrification, refer to Samuel Zipp, Jennifer Hock, and Nathan Storring, "The Forces of Decline and Regeneration: A Discussion of Jane Jacobs and Gentrification," in *Aesthetics of Gentrification: Seductive Spaces and Communities in the Neoliberal City*, ed. Cristoph Lindner and Gerard Sandoval (Netherlands: Amsterdam University Press, 2021).

38. Jennifer Hock, "Political Designs: Architecture and Urban Renewal in the Civil Rights Era, 1954–1973" (PhD diss., Harvard University, 2012), 132.

39. Hock, "Political Designs," 132.

40. Steven V. Roberts, "City Trying to Ease Impact of Renewal on West Side," *New York Times*, December 26, 1966, https://www.nytimes.com/1966/12/26/archives/city-trying-to-ease-impact-of-renewal-on-west-side-city-is.html.

41. Nicholas Dagen Bloom and Matthew Gordon Lasner, eds., *Affordable Housing in New York: The People, Places, and Policies That Transformed a City* (Princeton, NJ: Princeton University Press, 2016), 203–204.

42. Bloom and Lasner, *Affordable Housing*, 203–204.

43. Bloom and Lasner, 203–204.

44. Martin Arnold, "Relocation Especially Stirs Clash at City Hearing West Side Project Weighed," *New York Times*, May 18, 1962, https://www.nytimes.com/1962/05/18/archives/disputes-aroused-by-west-side-plan-relocation-especially-stirs.html.

45. Robert A. M. Stern, Thomas Mellins, and David Fishman, *New York 1960: Architecture and Urbanism between the Second World War and the Bicentennial* (New York: Monacelli Press, 1995), 733.

46. Thomas W. Ennis, "Civic Groups Back Mid-Income Co-ops," *New York Times*, May 13, 1962, https://www.nytimes.com/1962/05/13/archives/civic-groups-back-midincome-coops-final-plans-for-west-side-urban.html.

47. Ennis, "Civic Groups."

48. Sarah Chartock, "A Descriptive Study of the Programs Undertaken by the Riverside Neighborhood Assembly to Further Democratic Integration on the West Side of Manhattan" (PhD diss., New York University, 1957), 59.

49. Chartock, "A Descriptive Study," 109.

50. Elizabeth Halstead, "Many Local Units Aid Puerto Ricans," *New York Times*, May 21, 1954, https://www.nytimes.com/1954/05/21/archives/many-local-units-aid-puerto-ricans-adjustment-to-our-way-of-life.html.

51. Chartock, "A Descriptive Study," 56.

52. Chartock, 57.

53. Chartock, 98.

54. "Mid-Income Co-op Due on West Side: Plans are Made for 14-Story Structure on 96th St," *New York Times*, November 19, 1961, https://www.nytimes.com/1962/01/14/archives/midincome-coop-rises-on-e-96th-st.html.

55. Martin Arnold, "Nonwhites Decline to Quit the Slums and Live in Co-ops," *New York Times*, November 23, 1961; ProQuest Historical Newspapers, 1.

56. Thomas W. Ennis, "Sponsors Issue Primer on Co-ops," *New York Times*, November 20, 1960, https://www.nytimes.com/1960/11/20/archives/sponsors-issue-primer-on-coops-primer-on-middleincome-coops-is.html.

57. Hock, "Political Designs," 152–153.

58. Steven V. Roberts, "City Trying to Ease Impact of Renewal on West Side," *New York Times*, December 12, 1966, https://timesmachine.nytimes.com/timesmachine/1966/12/26/90252997.pdf?pdf_redirect=true&ip=0.

59. Wagner-RNA Groundbreaking1965.pdf—Text of Speech—At Dedication of Riverside Neighborhood Assembly Housing Project, Robert F. Wagner Documents Collection, Speeches Series, Box # 060057W, Folder #10.

60. Hock, "Political Designs," 176.

61. Anna Quindlen, "About New York," *New York Times*, October 14, 1981, B3, https://www.nytimes.com/1981/09/26/nyregion/about-new-york.html.

8. Two Utopias

1. Paul Vitello, "George C. Stoney, Documentary Filmmaker, Dies at 96," *New York Times*, July 14, 2012, https://www.nytimes.com/2012/07/15/arts/television/george-c-stoney -documentarian-dies-at-96.html.

2. Vitello, "Stoney."

3. Ed Halter, "Collective Memory," *Village Voice*, March 27, 2007, https://www.villagevoice .com/2007/03/27/collective-memory/.

4. Ali Gharib, "All in the Family: Farrell's Bar and Grill," *Brooklyn*, June 1, 2015, http://www.bkmag.com/2015/06/01/all-in-the-family-farrells-bar-and-grill/.

5. Margot Hornblower, "New York Marchers Protest Racial Attack," *Washington Post*, December 28, 1986, https://www.washingtonpost.com/archive/politics/1986/12/28/ny-marchers -protest-racial-attack/3a45e417-9db7-4035-a7f1-f6a578603858/.

6. Ernest Callenbach, *Ecotopia* (New York: Bantam Books, 1977), 55.

7. Callenbach, *Ecotopia*, 24–25.

8. Callenbach, 47.

9. Stephen Nessen, "Housing Generations, Life in the Projects: A Shift to Violence," WNYC, December 19, 2012, https://www.wnyc.org/story/258072-housing-generations-life-projects -shift-violence/.

10. Barbara Presley Noble, "IF YOU'RE THINKING OF LIVING IN: Upper West Side," *New York Times*, February 12, 1989, https://www.nytimes.com/1989/02/12/realestate/if-you-re -thinking-of-living-in-upper-west-side.html.

11. Sam Roberts, "Gap between Rich and Poor in New York City Grows Wider," *New York Times*, December 25, 1994, https://www.nytimes.com/1994/12/25/nyregion/gap-between-rich -and-poor-in-new-york-city-grows-wider.html.

12. Roberts, "Gap."

13. Kevin Baker, "The Death of a Once Great City," *Harper's*, July, 2018, https://harpers.org/archive/2018/07/the-death-of-new-york-city-gentrification/.

14. Callenbach, *Ecotopia*, 36.

9. Gentrification Turns into Revanchism

1. Mark Jacobson, "The Land That Time and Money Forgot," *New York*, September 7, 2012, https://nymag.com/news/features/housing-projects-2012-9/.

2. "How a Theory of Crime and Policing Was Born, and Went Terribly Wrong," *NPR*, November 1, 2016, https://www.npr.org/2016/11/01/500104506/broken-windows-policing-and -the-origins-of-stop-and-frisk-and-how-it-went-wrong.

3. Felicia R. Lee, "Coping; 'Quality of Life' and a Few Nightmares," *New York Times*, February 27, 2000, https://www.nytimes.com/2000/02/27/nyregion/coping-quality-of-life-and-a -few-nightmares.html.

4. "How a Theory of Crime and Policing Was Born."

5. Neil Smith, "Smith on Gentrification," August 4, 2011, http://vanishingnewyork.blogspot .com/2011/08/smith-on-gentrification.html.

6. Smith, "Smith on Gentrification."

10. Could I Ever Return to Utopia?

1. I. M. Pei quotes, *Goodreads*, https://www.goodreads.com/quotes/7789189-life-is -architecture-and-architecture-is-the-mirror-of-life.

2. Cara Buckley and Marc Santora, "Night Falls, and 5Pointz, a Graffiti Mecca, Is Whited Out in Queens," *New York Times*, November 19, 2013, https://www.nytimes.com/2013/11/20 /nyregion/5pointz-a-graffiti-mecca-in-queens-is-wiped-clean-overnight.html.

3. Lynsey Hanley, *Estates* (London: Granta, 2007), 85.

4. Jeremiah Moss, *Vanishing New York: How a Great City Lost Its Soul* (New York: HarperCollins, 2017), 38.

5. Renaud Le Goix and Loïc Bonneval, "Immobilier: La Propriété Devient de Moins en Moins Abordable, Même dans les Zones les Plus Pauvres," *The Conversation*, April 11, 2023, https://theconversation.com/immobilier-la-propriete-devient-de-moins-en-moins-abordable -meme-dans-les-zones-les-plus-pauvres-203255.

11. No Next Time

1. Interview with Gary Sloman, New York City Department of Housing, Preservation, and Development, April 5, 2013.

2. Michael Greenberg, "Tenants Under Siege: Inside New York City's Housing Crisis," *New York Review*, August 17, 2017, https://www.nybooks.com/articles/2017/08/17/tenants -under-siege-inside-new-york-city-housing-crisis/.

3. Jeremiah Moss, *Vanishing New York: How a Great City Lost Its Soul* (New York: HarperCollins, 2017), 162.

4. Russ Buettner and Ray Rivera, "A Stalled Vision: Big Development as City's Future," *New York Times*, October 28, 2009, https://www.nytimes.com/2009/10/29/nyregion/29develop.html.

5. John Leland, "In Williamsburg, Rocked Hard," *New York Times*, May 28, 2011, https://www.nytimes.com/2011/05/29/nyregion/gentrification-brings-discord-to-williamsburg -brooklyn.html.

6. Hilton Als, "The Sugar Sphinx," *New Yorker*, May 8, 2014, https://www.newyorker.com /culture/culture-desk/the-sugar-sphinx.

7. Julie Bosman, "Bloomberg Policy Blamed for Families in Shelters," *New York Times*, April 22, 2009, https://www.nytimes.com/2009/04/23/nyregion/23homeless.html.

8. Julie Bosman, "City Aids Homeless with One-Way Tickets Home," *New York Times*, July 28, 2009, https://www.nytimes.com/2009/07/29/nyregion/29oneway.html l.

9. Julie Satow, "Living in the Mix," *New York Times*, August 29, 2014, https://www.nytimes .com/2014/08/31/realestate/affordable-housing-in-new-yorks-luxury-buildings.html.

10. Emily Badger and Luis Ferré-Sadurní, "As Bloomberg's New York Prospered, Inequality Flourished Too," *New York Times*, November 9, 2019, https://www.nytimes.com/2019/11/09 /upshot/bloomberg-new-york-prosperity-inequality.html.

11. Luis Ferré-Sadurní, "The Rise and Fall of New York Public Housing: An Oral History," *New York Times*, July 9, 2018, https://www.nytimes.com/interactive/2018/06/25/nyregion /new-york-city-public-housing-history.html.

12. Katie Honan, "Sandy-Damaged NYCHA Developments May Not Be Fixed Until 2021, Official Says," *dnainfo*, March 1, 2017, https://www.dnainfo.com/new-york/20170301 /far-rockaway/nycha-hurricane-sandy-repairs-resiliency-projects-delays/.

13. Stephon Johnson, "Bloomberg: Fingerprint NYCHA Residents," *Amsterdam News*, August 22, 2013, https://amsterdamnews.com/news/2013/08/22/bloomberg-fingerprint -nycha-residents/.

14. Emily Badger, "The Lasting Effects of Stop-and-Frisk in Bloomberg's New York," *New York Times*, March 2, 2020, https://www.nytimes.com/2020/03/02/upshot/stop-and-frisk -bloomberg.html.

15. Michael Barbaro and David W. Chen, "De Blasio Is Elected New York City Mayor in Landslide," *New York Times*, November 5, 2013, https://www.nytimes.com/2013/11/06/nyregion /de-blasio-is-elected-new-york-city-mayor.html.

12. Relinquishing the Apartment

1. Larissa MacFarquhar, "The Mind-Expanding Ideas of Andy Clark," *New Yorker*, April 2, 2018, https://www.newyorker.com/magazine/2018/04/02/the-mind-expanding-ideas -of-andy-clark.

2. E. B. White, *Here Is New York* (New York: Harper and Brothers, 1949), 28–29.

3. White, *Here Is New York*, 54.

13. The Crucial Necessity of Affordable Housing

1. Dana Schulz, "Towers in the Park: Le Corbusier's Influence in NYC," *6sqft*, November 19, 2014, https://www.6sqft.com/towers-in-the-park-le-corbusiers-influence-in-nyc/.

2. Ian Frazier, "Utopia, the Bronx," *New Yorker*, June 26, 2006, https://www.newyorker.com /magazine/2006/06/26/utopia-the-bronx.

3. Matthew Haag, "Amazon's Tax Breaks and Incentives Were Big. Hudson Yards' Are Bigger," *New York Times*, March 9, 2019, https://www.nytimes.com/2019/03/09/nyregion /hudson-yards-new-york-tax-breaks.html.

4. Anna Fixsen, "Hudson Yards NYC: Everything to Know about Visiting, Shopping, and Dining at the Megadevelopment," *ADPRO*, September 22, 2020, https://www.architecturaldigest .com/story/hudson-yards-nyc.

5. "One in 10 NYC Public School Students Are Homeless, Report Says," Spectrum News, NY1, https://www.ny1.com/nyc/brooklyn/news/2019/10/29/one-in-10-nyc-public-school -students-are-homeless—report-says.

6. Tobias Armborst, Daniel D'Oca, and Georgeen Theodore, "Norcs in NYC," *Urban Omnibus*, March 17, 2010, https://urbanomnibus.net/2010/03/norcs-in-nyc/.

7. "Tempe Center for the Arts," *Architekton*, http://www.architekton.com/tempe-center -for-the-arts

8. Grace Dixon and Ben Weiss, "De Blasio's Record on NYCHA," *Gotham Gazette*, November 6, 2017, https://www.gothamgazette.com/city/7299-de-blasio-s-record-on -nychaDe%20Blasio.

9. Dixon and Weiss, "De Blasio's Record."

10. Dixon and Weiss.

11. Dixon and Weiss.

12. Dixon and Weiss.

13. Dixon and Weiss.

14. Dixon and Weiss.

15. J. David Goodman, "After Years of Disinvestment, City Public Housing Is Poised to Get US Oversight," *New York Times*, June 1, 2018, https://www.nytimes.com/2018/06/01/nyregion /after-years-of-disinvestment-us-to-take-oversight-role-in-city-public-housing.html.

16. Harry DiPrinzio, "State Finally Releases $450 Million Promised to NYCHA," *CityLimits*, November 8, 2019, https://citylimits.org/2019/11/08/state-finally-releases-450-million-promised -to-nycha/.

17. Sally Goldenberg, "City Considers Demolishing and Rebuilding 2 NYCHA Sites," *Politico*, April 21, 2019, https://www.politico.com/states/new-york/city-hall/story/2019/04/21 /city-considers-demolishing-and-rebuilding-2-nycha-sites-982098.

18. Goldenberg, "City Considers."

19. Noam Chomsky @noamchomskyT, Twitter, Aug 14, 2017.

20. Nicholas Dagen Bloom, "Hidden in Plain Sight: Billions in Potential Revenue for NYCHA," *Gotham Gazette*, December 2, 2019, https://www.gothamgazette.com/opinion/8948 -hidden-in-plain-sight-billions-in-potential-revenue-nycha.

21. Samuel Zipp, *Manhattan Projects: The Rise and Fall of Urban Renewal in Cold War New York* (New York: Oxford University Press, 2012), 255.

22. Charles V. Bagli, "Stuyvesant Town Said to Be Near Sale That Will Preserve Middle-Class Housing," *New York Times*, October 19, 2015. https://www.nytimes.com/2015/10/20 /nyregion/stuyvesant-town-said-to-be-near-sale-that-will-preserve-middle-class-housing.html.

23. Bagli, "Stuyvesant Town."

24. Bagli.

25. Bagli.

26. Elizabeth Kim, "City Spent $220 Million to Keep Stuy Town Apartments Affordable; Turns Out, It Didn't Have to," *Gothamist*, July 18, 2019. https://gothamist.com/news/city-spent -220-million-to-keep-stuy-town-apartments-affordable-turns-out-it-didnt-have-to.

27. Richard Plunz, *A History of Housing in New York City* (New York: Columbia University Press, 2016), 209.

28. "Mayor Dedicates Kingsborough Houses, City's 10th Home Project, 3d for Brooklyn," *New York Times*, September 10, 1941.

29. Mayor Dedicates Kingsborough Houses."

30. Mayor Dedicates Kingsborough Houses."

31. "Assessment of New York City Housing Authority (NYCHA) Properties," *New York State Department of Health*, March 2018. https://www.governor.ny.gov/sites/governor.ny.gov/files /atoms/files/FINAL_Assessment_of_NYCHA_Report.pdf.

14. Battle over Privatization

1. Philip S. Gutis, "Unfettering Mitchell-Lama," *New York Times*, February 23, 1986, https://www.nytimes.com/1986/02/23/realestate/unfettering-mitchell-lama.html.

2. Ronald Sullivan, "A Public Apartment Tower May Now Be a Private One," *New York Times*, August 24, 1991, https://www.nytimes.com/1991/08/24/nyregion/a-public-apartment -tower-may-now-be-a-private-one.html.

3. Sullivan, "Public Apartment Tower."

4. David Jones, "Witkoff Loses Rent Appeal at Columbus House," *The Real Deal*, January 4, 2011, https://therealdeal.com/2011/01/04/witkoff-group-loses-rent-appeal-at-columbus-house/.

5. "Apartments above Trader Joe's Skyrocketed in Value After Grocery Store Moved In,

Report Says," *West Side Rag*, August 25, 2019, https://www.westsiderag.com/2019/08/25 /apartments-above-trader-joes-jumped-in-value-after-grocery-store-moved-in-report-says.

6. Masha Gessen, "The Trial of Donald Trump Must Tell the Full Story of the Capitol Insurrection," *New Yorker*, January 15, 2021, https://www.newyorker.com/news/our-columnists /the-trial-of-donald-trump-must-tell-the-full-story-of-the-capitol-insurrection.

7. "Mayor de Blasio Announces New Program to Save City's Remaining Affordable Mitchell-Lama Developments," *The Official Website of the City of New York*, October 26, 2017, https://www1.nyc.gov/office-of-the-mayor/news/688–17/mayor-de-blasio-new-program -save-city-s-remaining-affordable-mitchell-lama-developments#/0.

8. "Mayor de Blasio Announces New Program."

9. "Mayor de Blasio Announces New Program."

10. Jeffery C. Mays, "Central Park's Scenic Drives Will Soon Be Car-Free," *New York Times*, April 20, 2018, https://www.nytimes.com/2018/04/20/nyregion/central-park-car-ban.html.

11. Open letter to the RNA House community. 2018.

12. "Bronx's Co-op City Refinanced for $621M," *The Real Deal*, November 29, 2012, https://therealdeal.com/new-york/2012/11/29/bronxs-co-op-city-refinanced-for-621m/.

13. Richard Rothstein, "The Neighborhoods We Will Not Share," *New York Times*, January 20, 2020, https://www.nytimes.com/2020/01/20/opinion/fair-housing-act-trump.html ?action=click&module=Opinion&pgtype=Homepage.

14. Rothstein, "Neighborhoods."

15. Rothstein.

16. Charles Grutzner, "Housing Is Sought for Middle Group," *New York Times*, May 12, 1952, https://timesmachine.nytimes.com/timesmachine/1952/05/12/84315905.pdf?pdf _redirect=true&ip=0.

17. "Big Changes Coming to Mitchell-Lama Program," *Real Estate Weekly*, June 8, 2021, https://rew-online.com/big-changes-coming-to-mitchell-lama-program/.

18. "Big Changes Coming."

19. Herman Wouk, *Marjorie Morningstar* (Garden City, NY: Doubleday, 1955), 2.

20. Gus Saltonstall, "New Data Shows Scope of Upper West Side Vacancy Crisis," *Patch*, July 29, 2021, https://patch.com/new-york/upper-west-side-nyc/new-data-shows-scope-upper -west-side-vacancy-crisis?utm_term=article-slot-1&utm_source=newsletter-daily&utm _medium=email&utm_campaign=newslett.

INDEX

Ackerman, Frederick, 96, 189

Bauhaus ideology, 3, 7
Baum, Charles (father), 4–6, 8, 14, 34;
death of, 32, 49–51, 59, 63, 68, 72, 107
Baum, Judy (mother), 80–81, 141, 147–48,
150–53, 214; Advocates for Children,
39, 133, 159, 161–62, 173; *Ask Judy*
column and, 133, 149, 156–57; death of,
154–57, 163, 173–74; education and, 69,
73; legacy of, 158–62, 173–77; letters
from, 77–78, 166–68, 177–78; stability
and, 157–58; Upper West Side and,
160
Baumbach, David (resident), 194–95
BC. *See* British Colombia, Canada
beauty, 117, 121
Bellamy, Edward, *Looking Backward*, 90,
114
belonging, 61, 128, 140, 149–50, 182, 200
Berelson, David (resident), 123–24
Beresford, 61
best friends, 22, 72, 79
Black community: activism and, 100–101;
housing and, 101–2, 208–9; Jewish
community and, 24–25; schools and,
24–25
Black families, 43–44, 53
Black kids, 29–30; private school and,
52–53, 56–61
Black Lives Matter, 213
blackout, in NYC, 76–78
de Blasio, Bill, 153–54, 184–85, 188, 202–3
Bloom, Nicholas, 185–86
Bloomberg, Mike, 133, 146; development
and, 150–51, 182; homelessness and,
148, 152, 182; housing crisis and,
148–49; infill projects of, 134, 152–53,
185–88
Bloomingdale's, 73–74
board of directors, of RNA House, 23, 124,
127, 194, 203–7, 210
The Boy Test, 28–29, 126–28, 130, 213
Bratton, William, 121
Brewer, Gale, 191, 200, 208, 213
A Brighter Choice (Hemphill), 39–40
British Colombia, Canada (BC), 130;
Vancouver, 60, 114
Broadway theater, 13, 67, 86

Broken Windows policing, 121, 152
Bronx, NYC, 94, 202, 207; South, 8, 12, 84
Brooklyn, NYC, 8, 93–94, 109–11, 173;
Coney Island, 144–46; filmmaking and,
112–13; Williamsburg, 151–52
Brooklyn-Queens Expressway, 93
Broom, Bobby (resident), 37–40, 198
Browne, Henry J., 42, 101, 199–200, 211
brownstones, 44, 100, 103
brutalism, 7, 9, 37, 61, 127
Bryant Park, 71, 118
buildings: cooperative, 3, 57, 90–91, 101–2,
106, 180–82; demographics of, 18,
41, 57; derelict, 31, 52, 119, 144–45;
elevators in, 13–14, 147, 181; high-rise,
7, 11, 98–99, 130; in Paris, 138–39;
postwar, 37, 94, 97, 176; prewar, 8–9,
47, 79, 109–10; rent-controlled, 44,
122; rooftops of, 10, 13–14, 127; social
hierarchy in, 19, 43–44; super-slabs,
3, 36–37, 213; walk-up, 105–6. *See
also* luxury buildings; maintenance;
Mitchell-Lama buildings
Bush, George W., 129, 135–36
businesses, 73; chain stores, 122, 133–34,
169, 196; local, 100, 109, 169, 196, 198
busses, 48, 73

Callenbach, Ernest, *Ecotopia*, 113–14, 117
Canada, 117; BC, 130
capitalism, 86–87, 202
care, 116, 128, 166; community and, 20,
174–75, 205, 208
cars, 5–6, 132, 155, 206–7
Castro, Fidel, 86
Central Park, 4, 9, 134, 137, 206–7; music
and, 183
Centre Pompidou, 140–41
CGPS. *See* Columbia Grammar and
Preparatory School
chain stores, 122, 133–34, 169, 196
Chelsea, Manhattan, 185
Chelsea-Elliot, 181
childhood friends: best, 22, 72, 79;
Daphne, 79–81, 120–21, 160; Dore, 15,
69, 106–7; Facebook groups and, 17–20;
Gabe, 160; Gina, 15, 36, 107, 132–33,

148, 203, 207; public housing and,
184–85; subsidized, 23, 36
The Mambo Kings Sing Songs of Love
(Hijuelos), 182
Manhattan, NYC, 61; Chelsea, 185;
Chinatown, 93; East Village, 115, 125,
181, 189; gentrification and, 133; Lower
East Side, 96, 109, 189; modernism and,
8; segregation in, 210–11; SoHo, 129;
Tribeca, 122. *See also* Harlem; Upper
West Side
Manhattantown, 98–99
Mao Zedong, 16, 86
Marjorie Morningstar (Wouk), 212
Mark (friend), 180–82
Marsh, Yvette (resident), 33, 198–99
Marx, Karl, *Communist Manifesto*, 88
matriarchy, 94
Mazzoni, Mario, 150–51
memories, 17–20, 40, 150–53, 170–71,
212–14
Mercado, Luis, 164
methadone clinics, 20, 106
Metropolitan Museum of Art, 67
Mets, NY, 66, 72, 76–77, 84, 126, 167
middle class, 4, 108, 117, 160, 198–99, 209;
Black families and, 53; suburbs and,
98–100, 121, 159
Mitchell-Lama buildings, 45, 51, 102–3;
Columbus House, 196; Columbus Park
Towers, 43–44, 194–96; 1199 Plaza, 56;
Esplanade Gardens, 52, 56–59, 61–62,
201; Goddard Towers, 16–20; Jefferson
Towers, 11, 37–38, 40; New Amsterdam, 33, 198–99; NYCHA projects
compared to, 61–64; privatization and,
124–25, 194–203, 211–12; Riverbend,
55–56; 700 Columbus Avenue, 38, 198;
Starett City, 108; St. Martin's Tower,
197–98; Strycker's Bay Apartments,
42–43; Tower West, 41–42, 122;
wait-lists of, 11, 70, 120, 126, 163, 180.
See also RNA House
Mitchell-Lama Housing Program, 3, 70, 90,
98, 217n3
Mitchell-Lama reform bill (2021), 211–12
mixed-race families, 6, 57, 76, 168–69

modernism, 8–9, 97, 127, 140; architecture
and, 3, 7, 63
Mollenkopf, John H., 154
Mondello (resident), 52–53, 56–63, 201–2
morality, 8, 114, 148, 210
Moses, Robert, 38, 53–55, 97, 99, 146, 150;
eminent domain and, 93, 98, 145
Moss, Jeremiah, *Vanishing New York*, 125,
150
mother. *See* Baum, J.
mothers, single, 57, 63, 81, 108, 111, 192
Mothers in Labor, 108
muggings, 80, 119, 124, 213
Municipal Housing Authority Act, 96
Museum of Modern Art, 67
museums, 67, 156–57, 184
music, Central Park and, 183
musicians, 75, 82; jazz, 15, 81, 85, 134
Mutual Redevelopment Houses, 98, 180

Nala (resident), 190–91
Naturally Occurring Retirement Communities (NORC), 174–75, 182, 201
need, for affordable housing, 11, 197,
211–14
neighborhood, 20, 26–31, 133; class and,
48–49; Columbus Avenue and, 36–38,
41–43, 100, 134, 214; gentrification of,
134, 142; play in, 9–10, 16–17; safety
of, 33–34
neighborhoods, destruction of, 8, 12, 54,
93, 147, 151–52, 171–72
neighbors, 5–7, 120–21, 124–25, 137.
See also cooperators
Nelson, Laurie (resident), 18–19
Nevada, 110–11
New Amsterdam, 33, 198–99
New Deal, 96
New Jersey (NJ), 80–81; Teaneck, 72
New York (NY): Long Island, 145; NYC,
11–13, 31, 115, 140, 142; White Plains,
153
New York City, NY (NYC), 11–13, 31,
115, 140, 142; blackout in, 76–78;
Bronx, 94, 202, 207; diversity of, 63–64;
filmmaking in, 126–28; fiscal crisis of,
63, 66, 75–76, 161; LA compared to,

Jennifer Baum is a filmmaker turned writer. Her writing has been published in *New York Daily News, Guernica, Jacobin, The Village Voice, The Phoenix Jewish News, Canadian Jewish Outlook, The Jewish Observer Los Angeles, MUTHA, Hip Mama*, and *Newfound*, which nominated her essay "A Different Set of Rules" for a Pushcart award. Baum teaches composition at Montclair State University and occasionally works as a freelance editor, most recently for a series of reports for the World Bank on poverty in Ghana.

EMPIRE STATE EDITIONS SELECT TITLES FROM EMPIRE STATE EDITIONS

Andrew J. Sparberg, *From a Nickel to a Token: The Journey from Board of Transportation to MTA*

Daniel Campo, *The Accidental Playground: Brooklyn Waterfront Narratives of the Undesigned and Unplanned*

Joseph B. Raskin, *The Routes Not Taken: A Trip Through New York City's Unbuilt Subway System*

Phillip Deery, *Red Apple: Communism and McCarthyism in Cold War New York*

North Brother Island: The Last Unknown Place in New York City. Photographs by Christopher Payne, A History by Randall Mason, Essay by Robert Sullivan

Stephen Miller, *Walking New York: Reflections of American Writers from Walt Whitman to Teju Cole*

Tom Glynn, *Reading Publics: New York City's Public Libraries, 1754–1911*

R. Scott Hanson, *City of Gods: Religious Freedom, Immigration, and Pluralism in Flushing, Queens*. Foreword by Martin E. Marty

Dorothy Day and the Catholic Worker: The Miracle of Our Continuance. Edited, with an Introduction and Additional Text by Kate Hennessy, Photographs by Vivian Cherry, Text by Dorothy Day

Mark Naison and Bob Gumbs, *Before the Fires: An Oral History of African American Life in the Bronx from the 1930s to the 1960s*

Robert Weldon Whalen, *Murder, Inc., and the Moral Life: Gangsters and Gangbusters in La Guardia's New York*

Joanne Witty and Henrik Krogius, *Brooklyn Bridge Park: A Dying Waterfront Transformed*

Sharon Egretta Sutton, *When Ivory Towers Were Black: A Story about Race in America's Cities and Universities*

Pamela Hanlon, *A Wordly Affair: New York, the United Nations, and the Story Behind Their Unlikely Bond*

Britt Haas, *Fighting Authoritarianism: American Youth Activism in the 1930s*

David J. Goodwin, *Left Bank of the Hudson: Jersey City and the Artists of 111 1st Street*. Foreword by DW Gibson

Nandini Bagchee, *Counter Institution: Activist Estates of the Lower East Side*

Susan Celia Greenfield (ed.), *Sacred Shelter: Thirteen Journeys of Homelessness and Healing*

Elizabeth Macaulay-Lewis and Matthew M. McGowan (eds.), *Classical New York: Discovering Greece and Rome in Gotham*

Mark Bulik, *Ambush at Central Park: When the IRA Came to New York*

Matt Dallos, *In the Adirondacks: Dispatches from the Largest Park in the Lower 48*

Brandon Dean Lamson, *Caged: A Teacher's Journey Through Rikers, or How I Beheaded the Minotaur*

Raj Tawney, *Colorful Palate: Savored Stories from a Mixed Life*

Edward Cahill, *Disorderly Men*

Joseph Heathcott, *Global Queens: An Urban Mosaic*

Francis R. Kowsky with Lucille Gordon, *Hell on Color, Sweet on Song: Jacob Wrey Mould and the Artful Beauty of Central Park*

Jill Jonnes, *South Bronx Rising: The Rise, Fall, and Resurrection of an American City*, Third Edition

Barbara G. Mensch, *A Falling-Off Place: The Transformation of Lower Manhattan*

David J. Goodwin, *Midnight Rambles: H. P. Lovecraft in Gotham*

Felipe Luciano, *Flesh and Spirit: Confessions of a Young Lord*

Maximo G. Martinez, *Sojourners in the Capital of the World: Garifuna Immigrants*

Davida Siwisa James, *Hamilton Heights and Sugar Hill: Alexander Hamilton's Old Harlem Neighborhood Through the Centuries*

Annik LaFarge, *On the High Line: The Definitive Guide*, Third Edition. Foreword by Rick Dark

Marie Carter, *Mortimer and the Witches: A History of Nineteenth-Century Fortune Tellers*

Alice Sparberg Alexiou, *Devil's Mile: The Rich, Gritty History of the Bowery*. Foreword by Peter Quinn

Carey Kasten and Brenna Moore, *Mutuality in El Barrio: Stories of the Little Sisters of the Assumption Family Health Service*. Foreword by Norma Benítez Sánchez

Kimberly A. Orcutt, *The American Art-Union: Utopia and Skepticism in the Antebellum Era*

For a complete list, visit www.fordhampress.com/empire-state-editions.